WeWere
There

Julie B. Wiest

TENNESSEE VALLEY
Publishing
2006

Published by:

> Tennessee Valley Publishing,
> P.O. Box 52527,
> Knoxville, Tennessee 37950-2527
> www.TVP1.com

Second printing, 2007

Library of Congress Control Number: 2006934551

ISBN: 1-932604-38-3

Contents

List of Photographs

The following forty photographs are located in a sixteen-page section between chapters ten and eleven.

Wartime headshots:

1. Fred Baumann
2. Wallace Baumann
3. John Bolinger
4. Joe Brownlee
5. Fred Cagle
6. Ed Coleman
7. Tom Evans
8. Al Holmes
9. John McAmis
10. John McDow
11. Frank Moore
12. Kay Ogden
13. Rob Schmid
14. Warren Sylvester
15. Jim Talley
16. Bill Tate
17. Vince Torbett

Contributed field photographs:

18. Ed Coleman stands in front of the *USS Pickaway* on January 20, 1946. (Courtesy Ed Coleman)
19. Tom Dempster receives the Air Medal from commanding officer Capt. John P. Owen at the U.S. Naval Hospital in Mare Island, California. (Courtesy Tom Dempster)
20. John Moore poses for a photograph with a friend. (Courtesy John Moore)
21. Frank Moore with two buddies. (Courtesy Frank Moore)
22. Tom Evans is pictured inside "The Forbidden City," the walled city in the middle of Peking, China, where the emperors lived. (Courtesy Tom Evans)
23. Rob Schmid enjoys the beach with his bombardier, co-pilot, and navigator in Okinawa after the war. (Courtesy Rob Schmid)
24. E.B. Copeland poses in front of a chapel. (Courtesy E.B. Copeland)

Introduction

My interest in World War II was sparked by my grandfather's death on April 5, 2004. Daniel William Geska was a member of the 299th Engineer Combat Battalion during the war. Although this unit wasn't one of the most celebrated or talked-about, its brave members were some of the foremost heroes of the war. My grandfather never spoke about the wartime horrors he must have witnessed, and I regret that it wasn't until his death that I learned of his great acts of bravery and heroism. But once I learned more about his unit and what specific role he played in the war, this book wasn't far away.

We Were There got under way in the summer of 2004, when I was approached by the Rev. Dr. Paul Rader, a minister at First Presbyterian Church in Knoxville, Tenn., to write a book compiling the World War II experiences of the veterans who are members of the church. Because of my newfound interest in the war and profound admiration for those who served in it, I jumped at the chance.

I began recruiting veterans at the weekly meeting of the church's James Park Bible Class. Initially, twelve signed up to be interviewed. Word spread rapidly, however, and the project continued to grow. I scheduled interviews and spent two to three hours on average with each veteran. When I finished, I had spoken with twenty-nine veterans from all branches of the service and one man who had worked in wartime Oak Ridge, all of whom had fascinating stories (and some that were surprisingly amusing) from their time in the war. In addition, I received nearly one hundred wartime photographs, along with other fascinating documents and mementos. Each chapter is primarily the veteran's own words, with minor editing.

Like my grandfather, many of these veterans told me they had never previously spoken about their time in the war, yet they have so much to share. I will always feel honored that these men, most of whom I had not previously met, were so willing to share such an important part of their lives with me. Hearing them relate (with the utmost amount of modesty) their unique experiences further fueled my excitement about this project. Each veteran played an important role in the war, and each story became an invaluable component to the book. I am grateful for this opportunity to help document and disseminate these extraordinary stories.

This project would not have progressed so smoothly without the generous help of many. First, I would like to thank the Rev. Rader and all the members of the James Park Bible Class, who helped get this project off the ground and supported it along the way. Thanks goes to Dr. Ed Coleman for the book's title and Tom Evans for the cover photograph. A very special thank you goes to the volunteers who transcribed the taped interviews – no small feat! Special recognition goes to Barb Wiest, who transcribed the majority of the tapes. Other transcribers were Paul Rader, Peggy Haglar, Sam Kincheloe, Vicky Whitaker, and Ailsa Schuller. Thanks also to Philip Nagy, Scott Barker, and retired Brig. Gen. Walter "Bud" Bacon for their editing and fact-checking assistance. I would also like to thank Mrs. Nancy McAmis for her generous donation toward the project.

Finally, thanks to everyone else who supported this project and offered assistance along the way. This was a big undertaking, but the hard work and generosity of many led to its timely completion. I am proud of this book and hope you enjoy it!

Dedication

We Were There is dedicated to my grandfather, Daniel William Geska, whose death inspired my interest in this project.

orn March 25, 1920, my grandfather was the second of four children and the only son of a poor family. Because his father wasn't able to work after suffering a spinal injury on the job, my grandfather, at age fourteen, quit school, lied about his age, and joined a CCC (Civilian Conservation Corps) camp to help support his family.

He married my grandmother, Agnes Barbara, on March 24, 1940, the day before his twentieth birthday. When the Japanese attacked Pearl Harbor on December 7, 1941, my grandfather felt a strong sense of obligation to his country and decided to join the Army. Because he was the only son of a father with a physical disability, he would have been excused from active duty, but that's just how he was – headstrong and loyal.

A native of Rochester, New York, my grandfather became a member of the original 299th Engineer Combat Battalion when it was activated in March 1943. Unlike most other military units, this one was almost entirely comprised of soldiers from upstate New York. Many of the unit's young members had known each other their whole lives. They attended school and church together; they worked together; they had the same friends; they dated the same girls; and their families were longtime neighbors. There must have been a special kind of camaraderie within the unit, more so than in other units in which soldiers were connected through the Army alone. I imagine this made the horrors of war all the more real and devastating for these men.

The 299th Combat Engineers trained at Camp White, Oregon, where the soldiers learned basic training and engineering specialties, including bridge building, mine detection, demolition procedures, construction, obstacle preparation, and invasion and beach assault techniques. But these young men had little idea what was in store for them once they joined the war.

This unit was responsible for clearing obstacles in the ocean and at the shoreline to allow troops to invade the shores. It was essentially a suicide mission. The unit arrived at Omaha Beach on D-Day, June 6, 1944, and worked under heavy enemy fire, with little food or sleep, until June 9. Their work was periodically interrupted when enemy fire became so extreme that they were forced to fight back. The difficult and hazardous conditions required incredible determination and heroism on each individual's part, and by the time the unit completed its mission, it had suffered approximately thirty-three percent casualties. During his service, my grandfather earned two Purple Hearts.

After returning home, my grandfather never spoke of the pain he experienced or of the suffering and death he witnessed; he only told funny stories about the good times he had in the

Army. And nearly every story I heard from my grandmother or mother cast him as a compassionate, honorable soldier and man, who would sacrifice himself to help others. I regret that it wasn't until his death that I learned of the heroic service and sacrifice he made for the country he loved.

The grandfather I knew was a loving, generous man who worked hard to provide the kind of life for his family he thought we deserved. He owned a successful company and was more mechanically capable than anyone I have ever known. He could fix or build just about anything and was constantly looking for projects he could complete for his family, neighbors, or others in his community. I always admired him growing up, but not because he was a decorated veteran or because he was a distinguished 32nd degree Mason, a member and past monarch of his local Grotto, and a member of the Scottish Rite – I didn't know much about all that then. He was just Grandpa, and, to me, he could do anything.

My grandfather started to get sick a few years before his death and, after a long stay in the hospital during late 2003 for a stroke and heart attack, was admitted to a nursing home. I hated visiting him there more than anything – to look at him then was almost unbearable, especially because I knew he was miserable. There lay a man who, during my childhood, was bigger and better than any superhero that I could imagine, a man who, at one time, could do anything he put his mind to, a man who was now confined to bed with virtually no mobility and in constant pain. When he died at age eighty-four, it was a compassionate ending.

After his death, I learned so much more about the man I had admired and loved so much throughout my life. The Rev. Dr. Paul Rader gave an excellent, moving eulogy, speaking of my grandfather's remarkable life and about how much love he must have had to sustain a sixty-four-year marriage. He also said that he was sure my grandfather saw a lot of himself in my brother, Dan, and me and reveled in our accomplishments. He did, indeed, pass on many qualities to members of my family. My brother is also incredibly mechanically inclined and possesses the same strong, generous spirit (and love for cheesecake). I have his love for challenges, problem-solving abilities, and drive to work hard. And my parents share his dedication and commitment to family and community.

Although I don't know much about his experiences during the war, I'll always be grateful for having the opportunity to know and love such a remarkable man, my hero. This book provides for thirty families an opportunity to know and forever hold these precious memories from an important time in these men's lives.

Chapter one
Fred Baumann

Fred Baumann was born in Knoxville, Tennessee, on August 28, 1923. He joined the Army Air Corps in 1943 and became a fighter pilot in the 15th Air Force based in south Italy. He completed twenty missions and earned an Air Medal. During his last flight, just before the end of the war, Fred's engine caught on fire, and he had to bail out. He subsequently crushed a vertebra and spent months in the hospital.

As a young boy, my dream was to be a fighter pilot. I always loved airplanes – and I still do. I told people I had achieved my hope for life at twenty years old when I graduated from pilot school.

When the war started, I was a senior at Knoxville High School. We had a military ROTC over there, and I was a lieutenant my senior year. I was going to graduate in January, but you know what happened on December 7, 1941. I remember it very well. The day after, on Monday, at school, we heard Roosevelt's address to the nation on the radio. It was the greatest speech I've ever heard.

So I said, "Well, I'm going down to enlist in the Air Corps." I mean, we were really mad as heck thinking that they would do that stuff to us. We were all going to go down to enlist, thinking, "Let's just get this thing over with." So, the principal of the high school, Mr. Evans, called a special chapel meeting, an assembly for all of those in my class. And his message was, "Go on and finish your school, and when they need you, they're going to call you." So that's how it was. And really, we thought it was nothing – you did your duty to your country, and I still believe that. So I enlisted in November 1942 when I was eighteen years old and was called to duty the following April. Then I graduated as a second lieutenant in May of 1944.

We were privates when we were called in April, and we were sent down to Biloxi, Mississippi. We were drilling and all kinds of other things, but not flying. Then we were sent to a CTD. Now, universities all over the country would have been devastated with all of the people going into the armed forces, but they sent us to a CTD – a cadets training unit – and we were there about a month. I was sent to a little school in Missouri, Southwest Missouri State Teacher's College. It was really very good for the universities because they had money coming from the government. It also was kind of like a large holding tank because they would need us later.

Then we were sent down to San Antonio, Texas, to a classification center, and that was where it would be determined whether you would be a navigator, a bombardier or a pilot. It was quite thorough down there, as far as the physical examinations. I didn't want to be a navigator, and I didn't want to be a bombardier – I wanted to be a pilot. So we did KP one time there, and we did a lot of other things, like drilling. When I went to my interview, they had psychologists and psychiatrists to interview very carefully with every kind of question you can imagine. I learned long ago that if you always tell the truth, you don't have to worry about what you're saying. I was asked some pretty callous questions down there, but when I was finished with my interview, he said, "All right, now which would you prefer – bombardier, navigator, or pilot?" I told him, "Captain, I have wanted to be a pilot all my life." And he said, "Well, I think you're going to make it." So then those of us who wanted to be pilots-in-training walked across the road. There were about 5,000 young men in each class of cadets for preflight training. We also learned some navigation. The thing that caused a lot of the guys to wash out of there was that we had to learn to copy Morse Code at eight words a minute. We were at long lines of tables with earphones on, and the instructor sat at his desk and sent messages. A lot of them had some trouble with "s" and "h" because they sound so much alike, but I got to twelve words with no problem – I've never been such a good scholar as I was there.

I guess it was about three months we were there in San Antonio. Then I was sent to primary flight school and was there several months. Then I went to a basic pilot school, which used a bigger and more powerful airplane, in Waco, Texas. When I finally finished that, the instructors would determine who would go to single-engine advanced pilot training – and probably get to be a fighter pilot – or to twin-engine training and fly bombers or transports. Well, we had a sergeant in the flight room – a fine fellow – and I heard that he was going to help the captain select who was going to the single engines and twin engines. But, before that, at the mid-point of basic training, they would select certain cadets for a special program in Temple, Texas, where they would fly a twin-engine transition, then come back to Waco, and then go on to fly B-25s. Well, my instructor came over one day and said, "I want to talk to you." So I came over there, and he said, "Now, you're aware of that program we have now that you can go down to Temple, Texas, and fly the AT-17 down there and then get back and fly B-25s. Now what would you think of that?" Well, I had never been asked what I thought – I listened to what I was told. I said, "Well…" And he said, "I want you to be frank because you're the only one I have in mind that I would recommend. If you want it, it's going to be yours." And I said, "Sir, my heart is set on going to single engine down there in Mission, Texas." He said, "It's all right. I just wanted to know. But, I can't guarantee you'll get there." And I said, "That's all right."

Anyway, time passed, and when we finished our training there, we were just standing around. When I first learned that sergeant was going to help the captain decide who was going where, boy, I brushed him up. I'd say, "Have a cigar there – single engine." And later, "Have a cup of coffee – single engine." I'd bring him a Coca-Cola and say, "You've got to help me." And he said, "Well, we'll see, we'll see." We were all sitting around in the barracks when he walked in and said, "I just came over here to tell you guys goodbye." I went over to him and said, "Sergeant, did I make it? Did I make it? Did I make it?" And he said, "You're going to Blackland (Army Airfield)." Well, that was where that B-25 class was going. I said, "Blackland?!" I mean, I was just foaming at the mouth. And suddenly he started laughing. He said, "Oh Baumann, I was just having fun with you. The captain said that you're going to be one hell of a fighter pilot." And I said, "Oh glory, hallelujah!"

So I graduated flight school as a second lieutenant. Then I was sent to Oklahoma to fly the P-40s, which were "Flying Tigers" – they had the single engine. We finally got overseas in February 1945, and I wound up getting my desire – it was a P-51 over in Italy, the best airplane in the war. You were handling a pretty powerful airplane, and you were flying in formation with others, so you were thinking about what you were going to do – that's it. We didn't get fired at as much as the bombers – I'll take my hat off to bombers. I mean, we used to tell them, "Well, you all *drive* your airplanes, and we *fly* ours."

I'll never forget when I was wingman for the squadron leader, and we were escorting a lot of B-24s. I was on the wing, and we would have our fighters up above come down, and if the Germans tried to get them, we'd go down to protect them. Now, at that time, it was really late in the war, and I never got a chance to do that. But I saw a B-24 off to my right, and I saw a lot of flak – that was horrible – the anti-aircraft the Germans put up. I thought, "Oh, good night." You could see those bombers just moving slow – I mean, it looked slow compared to us. I thought, "That next burst is going to hit us." And about that time, the B-24 hit one, and a ribbon of smoke came out behind one of his engines. I popped the microphone button to call my squadron leader to tell him we got one hit and that we should send two down to take him home. But it rolled over and blew up, and there just wasn't anything there. There were ten men in that thing and then ten men gone – it was just in pieces. But you got used to it; it's just part of the job, I guess.

Just before V-E Day, we were up in northern Italy. A good friend of mine, Bob Rochelle, was the only friend I ran into during the whole time I was in the Army. When you were a fighter pilot, you didn't have anything to do around the base if you weren't flying. So one of the guys – maybe it was me, I don't know – said, "Let's get a command car out and go down to south Italy and see some lights and some people walking around." We thought that was a great idea, so about six of us got into one of the command cars, went down there, and walked around. Well, I heard just before I went overseas that Bob was flying B-17s down there. So we went there and walked around, saw people, and bought some stuff. Then we thought, "Boy, we better get this thing back to motorpool," which was about seventy miles up north of us. So I was walking out the door, and Bob came walking in – five minutes one way or the other, and we would have missed each other. I said, "Bob, now one of these days, I'm going to bring down a P-51, and you're going to see a real airplane."

Well, maybe a couple of weeks later, the war was about over but hadn't quite ended yet when I went out and saw the operations officer one day. I said, "Jack, I'd like to check out a P-51 and fly down to see a friend of mine." He said, "Good, you do it. Get your flight time in." See, you had to fly four hours a month to get your flight pay. Well, my best friend, a boy named Gerry Carpenter, said, "Let me check one out, and we'll fly down there together." I thought that would be great, so he got a P-51, and I got one, too.

We took off going down the Adriatic Sea, and we were having a ball. We were buzzing around, and I don't think the Italian fishermen knew the war was over, so they'd get down on the ground when we passed. We were just two kids out there having a lark. But then all hell broke loose in my engine, and it blew out, caught on fire, and I had to bail out. Ah, the Lord was with me, and I say this seriously because when I bailed out – we didn't have ejection seats – you had to get out the best way you could. I was injured very severely and was in the hospital.

An excerpt about Fred's final flight from a document he wrote entitled "From Freshman to Fighter Pilot":

May the fifth, nineteen-hundred-forty-five: a day that (for me) will live in infamy, or with regret ... yet with indelible and unforgettable memories.

It started off like any other recent day. If I hadn't planned on flying down to see Bob, it would have been an uneventful day. Gerry and I went to breakfast together as usual. I had never taken my Argus C-3 camera with me on missions, but I took it along this time to snap a few photos of Bob and me.

The P-51B I would fly was "#4." Some of the fellows had flown that one when they had made their first check-out flights in late February, and I had flown a mission or two in it. The crew chief was a real character, the only one I can remember who wore a beard.

I looked over the Form 1, stuck my hat behind the armor plate, pulled on my helmet and goggles, slipped my hands into the leather gloves, stuffed the camera into my right knee pocket, and buckled up. Smitty was a real talker. He and I shot the breeze while I waited for Gerry to get set. While we were talking, Smitty pointed to another crewman nearby and said, "You see that fellow there, Lieutenant? He was the crew chief for the airplane Lt. Angle had to bail out of the other day. Now he ain't got no work to do and just takes it easy. So if you have any trouble with this one, please don't try to bring it back for me to have to fix; just tear it up real good." Laughing, I said, "Smitty, don't give it a thought; if anything goes wrong with it, I'll do it up right for you."

About then, Gerry signaled he was ready to go, so I started the engine, and in a few minutes, I swung out with Smitty sitting out on the left wing and taxied to the takeoff end of the strip, with Gerry close behind. Pressing the mic button, I said, "Dry Pond Tower, this is Cockney 5-1. You got a pair ready to go, over." "Roger, Cockney 5-1, you're both clear to go." "Roger, Dry Pond, we're gone." After making a climbing turn to the right, Gerry joined up on my left wing, just like he had done when we were flying P-40s back at Colorado Springs.

It was a beautiful day, our war was over, I was heading to visit a good friend in a hot fighter, and my best buddy was flying beside me. Throughout the time I had been in the Army Air Forces, I never had a day in sickbay, no accidents, no flak holes – life had been very good to me.

We were two young men flying the best U.S. fighter in the air, out for a lark, out to celebrate. I can't adequately describe how happy I was at that moment. Was "something" trying to tell me to enjoy it while it lasted, because there would never be a day like it again? Perhaps there is such a thing as premonition, which we are unable to recognize...

With me in the lead, we headed for the Adriatic Sea, and after reaching the coast, I took us down low and started beating up the place, down the beach at ground level. The poor Italian fishermen must have had the devil scared out of them, because they hit the sand when we bore down on them. We continued in this manner for several miles, occasionally breaking up and swinging around for a second blast at them. The poor souls probably didn't even know that the war was over.

Since Gerry had to remain above me, he couldn't get down as low as I was, so after several minutes, I pulled up and said, "OK, Gerry, you got it now." Down we went again. Man, that boy could sure fly; I'd be willing to swear that he was kicking up sand at times. After satisfying himself with the low stuff, he started climbing. Reaching about 11,000 feet, we started playing "can you top this?" He'd do something while I watched him, and then I'd try to do it better. Then it was my turn to show him something, and he'd try to top me. There we were, not a care in the world. Two kids playing games with 1,400 horses – and getting paid for it.

After a while, he told me to take the lead. By then we were well down the Italian boot, because a P-51 didn't know how to loaf along. This time, I picked some "dive bombing" targets: a bridge, a church spire, etc. With Gerry close behind, I peeled off and headed down in a 60-degree dive, using the K-14 gun sight to calculate the theoretical point of "bomb release." Pulling out of the dive, we zoomed up several thousand feet, and I let him take the lead again. He spotted another bridge below, so we peeled off and made a run on it, too. There were many other now-forgotten maneuvers and impulsive play that followed, the last of which was our engaging in several mock dogfights. First he'd get the best of me, and then I'd have him in my sights the next time, back and forth we went. Then I made another dive-bombing simulation. He bounced me as I was pulling up, and we went at it all over again. We pressed everything to the wall, 'round and 'round we went in a continuous circle, tighter and tighter, neither one of us getting enough "lead" on the other to yell "Gotcha!" One of my combat veteran instructors at Fort Sumner had said that when you were in a tough situation and needed to turn a little tighter, you could boost the rpm's, and the added torque would hold the nose up in a tight turn. That's what I did, and it was working, with the throttle advanced to the stop – just short of "war emergency" power.

I was gaining on him ... and then it happened!

My engine started shaking furiously in a pulsating frenzy. Chopping back on the throttle, it continued for a more few seconds before it seized up with a tragic shudder. Giving Gerry a call, I told him that I had a problem. At first he wasn't sure I was the one calling him, no doubt because my voice had a different edge to it now. We were close to 15,000 feet. Confirming that I was calling him, he came up beside me, easing back on his power, dropping a few degrees of flaps to remain close to me, since my engine had quit.

Glancing at the instrument panel, the first thing I noticed was that the engine temperature was past the red line. Ditto for the coolant temperature. Checking the oil pressure, I got a big fat zero. The problem: a broken oil line, confirmed by the heavy oil that had covered the floor and had soaked my shoes and flight-suit cuffs. Soon after flipping off the mags, the fuel supply, and the fuel booster pump, a cloud of steam blew from the cowling and streamed over the canopy – the coolant safety valve had blown. In a few seconds, smoke began pouring out. Gerry said that I was smoking bad, but he couldn't see any fire – yet.

I asked him if he could spot a place below where I could belly-in. By now, he had started circling, because my airspeed was too low for him to maintain close position. He said I was close enough to the beach to belly-in. Steadily losing altitude, I asked how it looked now. He said it looked bad and appeared to be getting worse; a few flames were now visible.

Perhaps I subconsciously remembered the time when I had learned about the fellow at Woodward, Oklahoma, who had waited too long to jump from a burning P-40. His parachute did not deploy, and he had been killed. I still remembered the words I repeated to my pals that, if they heard I had been killed in an airplane crash, they would know that I couldn't get out of it. I realized that I had only one option: a bail-out. Telling Gerry of this decision, he wished me luck and said he'd keep circling.

We had never made "practice" parachute jumps in training. Other than delaying pulling the ripcord until you were clear of the aircraft, there was not much to remember. Some went over the side, others rolled over and rolled out. Some had rolled in a lot of forward trim tab, unbuckled their harness, pulled way back on the stick, then suddenly released it – propelling themselves out of the cockpit. It was a matter of choice, based upon the situation. We had no ejection seats, and you had to get out the best way you could.

I flipped off the electrical switches and re-trimmed. You couldn't roll back the canopy on a P-51C (or B). The top lifted over you on hinges. Forward to my right was a red lever that would jettison the canopy. I pulled it back, but nothing happened. It didn't budge. Jerking it more strongly, several times, still nothing happened. The thought that I might not be able to get out and that I might have to take my chances on bellying-in flickered through my mind, but I rejected it. I had to get out of this thing! It was getting smoky, and it felt like I was getting a lot warmer.

By holding the control stick between my knees, I used both hands and started punching on the canopy with my fists. At first it didn't give, but after three or four strong licks, I felt it move a fraction. Good! After two more good licks, I felt it move about an inch, then the slipstream ripped it away. I didn't feel any panic, because I was too busy doing everything I could do to get out of there.

I slowed to about 110 miles an hour, re-trimmed, disconnected the microphone and earphones, and unplugged the oxygen tube. Glancing at the altimeter, I noted that I was passing through 8,000 feet. Time to go. Since the aircraft was under control, I had decided to go over the side. It seemed to be the best method because I was afraid the plane might explode if I rolled over and dropped out. Perhaps that's what I should have done, but why second-guess yourself after the fact? I slung my left leg over the side, but when I looked at my right knee, I noticed the camera. I thought about buttoning the flap but dismissed it with the thought that it might break my kneecap when the chute opened. Looking at the ground far below me, I believe that I have never felt so very small as I did at that moment. It was a weird feeling.

My goggles and oxygen mask were ripped off by the slipstream when I had put my left leg over the side. Before I could put the other leg outside and kick away, the aircraft rolled over and headed straight down, with me half-way in and half-way out. The airspeed was increasing quickly. For a second, the thought of pulling myself back inside to bring the aircraft under control did flash though my mind, but I dismissed it. I was losing altitude too fast. Then I made a silent prayer and kicked away.

One of the last things I remember was the realization that the horizontal stabilizer was going to knock the hell out of me when I let

go, but there was no alternative. It's difficult to describe what happened
– so much of it is fuzzy. The stabilizer caught me across the upper
thighs – that I do remember. The shock of the impact stunned me, and I
don't remember falling clear of the aircraft.

Then fuzzily, faintly I remember how quiet everything was,
like I was floating in a dream. Nothing seemed real, my arms and legs
were limp, and I was disoriented. Gradually, I became aware of what
had happened and feebly pulled the D ring. There was a "rustling"
sound, and all at once I felt as if I had been snapped on the end of a
whip. My back was stabbing me with pain, as agonizing as any I have
ever experienced. I was groaning, and the illogical thought of releasing
myself from the harness flashed through my mind – but was quickly
dismissed. I became aware of a faint sound; it was Gerry's aircraft.
Looking down, I saw #4 heading straight in, far below, then I saw the
huge fireball from its explosion. At some point during the descent, I
noticed that my camera was gone. A sense of regret was felt, because it
was gone with an irreplaceable roll of partly exposed film.

Firmly supported in the parachute harness, the sensation was
similar to sitting in a swing, high off the ground. A swaying motion
continued, and at first it seemed as if I were just hanging there. As the
ground approached, my speed of descent appeared to accelerate. The
pain had eased somewhat by then; perhaps nature had temporarily
deadened the affected nerves. I saw houses below and people running
around looking up at me. As stupid as it sounds, I recall saying, "Don't
go away, I'll be right down." I imagine that I was still in shock. Then
the ground seemed to jump up and hit me.

Although I knew better, I didn't remember to maneuver the
wind to my back, so I landed facing the wind and fell backwards.
Shouting Italians rushed at me as I attempted to spill the parachute. For
a moment, they had unintentionally frightened me. They babbled words
at me and gesticulated in their typical ways, but I could only say, "No
capish Ita-li-an." A woman approached with a fresh egg in each hand
and offered them to me, gesturing that I should crack them and "suck"
the raw eggs. Shaking my head, I muttered, "Multi gratz." She looked
disappointed, so in a gesture of reciprocation, I handed her my only
pack of cigarettes. Her eyes lit up, and she started passing them around.

I noticed a startling thing when I had unbuckled the parachute.
The ripcord D ring was only about four inches out of the metal spiral
tubing. The proper procedure was to pull it all the way out in one
motion, but in my confused state, I had barely managed to pull it. But it
had been enough to release the pilot chute, which pulled the main
canopy out.

Gerry made a low pass, and I gave him several waves, which he returned. He made one more pass, rocking his wings before returning to the base. One of the Italian men alarmingly asked if he was "Bosche," but I assured him that he was an American. Within a few minutes, an American first lieutenant in the engineers drove up in a Jeep and asked how I was and if he could take me anywhere. He said Gerry had guided him to me. I told him that I thought I was all right but would like to visit the crash scene. Fortunately, the aircraft had missed any dwellings, but people were milling around at a safe distance; the ammunition was still cooking off. The fire was burning furiously, and pieces of twisted metal were scattered around the huge crater. Nothing bore any resemblance to an airplane.

An elderly Italian gentleman, dressed all in black and wearing an unusual-looking hat, approached us. The lieutenant told me that he was a priest and was inquiring if anyone had been killed in the crash. If so, he wanted to administer the Last Rites. I thanked him and shook my head, saying, "No, seen-yor padro."

A few minutes later, a British truck appeared with an officer and an enlisted driver. He told the lieutenant and me that a British base was nearby and that they would be pleased to take me there. The lieutenant and I shook hands and said goodbye. I arrived at a small British base within 15 to 20 minutes. The officer introduced me to the commanding officer, a captain who cordially offered me a hot cup of tea.

I must have looked pale, for he remarked that I appeared to be injured and asked how I was feeling. I told him my back was painful, but I thought it was only a severe sprain. With that, he said there was a small British hospital within a few miles at Vasto and suggested that they take me there. Agreeing, he summoned the British equivalent of a Jeep and told the driver where to take me. Before leaving, he handed me a pack of cigarettes, and I thanked him for his hospitality.

The driver dropped me off at a small hospital, and after filling out a few forms, I was taken to a ward containing several cots – all empty. After being handed a pair of pajamas, I was left alone. Within an hour or two, a doctor examined me. Before he left, he remarked that he was sure that I would much prefer to be placed in an American hospital as soon as possible. In that respect, I was lucky, because a south-bound military train came through once a week and would take me to Foggia. Fortunately, it would be coming the next day.

The next morning, the nurse said that the doctor would like to speak with me before I left. She escorted me to his small office, where he handed me some papers, after which he made a few comments. I had been insisting that my back was only sprained and that all I wanted was to get back to my squadron. One of his last remarks was: "…and I do believe you will discover that you are much more seriously injured than you think you are."

The drive to the train station at Vasto didn't take long. It was old and small, and most of the personnel were British military, because the British ran the railway. I handed the officer in charge my A.G.O. card and told him that I needed transportation to the American Army Hospital at Foggia. He pulled out a form, filled it out and handed it to me. He was not certain when the train would arrive, but he said that it shouldn't be too much longer. I hoped not.

When I got out of the hospital, they put me on a ship to go home. I could not wear a uniform because I was walking with that cast on, so they carried me. I was on an American luxury liner – the *America,* I think. It was then run by the Navy to carry troops. They carried me to where the officers ward was, and I was lying there on the lower bunk while they were bringing different guys in. I saw them bringing in a black guy, and, as a Southern guy, I thought, "A black guy in a white officers ward?" Well, he was a pilot and had been shot. He was a nice fellow. His name was Charlie Jones, from Chicago. And it turned out he and I were the only two fighter pilots in that whole ward. He was a second lieutenant, and I was a second lieutenant; he flew a P-51, and I flew a P-51. So we became great friends. He could not walk much, and I would bring him things. When we both got to Norfolk, we were taken to a hospital. You know, I would say if they had had a vote on the most pleasant pilot in the war, I would say it would have been Charlie. He was a fine, fine fellow. I've often wondered what happened to him.

The second lumbar is a big lumbar, and mine was crushed, so they had me in a cast. They injected something in my vein and said, "Count down from one hundred." I think I got maybe to ninety-six, and I was out of it. But when I woke up, I was back in my bed, and I had a cast then that had me bent way back. Then the doctor came by again, and he had the X-ray. He was very proud of it because he got what was called a "one hundred percent reduction." Then he explained what they had done when I had had the anesthesia that put me way under. They ran an oxygen tube and an ether tube down my throat, then put a harness around my ankles. Then he bent that lumbar back and manipulated it until he found out that he could pull it open, but it was going to have to be filled. So, when I was in Augusta, Georgia, they took me down to where the orthopedic wing was, down below the hospital. And they said, "Well, let's get the cast off." They had big cutters, and then they took some X-rays. Then the surgeon said, "Which one was it?" He couldn't find it, couldn't see what vertebra it was. So they kept me out of the cast and made a brace for me. Then I went home for leave. So I had a thirty-day medical leave, and then I went back and they took the brace off. So it worked out all right.

When I heard about the atomic bomb, I was still at the hospital in Augusta, Georgia, convalescing before I went home. I was walking down one of the halls, and I heard everybody yelling, "Throw your crutches away; now you don't need them," and all this kind of stuff. But nobody knew what was in Oak Ridge. Can you picture the press today keeping something under lids like that? And the Internet – they'd probably show you how to make an atom bomb. But nobody knew what was there, and when I heard, I said, "That's what they were making at Oak Ridge!"

Later I got to go home on leave, and then I went back down there and got my orders. So I went to Miami to a convalescence center there, then came home, and that's when I wound up deciding that I would go back to college. So I did.

During the war, I never got to fly a jet fighter – that's my one regret. After the war, I flew a little while. The reason I did was that I learned about the GI Bill, which was probably the finest thing that was ever passed. With the GI Bill, they would pay all the tuition for any school you wanted to enroll in that would accept you. It would also give you free books. And you got $65 a month, which back then wasn't bad. I had planned to stay in the service, but when I found out about the

GI Bill, I decided to finish school. See, I had two quarters in at
The University of Tennessee when I went in. So I got a degree
in business administration.

After the war, most veterans were about the same age I
was, and usually we had a lot to talk about girls – we loved to
talk about the girls. Well, I was discharged in November of
'45, and you couldn't enroll in the university until January. So
I let it be known to the girls that "I'm around and I'm
available." Frances McAmis – a member of the church – was
the pledge mother for the Chi Omega sorority house, and I was
dating her. And one night she said, "Fred, would you do me a
favor?" And I said, "Sure, what would you like?" And she said,
"Would you take one of my new pledges to the pledge dance?"
I said, "Sure, I'll put her on the list." Her name was Mary
Shankland, and I found out that she was living in a private
home close to the university. I thought, "Boy, that's good – no
dormitory." So one afternoon I called her up, asked for the
honor of taking her to her pledge dance, and, just casually, I
said, "What did you do today?" And she said, "Well, I was out
at the Island Airport having a flight lesson." I thought, "Bingo!
A flight lesson!" So I met her, and I had never met anyone
quite like her. At first, she shot me down. But we became very
great friends, and we married after I graduated.

My mother told me something after I got home. I had a
brother-in-law my sister had married, and he was a P-38 pilot
in the southwest Pacific. Well, I grew up right off Clinch
Avenue in Knoxville, right above where the hospital is.

I heard after he and I were both back that my mother
was up on the second floor looking out of her window to the
street and saw this automobile drive up right in front of our
house. My sister was also living there while her husband was
gone. And my mother had heard that when they delivered the
telegram that your husband had been killed, they would come
to your house. When she saw the woman going around to get
something in her seat, she was wondering, "Oh, is it Fred or is
it my son-in-law?" And she was very emotional. It turned out it
was papers for somebody else.

But that must have been terrible. See, that is what they were always concerned about – is it going to be our boy?

Chapter two
Wallace Baumann

Wallace Baumann was born in Knoxville, Tennessee, on April 19, 1925. He joined the Army in 1943 and was a member of the 10th Armored Division. He crossed the Siegfried Line and fought at Bastogne and Bavaria and during the Battle of the Bulge. He was never injured but earned various commendations for his time in the war.

I was drafted in August of 1943 when I was in summer school at The University of Tennessee. They wouldn't even let me finish summer school. See, you did it in six-week increments. I finished the first six weeks, and then I wanted to do the last six weeks, which I would have finished in August. They said, "No, you can't finish. You're going to report for duty at Fort Oglethorpe." So I went into the Army then, like so many. I remember we marched down Gay Street, and, because I had a little military training in prep school, I was supposed to be in charge. I was eighteen years old, scared to death, and I was supposed to be in charge of thirty-five or so men. We paraded down Gay Street, got on the train at the Southern station, and went down to Fort Oglethorpe. From there, we went to Fort Benning for basic training, and in January 1944, I ended up in the 10th Armored Division.

Basic training was really something. They had you run an obstacle course, and they would shoot real bullets over your head. And they had you crawling under barbed wire, trying to make it like what you might do in combat. We had to go to the firing range and learn how to fire an M1 rifle and even a machine gun. They would test your shooting ability, and I was a really good marksman. I think I earned a badge for being an expert rifleman – I could usually hit the bull's-eye. Luckily, I didn't have to shoot anyone in Germany. Most of it was done with artillery and mortar shells.

The 10th Armored Division was being trained to go overseas and fight in Germany, so it was a full division of 10,000 men. We had field artillery and tanks; we were in armored infantry and rode in half-tracks. That was the difference from foot soldiers – I think they took them in trucks, but we went ahead in half-tracks. So, from January, I was in the 10th Armored Division. They told us we were going to go overseas and not to tell anybody – it was a big secret. We couldn't even tell our folks because they thought spies might be around.

So I trained at Camp Gordon, Georgia, where the 10th Armored Division was, which was right outside Augusta, Georgia. We all got on this big, long troop train in the middle of the day. So right in the middle of the morning, we went across the main street of Augusta, Georgia – Broad Street – and all the people in town were looking at us. We were hanging out of the windows, and all the people were waving "goodbye." I'm sure they hated to see us go – we were a big boost to their economy. Every weekend we'd go into town and go to the movies, restaurants and wherever we wanted. But it was no secret. I often said it was the worst-kept secret of the war.

We ended up at Camp Shanks that evening, and we were there about three days. I know we had a couple of leaves to go into New York City, and I got to see "Oklahoma" one night. And we looked around, of course; New York was very busy with soldiers. Then, on September 12, 1944, they took us down to a train in New Jersey, and we went on ferryboats to get across the Hudson River. Then we went on the ships that would take us overseas. We all got so excited. We looked across the New York skyline, and there was the *Queen Mary*. We thought, "Isn't that wonderful, we'll go over to France on the *Queen Mary*." We pulled right up by the *Queen Mary*, and it was huge. They told us to disembark on the right side – not on the *Queen Mary* side, which was on the left. We got on this little old ship called the *General William H. Black*. The ferry pulled out, and we could look up and see that the *Queen Mary* was way up there.

I think we sailed about 1 a.m., and some of us stayed up on deck to watch as we sailed out of New York harbor, past the Statue of Liberty, because we knew we might not ever see it again. We were told that we were the first division to ever sail directly to France. Before that, they had all landed in England first and then went over across the channel. But this was September, and D-Day had been over three months before, so the Allies were well inland. I remember that the Atlantic Ocean was the roughest you can imagine – we never had good weather – and practically everybody on our ship got sick. We were on perpetual clean-up duty to clean up where everybody had thrown up all over the ship. It was enough to make you get sick. The ship was rocking one day as I was trying to mop up, and I felt like I was going to get sick. They had us crowded in the ship four bunks high, with just enough space to slide in. I bet the bunks couldn't have been more than two and a half feet apart at the most. You couldn't sit up; you just would slide in. I was lucky I was on the second bunk high, so it was easy to get in. I would just get in and hope that I wouldn't get sick. We didn't have much appetite either. Of course, not all of the division was on that ship – it just wasn't that big of a ship. We could look out and see a huge convoy of ships, which was trying to protect us because they were afraid of submarines trying to sink us.

We bivouacked in a little French town, and I still have some old postcards of it. We got off the ship, and those duffle bags were the heaviest things. They had in them everything we had in the world. So we had to put them over our shoulder, go down the ramp, and get off the ship. We were struggling, but we got there. They took us to several locations while we were bivouacking, and we were just in pup tents, literally. I remember one day, when we were waiting to go to the front, they took us to one of the beaches and showed us where one of the landings had taken place – I think it was Utah Beach. We were all amazed, of course. Omaha Beach was way up above, and that is where the Germans killed so many of our soldiers. Omaha was the worst – I think they told us that, of the two hundred eighty-something Rangers who had to climb up there, only about eighty made it to the top. The Germans were just right up at the top shooting down on us. It was terrible. But we missed all that, thank goodness.

So we bivouacked near Paris, and about four days later, we had our first action with the Germans at the front lines. I had a good friend – we were all so fond of him – in my company, and a rumor got around that he had been shot. We just couldn't get over that; it was the first casualty that we knew of. As we went through the woods, we passed him lying there – he was facing us, just lying there – and you couldn't see any blood or anything. He was lying in his winter overcoat, with his steel helmet and his rifle. We stopped for about three minutes, and our lieutenant, Lt. David Cook, went over and pulled out his bayonet, stuck it in his rifle, and stuck it in the ground – this was the procedure you were supposed to do. And then he took his steel helmet off and put it on top of the rifle, so the medics could come and take his body to the rear and make sure it was taken care of. That was a pretty emotional experience for all of us as we stood there and watched. I remember the boy so well, and I thought it was just awful; he was just nineteen years old.

I remember we were told that we were the first division through the Siegfried Line. There may have been other divisions that claimed it, but I just know we went through the Siegfried Line in a little town in Germany called Borg. I'd seen newsreels at the Tennessee Theatre several years earlier, as a young teenager, of the Siegfried Line, with all these dragons' teeth and pillboxes, never thinking that I'd be there. Then, all of a sudden, I was right in the middle, and mortar shells were coming in on top of us, so I ran to jump into a foxhole. I looked down, and there was a German soldier lying there with his guts all blown out. It was an awful sight. I quickly did a push-up and rolled over the ground, or I would have gone in right on top of him. So I crawled with my M1 rifle about ten feet away, and I found another foxhole that was empty and got in it. Within a few hours, we had gone all the way through and pushed the Germans back, and we had used one of the pillboxes as our company headquarters for the night. We kept guard duty for that night, and it was pitch black. I remember there was no moon, no stars, and we were relieved of guard duty every four hours. It was so dark that I couldn't see where to go back to the pillbox. I thought that if I went the wrong way, I may go towards the Germans. I went very slowly, found the pillbox, and got in there. So that was my first experience in the Siegfried Line, and it was just like I had seen in the movies. That was November 22.

In between these actions, they would occasionally pull you back a little to a rest area to clean up, clean your weapons, and if you were lucky, maybe get a shower. In December, of course, we didn't know that the Germans were advancing to the Battle of the Bulge – we'd never heard of it. We were just Combat Command B of the 10th Armored Division, and my battalion was sent to Belgium. We arrived at dusk on December 18 in a little town in Belgium. As luck would have it, my half-track was stopped right at an intersection. Lt. Cook told me to get up on the back seat and see if I could read the sign. I got up, looked, and said, "Lieutenant, it says 'B-a-s-t-o-g-n-e. I guess that spells Bastogne." He said, "Yes, I guess it does." And we both agreed that we had never heard of it – of course, we did later.

We heard gunfire in the middle of the night, and we were just in bedrolls on the ground. So they moved us early in the morning of the nineteenth to the west of Bastogne. We went to a tiny place called Sans Souci, which means "without care" in French. It's about two miles outside the city of Bastogne. When we got there, we were up on a hillside, and there was a huge, open pasture area before you saw any farms, about three or four hundred yards away, and the Germans were supposed to be over there. They would shoot mortar shells up in the woods where we were, and we thought, "Oh boy, we'll just stay in the woods where we will be protected from the elements." They said, "No, mortar shells could cause shrapnel to come down and kill you from the tree tops. They will explode above you. You have to go out into the field there and dig foxholes." They put two of us to a foxhole. Someone later asked me, "Where did you stay during your time in Bastogne? Where did you live?" I said, "In a foxhole!" It was pretty deep; I would say it was at least three and a half to four feet high, because when you looked out, you could put your elbows on the top of it. There was a little building, like a hut, down the bottom of the hill, and the company headquarters had set up a little post inside. I think that's one place where they made some hot coffee on occasion, and we could go down there and get a little hot coffee. But mostly we just had to use C-rations or K-rations. We didn't have any hot food.

On December 22, it began to snow early in the morning, and it was very cloudy. The bad weather is why our air force couldn't send any planes over to attack the German positions. It was on that same day, December 22, that the Germans demanded that we surrender. Well, the word got around that Gen. McAuliffe had said to that, "Nuts." He was in charge of the 101st Airborne. He was in charge of our 10th Armored, too, because our general wasn't there – he was with Combat Command A and the Combat Command Reserve in another area near Luxemburg. Just Combat Command B, a third of our battalion, was at Bastogne. So I guess we had about three thousand men or so. All you hear about is the 101st Airborne, and nobody every mentions the 10th Armored, but later Gen. McAuliffe said – I saw it on the History Channel – "If it had not been for the 10th Armored Division, Combat Command B, the 101st Airborne Division couldn't have held Bastogne because they were rushed in there without any winter clothing and without enough ammunition." But we had winter clothes and tanks and field artillery, and we could hold the Germans off, so I think we made the big difference.

Amazingly, on December 23, the skies cleared, the sun came out, and I heard a distant roar in the sky. I looked way off, and from one side of the horizon to the other, here came this huge air armada of planes. I said, "I hope to goodness those are our planes," and they were coming from the right direction. As they got right overhead – they couldn't have been more than one thousand feet above us – they began to drop parachutes with all kinds of supplies – ammunition, medical supplies and some food. We were getting low on ammunition, field artillery and tanks, and pfcs like me didn't have much left in the way of bullets. Well, Bill Dickey was in one of those planes that dropped us supplies. I still have a little piece of a red parachute. We sure were glad when we looked up and saw those planes with the white stars on the bottom of the wing; we knew they were ours, and we were awfully glad. I think that was the beginning of the end for the Germans.

Christmas Day came, and *The Stars and Stripes* said every soldier would have a turkey dinner. Here we were in foxholes, in the snow, and it was as cold as it could be. But Christmas Day was a pretty day just like the twenty-third was, and at about noon, they took one company at a time in our half-tracks back into Bastogne, got into a house, and we were served cold turkey sandwiches — but they were good. When we were done, they put us back into half-tracks, and we went back out to our foxholes.

I think it was the next day, December 26, when the word got around that the 4th Armored Division, under Patton, had broken through the German encirclement and lifted the siege at Bastogne. So by then the Germans had begun to move backwards and retreat.

Then they moved us to the other side of Bastogne, toward the east, where the Germans were moving backwards. We had heavy snow still, and we found a lot of foxholes as we went – some were big holes that were covered with logs. We thought they were better than what we had, and we were about to go in when we looked in, and there was a German soldier sitting in it just as dead as he could be. So we did not go into that foxhole. I think the only time at Bastogne that any of us had seen any German soldiers was in the distance in the snow, maybe four hundred yards or so up on the hill, running away. I think that's the only time anyone in my company shot at them because we really hadn't seen them.

One time, tanks were going toward the woods where the Germans were. It was a long distance, so about three of us hopped on the side of the tank and rode on it all the way across the pasture into the woods because it saved us from walking. When I did it, I thought I would never be on the side of a tank in this kind of situation.

They needed a runner from each company to the battalion headquarters, so while we were at Bastogne, they had me be the runner for Company B, and I guess there was someone there from Company A and Company C. So there were three of us, and here we were in the woods with Col. O'Hara and this real pompous Capt. Wilson, who just loved to look important and be important. So, whenever we would have a parade to be reviewed by the general at Camp Gordon, we would have a dress rehearsal the day before, and Capt. Wilson would stand in for the general and take all the salutes. We all just laughed and thought, "Isn't he a pompous somebody?"

Attached to the battalion headquarters, here Capt. Wilson was with Col. O'Hara and the three of us pfcs, and a German 88 tank began to shell us from close by. An 88 had a crack to it like no other shot you ever heard. It scared the daylights out of you because it was the German's most powerful weapon. It could outshoot our tanks. We immediately jumped down to the ground and began to dig, and I'll never forget that Capt. Wilson turned to one of the other pfcs and said, "Dig me a hole." Can you imagine that? We all, with out mouths open, thought, "How could he?" And Col. O'Hara, bless his heart, was digging a hole, and he said, "Capt. Wilson, you'll have to dig your own hole." From then on, we thought Col. O'Hara was wonderful. I've never forgotten that. I've often wondered what ever happened to Capt. Wilson. He sure was a pompous one, and I bet he was the same way as a civilian.

We were in Bastogne almost a month. It was January 17 when, finally, we were allowed to leave. Patton didn't want us to go; he wanted us to stay up there and keep pushing the Germans back. But the colonel who was in charge of us figured out a way to get us pulled back. The word came out on maybe the sixteenth that the way he was going to get us back was that we should all gradually leave our foxholes, walk into Bastogne, turn ourselves in at this building, report to the medics, and say that we had frozen feet. Some may have, but I didn't. So I thought this seemed wrong to just go back in there.

I looked around at about four in the afternoon when the sun was setting, and just about everybody in my company had walked back into Bastogne. And I thought, "I don't want to be the only one left here." So I got my M1 rifle and trudged back up the snowy roads, which took me about thirty minutes. I walked down the main street of Bastogne, found the building, walked in the basement level, and there was all my company. The medic said, "What is wrong with you, Private?" I said, "Frozen feet." I think I held my face down and thought, "This is not true." He told me to take off the boots and socks, and then he looked and told me to put them back on. Later on, we had something to eat that night and slept in bedrolls right there on the floor of this building. The next morning, they said, "Mount up." So we got in our half-tracks, and the tanks got up in the front, and we rolled out of Bastogne. We went back to the rest area in a small town near there. We were awfully glad to get back.

We arrived in a little town. I remember we were on an autobahn – those autobahns were wonderful things, but you could only go so as fast as the tanks could go, which were in front of us. The half-tracks could go pretty fast, about fifty miles per hour.

One time we stopped and there was a big bank on the right side. They had us all dismount, get out of the half-tracks, and go up into the woods to be sure that the enemy didn't come and shoot down on our vehicles and tanks. So we were in the woods, and I could hear some people – German soldiers, I guess, but we never knew – creeping towards us in the woods. We could hear leaves rustling, and I thought, "What are we going to do? Are we going to have bodily contact with them right here in the woods?" When I was really getting nervous about it and they were really getting closer, all of a sudden the order came: "Mount up." And we came down the hill, jumped back on our half-tracks, and moved out. I was awfully glad to leave because I can't imagine who it would have been except Germans. They were probably creeping up to see what we were doing and what was down there. But they could have easily come, and when they are coming towards you in the woods, you can't see them until they are right on top of you.

We took Mannheim, and we were there a couple of days. Many years later, I took a tour of Europe and stayed at a hotel in Mannheim, and I got out and walked around a little after dinner. I found this great big, high, round monument that probably went back to World War I, and I remembered passing that in my half-track in 1945. We also took Heidelberg, and then we were sent into Bavaria, which is where the 10th Armored Division's last actions of the war took place.

We advanced down into Bavaria and ended up on April 30 in Garmisch-Partenkirchen, absolutely one of the most beautiful places that you can imagine in Bavaria – right at the foot of the Alps, which are the tallest mountains in Germany. The Alps are unlike the Smokies; they are, of course, a lot taller, but they rise abruptly from the valley floor straight up.

The Germans surrendered, of course, on May 8, and we had a victory parade in Garmish. I remember when we came into Paris, we came down one of the main arteries toward the Arc de Triomphe, and we could see it. The five flags of the Allies were flying under the arch.

The French were awfully nice to us, and we got to go see some of the sights in Paris. We were there four days. I took a Kodak picture of the Arc de Triomphe. At the time, I was in the Headquarters Squad, Company B, of the 54th Armored Infantry Battalion. When you were in the Headquarters Squad, you were in the front half-track, and there was a .50-caliber machine gun mounted behind the front seat. The lieutenant sat up there with the sergeant and the driver of the half-track, and I thought that would make a good picture – it showed the big .50 mm gun and the scene down the street.

When we heard they surrendered, we couldn't believe it. Actually, I think we kind of knew – we heard that Hitler had died, but it took forever to be sure of where and how. Later, we found out. Then the Germans surrendered, and it was just amazing. This was the first time we came face to face with German soldiers. We saw an awful lot of them at the end of the war, and, boy, they were very young and very down-trodden, with hands up and faces down. We saw thousands of them being taken back to prisons and stockades. At the time, we seemed to forget about the fact that there was still something going on in the Pacific. We felt that it was over, at least here. Nobody else was going to get killed. And we couldn't have landed in a better, more beautiful place because there were so many beautiful, scenic places to visit.

We were in Garmish from the last of April until we were ready to come back to the States. We still had guard duty there, but we were able to stay in buildings. They put two guards in each place, and we had to guard it and make sure nobody got back in and did anything. We'd go through it, and I'd have to go back through and walk all the way through all the plants. They had all these drawing boards of designs, and it was interesting. To think this was where they were designing some of those weapons that they fired off at England.

While we were in Garmish, there was a wonderful big hotel atop Mount Zugspitze on the back slope. There was a cable car that went into the hotel, and another took you right up to the tippy-top of the mountain, where there was a steel rail to hang onto, and you could look straight down into the valley and see Garmish ten thousand feet below. You could walk along the top of the mountain to the Austrian line. The border was right there. There were Austrian guards, and they would let you through to see the rest of the observatory that was on the other end of the mountain. You could walk back again and take the cable car down. They claim that you could see seven countries from there. It was a wonderful view, and we did that a couple of times.

Then we got the word that a lot of us were being sent back to the States. So they put us on a train in Garmish and sent us to Le Havre in France. They had named all of these camps at Le Havre where you stayed after cigarettes, and I was at Camp Philip Morris. There was a Camp Lucky Strike and I guess others. This was where they put all the soldiers on their way back to the States. You'd be there maybe three days waiting for your ship to come.

We got passes and went down into Le Havre. They had a little playground with swings, and we could get some ice cream. People were very nice to us – they were so glad to be liberated. The French were always very nice to us everywhere we went. Even the Germans in Garmish were pleasant. Every night or so, they'd have a movie in a tent – first-run movies. The movies were sent to the Army sometimes sooner than they were shown in this country. I can remember seeing the brand new movie "Laura," with Gene Tierney and Dana Andrews, and we also saw "Rhapsody in Blue," the story of George Gershwin. Those movies have been on television a lot lately, but I always think, "I saw those two movies at Camp Philip Morris in a tent."

We finally left about August 2 or 3. Coming back, we were on the *Santa Rosa*, which had been a luxury liner. It was a big ship and very nice – much nicer than what we went over on. They gave us a stateroom with about four of us in each, so it wasn't too crowded. It was just double-deck bunks in those. The weather was good, and I imagine we got back in less time than it took to go over there, about nine or ten days.

We had the Glenn Miller Band onboard – Ray McKinley had taken over the band when Glenn Miller died in the war. Every afternoon at about five-thirty, the band would play for about an hour for us on the top deck, and then we would get in the mess line, have our supper, and then you could go back and listen some more. They played for us every afternoon, and it was wonderful.

We arrived in New York on August 12. We'd been gone almost a year. It was right after the atomic bombs had been dropped on Hiroshima and Nagasaki, and we heard about the atom bombs onboard ship. The word came out that they had dropped them, and we felt that this might bring an end to the war. So, of course, they took us back immediately by train to Camp Shanks, where we had been before we went overseas, but they didn't let us go into New York that night. I would have loved to have gone in, but they weren't going to take the chance that you might not get back. They wanted to get us right back to Fort McPherson, Georgia, so we could be deactivated and given a leave.

The next morning we went by train to Fort McPherson, which is near Atlanta. We got there on the 13, and on the 14, I remember I was in my barracks when I heard a lot of GIs yelling and whooping it up. I said, "What's happening?" And they said, "The Japanese have surrendered."

I called home, and I was going to go home the very next day. I got my thirty-day leave. As I went up there, there was a man from one of the Atlanta radio stations interviewing people. He grabbed hold of me, and I just told him how I had heard it and how I was excited to know that the whole war was over. He asked where I was from, and I told him I was going home tomorrow for a thirty-day leave. It just happened that a good friend of my uncle was listening to the radio, and he told my uncle that he heard me being interviewed. I got to Knoxville on August 15.

You know, they discharged you from the Army by the point system. They gave you five points for this and five points for that. You got points for whatever combat ribbons you had been given in your division. I'll be honest, I really don't remember the names of some of the ribbons – we got a lot of ribbons. There was a combat command infantry badge, and all of us in combat got one of those; I still have that. And you got an ETO ribbon, which was for the European Theater of Operations. My whole division got three Battle Stars – one for going through the Siegfried Line, one for Bastogne, and one for Bavaria. Each one of those had five points or so, and I think you got some points for good conduct. You know, we had these little ribbons, and I don't even know what they were anymore; I just have them in a box.

The government could have saved a lot of money when the war was over if they just processed my papers while I was at Fort McPherson and said, "All right, you're discharged. Go home." They didn't need me. But, they had to use the point system, and so they sent me to Camp Shelby, Mississippi, for two weeks, and then they sent me to Fort Missoula, Montana. I was there for three months – October, November and December. It was a disciplinary barracks for wayward GIs that had gone AWOL or done something bad, so we were sort of on guard duty.

Because I had high school chemistry, they put me in Fort Missoula's pharmacy, helping a really nice sergeant there. He made me a corporal because I had done a good job for him. I think it's funny that I got promoted after coming back from overseas. See, when you went overseas, you were a private, but the minute you got there, everybody was made a pfc. That gave you a little more pay, probably about $5 a month or so. I don't even remember what we got paid, but it wasn't much.

I got the word that I could be discharged the first of January, so I headed back home, spent some time there, and then I went back to Fort McPherson and got my final discharge papers and came back for good. Some people say they still have their uniform. I guess I came home in a winter uniform since it was winter. I hung it up in a closet, and moths got into it and ate a lot of holes in it, so I threw it out.

So I don't have an old uniform, but I did keep the stuff that was sewn on it. I have my 10th Armored Division patch that we wore, and we had a little bar for each six months that we were overseas. I had two little bars and all the little ribbons

– I don't remember what they mean, but I guess I knew at the time.

I was so glad to get out. When I came home – you know, it's funny – nobody in my family ever asked me to tell them what we went through, what we experienced, what we saw. We really were so glad to be home that we really didn't care to talk about it. I guess, on rare occasion, my cousin, Fred, told me a little bit and must have asked me a few things. But my mother, father and grandfather never asked – and I never discussed it. I guess they were so glad to have me back that we just never talked about it. If we did, I don't remember.

When I was overseas, we got mail all the time from home, and I wrote whenever I could. But you could never tell where you were located in the war. When we were in Bastogne, we couldn't say we were in Bastogne. But, when the encirclement had been relieved by the 4th Armored and the German lines had been broken and we knew we weren't going to be taken prisoner or anything, the general in charge sent a mimeograph bulletin and congratulated all of us for our activities in Bastogne. He was congratulating us on the fact that we didn't let the Germans take Bastogne. They did allow us to send that bulletin back home. So, in my letter that I sent, I said, "We are not allowed to tell you where we are or where we have been, but this bulletin may explain it." By then, it was all right.

While I was there, I started many letters and never got to finish them. Sometimes you were called out to do something, and you couldn't mail the letter. But we got mail all of the time; we got mail call, and I took the Knoxville papers. We were driving in Germany at the time, and everybody in my half-track was reading a *Knoxville News-Sentinel*. I thought that would be a good ad for the *Sentinel* if they could ever get a picture of us – steel helmets, uniforms and rifles, and here we all were reading the *Sentinel* as we rode along on a German road.

Nobody with me was from this area; they were from all over. There was a fellow, a really close friend of mine, from Danville, Illinois, and we had been in basic training together.

His name began with an "A" and mine with a "B," so we were in the same barracks, and we went to the 10th Armored together and overseas together, but I haven't seen him since I left the Army. We stayed in touch by mail, and I called him once on the phone. To this day, I would love to know what happened to him because I have tried to find him, but he didn't go back to his hometown. He could easily have found me because I have never left Knoxville. I often wonder if he is still alive or what happened to him. In basic training, they were from everywhere – Pennsylvania, Michigan, Brooklyn, all over. It was a really interesting experience. You know, I never saw my lieutenant that I liked so much after the Battle of the Bulge; I often wonder what happened to him. And I never saw our captain again that we liked so much from Kentucky. I don't remember seeing him after we went overseas, and I often wondered what happened to him – because in Bastogne, we had another captain.

I think being in the service matured us a lot – we grew up in a hurry. Most of us went in at eighteen years old, and I was a very young eighteen. Basic training really made you grow up in a hurry. At Camp Gordon, they had us go on these forced marches. We'd go a lot of times at night and get back at four or five in the morning, and I'd see many of the soldiers dragging. I learned quickly to get up at the front of the line on one side, and if you kept your pace up and stayed at the front, it's a lot easier to get through it, and when it ended, you'd get back to the barracks first. I had long legs, so I could walk pretty fast.

After I got home, it wasn't very hard to readjust. We sat around sometimes and were worried. And it had been so long, and you heard all kinds of bad language – you must have heard all the bad words constantly. We thought it would be so embarrassing if we came out with a bad word in front of our family. But, you know, the minute you got home, you just reverted right back to where you were before. I know we used to laugh about it, but it didn't happen. We just acclimated right away.

Of course, as soon as the next quarter began at UT, I enrolled in school. I couldn't get in until March, but I did and graduated in 1950. I have a BA degree in political science, with a minor in history. I never went back into the Army, and I was not about to – I had my fill. I stayed right here in Knoxville – I grew up in this church. I was in the retail business for years with our store on Gay Street. It was a family business, a home furnishings store called Woodruff's. It was founded by my great-grandfather in 1865. I just wanted to stay in Knoxville. Before the war came along, I'd always wanted to go to Washington and Lee University, but after being away so long, I just wanted to go back to UT. I was in a fraternity at UT, and I'm afraid we had an awfully good time. Those were simpler times – there wasn't a lot of drinking, no drugs, and most of us were veterans at the time.

The 10th Armored had a reunion here in Knoxville, and I went. A lot of them go every year, and they knew each other. But they didn't know me, and I felt like the odd man out. Someone asked me, "When did you join the 10th Armored?" I said, "I joined it in January of '44. I went overseas with them." Well, a lot of these guys had come over as replacements in December, January or February, so they didn't go over with the division. At the end of the war, I was the only one in my squad still left. I don't remember anyone in my squad getting killed, but one by one, they just kind of vanished from the scene. We had new replacements, who would have been one year younger than me because in '45, they were eighteen and I was nineteen. It's been so long, but you wonder what happened to them all. If somebody had been killed, we would have heard. I guess some were transferred here and there.

I remember one time, the Germans were way up ahead, and they had us down on our elbows – you cradled your M1 rifle in your elbows and crawled with your elbows. We had a replacement who joined us named Walters from Brooklyn, and we were going forward toward the woods. We were all abreast, and then I looked, and he was getting farther and farther behind. He was doing his elbows backwards – he was going backwards instead of forward. He didn't want to go up there. Shortly thereafter, we all knew he turned into a coward, and they transferred him. He was no longer with us. I thought that was so funny – he was going backwards. Good thing Patton didn't come along; he might have slapped him.

Someone asked me if I had ever seen Patton, and I said, "No, but I was scared to death he might drive by in a Jeep in Bastogne and I would fail to salute him because you were always so preoccupied." I never did see him.

Gen. McAuliffe did come and review the 10th Armored Division at the end of the war. He thought a lot of the 10th Armored. It was referred to as the "Ghost Division" because they would throw it into the line, and the Germans never did know where we were going to show up. The official name for the 10th Armored was the "Tiger Division." We had a good sergeant – the platoon sergeant, Sgt. Yost – who was a nice fellow.

I later found something among my papers, and it's signed "A. Hitler." We found it in a German home. I guess it's valuable; I don't know what to do with it, but I've got it. I also have an old swastika banner that members of my platoon signed.

I went back later, in the '60s. Well, you wouldn't have known that there had ever been a war there. Well, actually, Garmish wasn't really damaged at all. By the time we got there, there was little resistance, and the Germans surrendered shortly thereafter.

The vacation areas in Bavaria were pretty much spared. It was really interesting to be back where I was for almost three months. It still was a beautiful place, but it had grown a lot. Big buildings had sprung up, and it was a little hard to find some places that I remembered. In Garmish, the building across the street from where we were was still there, but the factory I remembered was long gone. They had widened the streets, and I couldn't find the building where we had been. I went in the general direction, but, of course, it had been a long time. From

'45 to '68 – that's twenty-three years – and a lot could have happened, but I did find a lot of familiar places.

Chapter three
John Bolinger

John C. Bolinger, Jr., was born in Knoxville, Tennessee, on February 12, 1922. He received his commission as a second lieutenant on January 21, 1944 and was assigned to the 26th Division. He later attained the rank of captain. During World War II, he participated in four battle campaigns and earned a Purple Heart, a Bronze Star, and a French Croix de Guerre. He graduated from The University of Tennessee with a bachelor's degree in finance in 1943 and from Harvard Business School with an MBA in 1947. He married his wife, Helen, on January 26, 1944, and had three children. He is an elder at First Presbyterian Church and had a long and distinguished business career. The following account is taken from a document he compiled entitled "A Glimpse into my Life."

At OCS at Fort Benning, there were 200 in my class. In the adjacent bunk was a person by the name of John Belk (Belk department stores). John was a tall, angular guy who played basketball at Davidson. In the fifteenth week of the seventeen-week school, the powers that be decided we had too many second lieutenants – this was before D-Day – so they decided to bust half of our class. Practically all of us were college ROTC graduates. John Belk was one of the "unfortunate casualties." He got to stay at Fort Benning playing basketball, and then re-enrolled in OCS again and got his commission and never went overseas. I thought what a lucky break I had not been one of the "casualties" – ho ho.

I joined the 26th Division in early February 1944 on Tennessee maneuvers as a section leader in an 81 mm mortar platoon. On one of the first problems, the company commander, a fellow we called "The Bubble" because he had a big red nose, pointed on the map with his gloved finger, saying "Camouflage your Jeeps in that draw." We had had a lot of rain. When I got to the particular place where I was supposed to put the Jeeps, it was a river. So I put the Jeeps on a little, narrow country road, spaced and camouflaged properly. The next time I saw the captain, he asked, "Did you put the Jeeps in that draw?" I said, pointing to a map, "No, captain – that draw was a river. I put them on this little road up here." He looked at me and said, "Lieutenant, you have got to learn right off the bat to obey orders." I knew then that I had a problem with the captain. Incidentally, he was a captain when the division was activated in 1939, which was one of the first divisions that was activated in World War II. He was a gas meter reader in civilian life – nothing against gas meter readers; I have been in the gas business – but it didn't qualify him for leadership as a company commander. He was also a captain when the war ended, so he was a captain when he went in from the National Guard in 1939 and stayed a captain until the war was over, which was a pretty good indication of his ability.

It rained and rained and rained – it was a cold rain – all the time we were on maneuvers. Most of the men were from the Boston, Massachusetts, area. They cussed the state of Tennessee and the weather. I never admitted I was from Tennessee. As a matter of fact, I never could understand why I was assigned to the 26th Yankee Division from Boston. Here I was, a Southerner in a Yankee division, a Reserve officer in a National Guard outfit, and a Protestant in a predominately Catholic outfit.

On Tennessee maneuvers, I didn't have an opportunity to see Helen very much. She rented a room with a bath at a large home across the street from Vanderbilt University on West End Avenue. At that time, there were no commercial buildings across from Vanderbilt University. The weekly problems on the Tennessee maneuvers were over on Friday evening and began on Monday morning. I would generally be able to leave the company sometime Saturday afternoon, hook a ride into Nashville from generally around Carthage, Tennessee, and be with Helen Saturday evening and usually up to noon on Sunday. This was half of the month of February and all of the month of March 1944.

We moved to Fort Jackson in Columbia, South Carolina, around April 1. Helen was fortunate enough to find a small apartment that a couple had built at the rear of their home for one of their kids. Their names were Irene and Pierre Laborde. He was a lawyer. Upstairs in the same large home was another lieutenant and his wife from Mississippi, Frank and Dottie Harrison.

The Labordes insisted, and it didn't take much insisting, that we have Sunday lunch with them. It was always a large, fancy, formal lunch in the dining room. Mr. Laborde had this long, involved blessing, which became sort of a joke between us and the Harrisons. Dottie was sort of a giggly gal, and finally during one of Mr. Laborde's blessings, Dottie started giggling. Promptly and calmly, he said, "Dear Lord, forgive Dottie for laughing at my blessing," and kept right on going.

Although we were only together at Fort Jackson from April until July, it was a lot of fun. I remember very well on Sunday mornings catching a bus, with a paper bag containing our swim gear, to First Presbyterian Church in downtown Columbia, South Carolina, and storing the paper bag behind the door as we entered the church. After church we would catch a bus and go out to the officers club for a swim and lunch. Incidentally, I was not a swimmer, so Helen on these occasions at the officers club actually taught me how to swim.

Another interesting event we engaged in was going to the movies at the Palmetto Theater in downtown Columbia every Sunday night. Before the movie started, Walter Winchell always appeared on the screen. I will never forget his newscast.

I do not know if it was love or macaroni and cheese and bran muffins or a combination of it all, but during that four-month period, I gained about fifteen pounds. Actually, in the one-year period – August '43 (my induction date in the Army) to August '44 (when I went overseas) – I grew a couple of inches and my weight went from one hundred fifty-five to one hundred ninety pounds.

From Fort Jackson we were shipped to a camp near New York City called Camp Shanks. Most of the wives from Fort Jackson followed us, thinking we would have some free time in New York. Helen was included in this group. We actually got on the boat August 23. They wouldn't let us off, though, and here our wives, dates, etc., were only a few blocks away in New York City. For security reasons, they made us stay on the boat. We finally set sail on August 26, 1944, for Europe. It took us seventeen days by zigzagging across. There were a number of ships in our convoy. We were the first convoy to go directly to the mainland of Europe, rather than a stopover in England. My ship was a converted Italian luxury liner called the *SS Saturnia*. It was a gorgeous ship. The dining room was absolutely beautiful, I thought. The staterooms had been converted into upper and lower bunks. I think there were about six second lieutenants to a room.

One interesting thing going over: I was a section leader of a mortar platoon. Another section leader, a Lt. Havard from Louisiana state, went into these antics on how he was going to conduct himself when he first got into the front lines. Mockingly, he picked up the telephone, calling his mother. "Mother, I am here. Mother, I want to come home." Anyway, he actually did this when he got into combat, and they sent him back, relieving him of his duty, because they thought he was crazy.

We landed in Cherbourg in Normandy, and for about two or three weeks, stayed there waiting for our equipment to catch up with us. During this period, we had these afternoon marches of four or five miles around the beaches. Looking up at those fortifications, I could never understand how we ever secured the beaches. This was only a couple of months or so after the landing, so there were still a bunch of landmines around. We had eleven people injured or killed during that two- or three-week period, just from these afternoon marches, stepping on mines.

After the war broke out, the lieutenant came into our classroom in ROTC and stated, "Anyone in the college of business administration can transfer from the infantry to the Quarter Master Corps." And anyone majoring in finance – I was a finance major – could transfer either to the Quarter Master or finance. I was crazy enough and dumb enough to say, "No, I'm staying in the infantry." Well, I finally got there. We relieved the 4th Armored Division in Patton's 3rd Army just east of Nancy, France, in October 1944. The first thought I had after getting into my first foxhole was what in the hell am I doing here, knowing the only way I could get out of this thing was to get hit or get killed.

After nearly a month in a holding position where we would lob over a few shells and they would give us a few in return, Patton's offensive drive, which was stalled during his big summer offensive, was resumed. We jumped off about November 5, and while we were on the offensive, we went about three hundred to four hundred yards a day.

On the first night of the offensive drive, I saw my first dead German. I looked down at him. He was a young, handsome-looking guy – looked just like an American – quite a contrast from the mean-looking Germans we had seen in training films. It was a real shock.

We continued on that first day and holed up in a big barn with holes in the ceiling from artillery shells. The next morning, we went another two hundred to three hundred yards only to find our sister regiment, the 328th, was a victim of a counterattack the evening before. We found all these guys bayoneted and shot in their foxholes. That was a good lesson for me. Even though I instructed my men to do so, I never dug in. I always was under the pretense of checking all the guys and making sure everybody was OK. It seems as though when I moved from one place to another, shells would come in right where I had been. I thought, with fate on my side, I am going to keep up this habit, and I did all through the war. The following day, we made it a few hundred yards farther, and I saw one of the officers in the 2nd Battalion hanging over a barbed-wire fence, and he had a pistol. I took the pistol out of his holster, took the holster off from around his stomach, and wore that with the pistol the rest of the war – for close contacts, just in case. I never used it.

I remember those first few days vividly while we were on the offensive. It is quite different from a holding position or being on the defensive. You are subjected to many more casualties on the offensive. A single machine gun in a pillbox can kill off a company of men before you can circle the pillbox and get the culprit. I remember the third or fourth day, we were down just to our field jackets for some reason and it started to drizzle rain, which turned to snow. We ended up in the woods at nighttime, which I did not like to do. When artillery comes in, you get tree blasts, and it is hard, even when you are dug in, to dodge those blasts because they come straight down. Whereas in an open field, if artillery hits nearby and you are lying flat, the shrapnel goes over you – unless you get a direct hit. In these woods, there was a great big, I guess fifteen- to twenty-foot long, concrete culvert pipe about four to five feet in diameter. Lt. Lewis, the platoon leader, and I got in this concrete culvert and breathed on each other to stay warm. About every thirty minutes, one of us would get up and make all the guys kick trees to keep from getting trench foot. We did the same, of course. We stayed on this offensive, taking yards and hills at most a half-mile a day, until December 10, about thirty-five days. The biggest town we took was Sarre Union.

After we crossed the German border into Germany about December 9 or 10, we were relieved by the 87th Division. This was the division that was at Fort Jackson with us. We went back to Metz for rest, and they immediately lost ground the first day. It was after the Bulge before American troops re-entered German territory.

During this thirty-five-day offensive, I never had my shoes off. We had a lot of casualties, including Lt. Lewis, who got a direct hit the day after we spent the night in the culvert.

During this thirty-five-day period, I took over the platoon and was awarded a Purple Heart, a Bronze Star, and a battlefield promotion to a first lieutenant.

It was wonderful being at Metz. All kinds of rumors were flying around that the war was about over, that we would never be back in combat again. After about a week in Metz, at our morning briefing, we were told that this new German offensive was just a sputtering one and did not amount to anything. But three days later, we were on trucks and Jeeps and many walking en route to the southern flank of the Battle of the Bulge.

It was more than just a sputtering German last-ditch offense. We were one of three divisions assigned to go north and hit the southern flank of the German offensive. The three divisions were the 26th, 80th and 4th Armored.

With snow on the ground, the Germans came up with a new tactic of putting white capes on. This was a real smart move on their part. We couldn't detect them. They blended right in with the snowy terrain, and we lost several guys when we got near the southern edge of the Bulge.

Our sister regiments, the 328th and 104th, were the first to hit the southern flank on December 24, 1944. We were in a so-called reserve, about a mile behind the front lines. There is a big difference being in "reserve" and being on the front line.

Most of the people in the infantry were not front-line troops. For instance, in nine months of combat in Patton's Army, I never saw Patton; I never saw my division commander. I saw my regimental commander three times. Everybody on their staffs were so-called infantry. They were back far enough to avail themselves of typewriters to write up their medals. This is why I never wore my medals. When I see senior officers wearing medals from their shoulder to their stomach, it makes me throw up. I had a few guys in my company who were exposed twenty-four hours a day and never got close enough to a typewriter to get a medal.

In the infantry, officers on the front line received in their weekly ration a fifth of whiskey. You never knew what

brand it was going to be, whether it was going to be gin or
bourbon or whatever, but you received that every week.
Sometimes it was two or three weeks late, but you received two
or three bottles then. I didn't drink when I went overseas.
People thought I was crazy because I always gave my weekly
ration of booze to my sergeants.

Finally, on New Year's Eve, with another officer, John
Mohney, I took my first taste of alcohol. We had just received
our weekly ration. It was a bottle of Gordon's gin, and there
was orange powder in every package on C- and K-rations. So
here we were, knowing that the following day we would be
relieving our sister regiment on the front, a mile ahead. We
opened up all this orange powder and Gordon's gin. We
finished the bottle about midnight. It was a moonlit night with
snow on the ground. It was almost like daylight. We decided to
check the guard of the machine gun platoons. We jumped in a
Jeep, circled around and got lost. Finally we went into this little
village, thinking that was where the machine guns were.
Instead we stared at a big German tank. They were as surprised
as we were. We twisted around the Jeep quickly in the snow
and got out of there. Probably, had we been sober, we wouldn't
be here today.

In the Army Field Manuals, there are several sacred
rules. One is never make your observation post on the highest
peak, highest hill or highest building. Two, never go after and
try to save your falling comrades. There are many other rules,
but I remember those two distinctly. They didn't remember it
in filming *Saving Private Ryan*. Unfortunately, I broke those
two rules myself, and both mistakes ended in disaster.

The first was on November 19, 1944. A couple of
weeks after we started the offensive, we entered the little town
of Lohr, France. We were pinned down by what we knew to be
German 88 artillery fire. We could tell it was the 88s because,
by this time, after being veterans of a couple of months in
combat, you could tell by the sound of the missile coming in,
as it had a distinctive whistle to it. The German 88 was their
most effective piece of artillery. Also, you could tell by the

degree of loudness as it approached how close it was going to be to you. Sometimes when you heard it coming, you didn't hit the ground because you knew it was going to hit too far away from you, say over fifty yards or so. But when it started really squealing, that's when you started biting the ground. At any rate, we were pinned down by these 88s in this village of Lohr. The only high place in town where you could see was this church steeple. I climbed up through the balcony into the attic and up a straight ladder against the wall into the steeple of the church. It was not a pointed steeple – it was a big square, about four or five feet, with great visibility of the battery of German 88s on the edge of town.

Unfortunately, they saw me too. As soon as I started firing – we eventually knocked it out – they got me first. I had taken an artillery observer up with me because I knew my mortars would not fire that far. Mortars only fire, say, effectively, a little less than a mile. They hit the steeple, and we both went tumbling down through the attic into the balcony of the church. He was severely wounded, and I don't know what ever happened to him. I looked down – I had a raincoat, trench coat, field jacket, sweater, shirt and thick underwear – and I saw that the sleeve of my raincoat had been sliced and was lying at my feet. I also had pain in my arm, and I thought, "Oh, my God, I have lost my arm." It turned out to be a superficial wound, but I had a terrible ringing in my head from the concussion. I didn't want to go back to the hospital because I did not want to come back up as a casual officer. I wanted to stay with my unit. I went back to my regimental headquarters and stayed there four or five days until the ringing stopped in my head. I got back to my unit knowing I had hurt my back and my neck, but at age 22, so what?

I remember Thanksgiving night 1944 – I don't think I had ever felt closer to God than that particular night. I was surprised to find recently a copy of a letter I had written Mother and Dad, which did not sound like me at all. I was just amazed that I could feel that deeply.

THANKSGIVING NIGHT
November 23, '44

Dear Mother & Dad:

As I sit here in the quiet by candlelight, I find so much to be thankful for. I know that He has watched over me, and has held me steady in times of despair. May I be worthy forever, that is all I ask.

How wonderful it would be if people were only conscious of how little it takes to be abundantly thankful. This experience has made me deeper and richer. The simple things are truly the significant things in life.

We would all like to be with our loved ones. But our regrets are not perceptible; they are engulfed with hopes and dreams of tomorrow.

Your loving son,
John

The second time I ignored one of the rules of the Field Manuals was during the Battle of the Bulge. The date was January 4, 1945 – the worst day of my life. We were at what we called "screaming meanie" corner. The night before, unbeknown to us, the battalion on our right was driven back by a German counterattack, which exposed my mortars. (Incidentally, Helen and I have revisited "screaming meanie" corner and also Lohr, France. The church steeple had been rebuilt.)

Being exposed, we were confronted with what we later called "screaming meanies." They were artillery shells, say, two pounds in weight. When they came tumbling at you, it was a terrifying sound, like somebody screaming. Thus, the name "screaming meanie." Anyway, a couple of my guys were hit with "screaming meanies," and then I got a call from the OP (observation post). The guns were usually located in a ravine maybe one hundred to two hundred yards back from the observation post. I always made it a point to set up the observation post myself and be familiar with it. From then on, if we were in the same position, the sergeants rotated manning the OP. I got this call at the mortars from Freddie Dinardo, one of my favorite sergeants, saying, "Lieutenant, I have been hit." I immediately left the mortars and ran up the hill to see if I could be of any help – a mistake.

I found him, and the first thing he asked was, "Can you give me a cigarette?" He also said, and I'll never forget, "My hand is cold, and I don't have an arm." I lit a cigarette and gave it to him. I examined him, and he had a big hole in his hip, and his left arm was hanging by the skin. I cut it off with a bayonet. I put him on an Army blanket, and four of us tried to get him down off that hill, each of us holding a corner of that blanket. One guy, Bill Mahle, was hit going down the hill. Snow was up to our knees, sliding down this hill with him. Another guy got hit – I have forgotten his name – and Freddie Dinardo was dead when we got him to the foot of the hill.

So they who wrote the Army Manuals were right – avoid an obvious OP and don't go after a falling comrade.

I must mention Douglas Briggs. He was a pfc in one of the mortar squads. He carried a base plate – that was his job, a base plate mortar carrier. He was a very clever guy. I remember I was supposed to censor all the outgoing mail, and I never did. I thought it was silly. We never knew where we were anyway. But I always read his letters because they were so interesting. He also kept a diary unbeknownst to me or to anybody else because you were not supposed to do this.

After the war was over, he wrote a book, about a hundred pages on ditto paper, that he mailed me – I was working in Philadelphia at the time, and I had a copy made of it. He labeled it "Europe Under a Base Plate." I sent it to all the addresses I had of the company at the time.

"Europe Under a Base Plate" is a masterpiece, as far as I am concerned. It was very helpful to Helen and me as we have retraced on a couple of occasions my day-to-day travels during World War II. Taking his book along with us was most, most helpful.

Towards the end of the Bulge, around January 12-15, 1945, we entered the town of Clervaux, Luxembourg. It was reported that Mrs. Roosevelt's family vacationed in this resort city from time to time. As we were going down the hill going into Clervaux, we were exposed to machine gun and rifle fire coming from the hill on the other side of the town. There was a monastery on my right with a big wall around it. We ducked into the monastery, which had a courtyard and a basement. We got in the basement. It was bitter cold. It was about dark, so we took some furniture and built a fire to try to warm up.

I was awakened about midnight from a battalion headquarters runner who said I was wanted by the battalion commander. The battalion commander said, "Effective immediately, you are the company commander." I asked, "What happened to Kneeland, the captain?" He said he was sent to the States for a thirty-day rest period. I thought this was a joke, as he was a 100 percent goof-off.

My first questions was, "Where are the machine gun platoons?" The battalion commander said, "We don't know." At daylight the next day, I went to the other side of town looking for the machine gun platoons, where I thought they should be. I bumped into one of the machine gun platoon commanders, a Lt. Cossman. He looked at me and said, "What are you doing here?" I said, "I am your new company commander, and I wanted to find out where you were and what you were doing." He said as he started laughing, "This is the first time since I have been in combat that I have seen my company commander on the front line."

I have already mentioned that Helen and I have retraced my World War II footsteps during my nine months of combat. When we got to Clervaux, we visited this monastery. The priest was showing us around and telling us all the fine things about the monastery. He mentioned that both the American and the German troops occupied this monastery during World War II. "Would you believe that either the American troops or German troops destroyed a lot of our valuable furniture?" he said. I replied, "It had to be the Germans."

The only major battle that I recall after the Bulge was the Battle of Fulda, Germany. It lasted about three days and started on April 1, 1945, but it certainly wasn't an April Fool's joke. After that, it was mostly a rat race, a matter of logistics, trying to move troops in a massive way as many miles as you could in a single day.

We divided up into task forces. We had two task forces in our battalion, and I was the head of one of them. We were trying to move as fast as we could.

There were many obstacles at that time trying to move a mass of troops as fast as possible, as far as possible, in the shortest possible time. First there were logjams – people who were either mixed up or so involved with so many vehicles with inadequate roads. It was just impossible to move as fast as you wanted to move. Secondly, the Germans had the tricky habit of reversing road signs. This became a real problem because we didn't believe all the time that the road signs gave you the right directions. Third was the inaccuracy of available maps. We had been used to using contour maps all through the war, which generally extended at most over a four-mile area. It seemed strange that there was a shortage of regular road maps.

One thing I saw in every village you approached were many white flags hanging out the windows. The date was April 23, 1945. We were going down this hill toward a little town, and I noticed there were no white flags, which was extremely unusual. I stopped the convoy and got my machine guns and mortars off the vehicles. I instructed one of the rifle company commanders to form a patrol and search out the town before we entered it. As I was doing all of this, along came a brand-new battalion commander by the name of Maj. Boucher. He was a very impatient kind of guy. He stopped alongside my Jeep and said, "John, for Christ's sake, you are holding up the whole convoy. We need to make another ten miles before nightfall (this was about four o'clock in the afternoon), and you are holding up the whole works." I said, "Major, I don't like the looks of the town. There are no white flags. I don't think we ought to put all these troops in there without investigating." He said, "Ah, come on." He waved his arm and told his driver to go forward. He said, "Follow me." He got to the little bridge entering the town, and he was ambushed. Both his driver and he were killed.

One reason I was so cautious at this stage of the war, I am sure, was I would look around and say, "Gee, I am the only one left here. I sure don't want to get banged up when the war is this close to being over."

There were seventy-five guys in my regiment that were company commanders or platoon leaders ("follow me" guys). At the end of nine months of combat, there were five of us left out of the seventy-five, and all five of us had been hit at least one time. Those are your odds in the infantry, particularly if you are a "follow me" guy. Of course, not all these guys were killed. A lot of them got sick, trench foot, battle fatigue, etc. – but those are your odds in the front-line infantry. Maj. Boucher and his driver were the last fatalities we had in World War II in our outfit.

I might add, and I am not proud of this, after Boucher and his driver were killed, I took my guns back off the Jeeps and I leveled the town. Thereafter, until the end of the war two weeks later, we approached no village that didn't have their white flags waving. Word got around.

About May 1, 1945 (the war was over on May 5), we were approaching Czechoslovakia and were aiming toward Prague. I thought we would surely end the war in Prague; however, they slowed us down and practically stopped us before we got into Czechoslovakia and let the Russians take Prague, much to our disappointment.

Our headquarters were in Pilsen, Czechoslovakia. Our particular unit ended up just inside the borders of Czechoslovakia. Our destination for this last day of the war (we had gotten the word the war was already over) was such that I had to cross a river into Czechoslovakia and then turn back southwest towards the little town of Horna Plana. En route, after entering the inside of the borders of Czechoslovakia, I saw in the distance a bunch of German tanks. I thought, "Oh God, I hope they have gotten the word that the war is over." It was too late to turn around, and here I was at the head of the column. As I got closer, I saw they were all sitting on the steps of buildings. A lot of girlfriends were around, and they were living it up. I thought, "Well, they have gotten the word." As we passed them, we waved at each other, and I was so relieved. I thought that, instead of Boucher, I was going to be the last fatality of the war. Thank God they had gotten the word.

The big deal just after World War II in Europe was the I. and E. Program – Information and Education. A few days after the war ended, I was summoned to regimental headquarters and told I was selected as the regiment I. and E. officer. I was immediately dispatched to Paris to attend the University of Paris to learn how to be an I. and E. officer.

This was my second trip to Paris and much more pleasant than the first one. During the fighting after the Bulge, we were at a place called Sauerlautern fighting the Germans across the street from each other, living in cellars. You can imagine the filth and stench of men living in one place in cellars for several days. We were all filthy.

After the Bulge, every weekend, an officer took back twenty-five enlisted men for a three-day trip to Paris – all in a two-and-a-half-ton truck. It became my turn on this particular Saturday night while we were in Sauerlautern, and I was absolutely filthy, along with all the other guys that were selected.

I was sitting next to the driver in this two-and-a-half-ton truck with twenty-five GIs in the rear, getting into Paris on a Sunday afternoon. As we pulled up in front of the hotel we were supposed to stay in, I got out of the cab of the truck with my helmet in my arms. This smart MP with a sharp uniform came up and said, "Lieutenant, put your headgear on," and I said, "If you want it on bad enough, let's see you put it on." That ended the conversation. On Monday, I went to the PX, cleaned up, and got new clothes, or fresh clothes. The next three days I was there, I walked down the street to the Opera House where Glenn Miller's band was playing. Of course, Glenn Miller was already missing in action – this was in February 1945. He was missing in action December 1944. Ray McKinley was leading the band. Johnny Desmond was his vocalist. It was just beautiful. I went there three straight afternoons, and it was the highlight of my first visit to Paris.

The second time I never really quite understood what they were trying to teach me at the University of Paris. I think it was mostly a deal where this group had been trained by the Pentagon to set this up after World War II in Europe and gave them an opportunity to spend a couple of weeks in Paris. I didn't get much out of the meetings, but I went back, and strangely enough, most of the teachers I found qualified were privates and sergeants – not officers. There were a few. It was mostly high school- and college freshman-type courses. The most popular school we had, though, was led by an officer from Texas A&M. The principal activity at the agri college and one that created the most excitement was watching horses breed. Great fun.

It was August 1945, and the war in Japan was still going on. We were getting ready to go to Japan, and unfortunately, we were not going to be able to stop in the States en route, as many of the outfits in Europe did. We didn't particularly like the idea of going to Japan, of course. Here we won the war in Europe, and now we were going back to get shot at again. One night at dinner, mail call came, and I had a letter from Helen, who was working at Oak Ridge as a chemist. One of the things she said in her letter was, "If what I am working on works, you will never go to Japan." I read this little sentence to a bunch of officers sitting at the dinner table and said, "Look what the civilians are doing," and we all had a big laugh. Sure enough, the next day they dropped the bomb on Hiroshima.

After the war had ended in Japan, we were immediately sent into Austria for occupation. Regimental headquarters was at Steyr, Austria. It was a lovely little town and the headquarters for the Steyrwerks Company, which made the Steyr automobile. We had all of our Jeeps winterized as a result of this. We, or at least our regimental commander, became great friends with the former head of the company. After being so friendly for several weeks, they all of a sudden came in and swooped him up as a Nazi sympathizer.

I stayed on staff level at regimental headquarters − I never went back to a company and was regimental S1, which in the corporate world would be the assistant to the president.

I was assistant, really, to the regimental commander. His name was Robert H. York, a wonderful guy and the best field officer I met during World War II. He was a cross in appearance between Robert Taylor and Clark Gable − a handsome guy. Unfortunately, he had an eye for the women. We were under strict orders, and I was the one ultimately in charge of enforcing the order of non-fraternization. He shacked up with a countess − or she shacked up with him − in his hotel suite, where we all stayed. Other than that, he was just a great leader of men. He was a West Pointer, class of '38. He went overseas as a second lieutenant in Africa, and he commanded a platoon, a company, a battalion, a regiment and a division during the course of the war. He had five Purple Hearts, and although I didn't fight with him, I was told he was an outstanding leader. At any rate, I admired the guy very, very much.

It was a custom to have a dance party every Saturday night. In Steyr, there was a big auditorium and a theater on top of a hill overlooking the town. They would have this party at the auditorium. My office was in charge of arranging for the band, the booze, the food, and all this stuff, but I don't recall going to any of the dances personally. I always went to a movie rather than the dance.

There were about eight or ten of us that got promotions in early December 1945. I was promoted to captain, and we were going to have this big party called a "promotion party." I got the word going around that they were going to get me drunk at this promotion party. Anyway, I went to the party knowing what was happening. They kept pouring me drinks. Col. York was dancing with his countess, and I went up and tapped him to break in. He said, "Bolinger, I now know you are drunk." Anyway, when the party finally ended, everybody was looped, and I had to hold the colonel up by one arm, along with another guy, almost carrying them down the hill. They did themselves in trying to do me in. But it was a wonderful promotion party.

The outfit finally broke up in March 1946, going home. Another captain and myself lacked two points (we went home by the point system). The old man, Robert York, told me and the other fellow who was a personnel officer, "You two guys know your way around. I am not going to cut any orders for you for a new assignment because by the time the paperwork gets done and they shuffle you around, the points will drop to your level. I am going to give both of you a three-week pass to London – a week to get there, a week to get back, and at least a week in London."

This other captain and I took one of the winterized Jeeps with a trailer full of rations and gasoline. We got as far as Paris, and the clutch was slipping badly. We barely could keep the thing going. We pulled into a civilian garage and parked the Jeep. We took the keys and went to this officers hotel in Paris. Lo and behold, the guy behind the counter was an old friend of this captain companion of mine. We gave him the keys to the Jeep and told him where it was. He was, of course, elated. The Jeep had no records. It was a land-leased Jeep to Russia, then captured by the Germans, and then captured by the Americans, so it didn't belong to anybody. He gave us the bridal suite of the hotel. We stayed in Paris a few days and then went by train into Le Havre. Here again, luck was on our side. A guy from Knoxville was the head man at Camp Home Run in Le Havre at the time. He assigned us orders at Le Havre, and then we went on to London and stayed there about a week or ten days. Both of us were in London for the first time. When we returned to Le Havre, sure enough, the points dropped, and we were eligible to go home.

On top of this, they were closing the camp. Here we had been automatic members of the officers club. The membership, of course, was very short-lived since they kept rotating people through there to go home. Anyway, we were the current members when it broke up, and the current members got all the inventory of booze. I had two footlockers. I filled them up with champagne and booze and threw most of my Army clothes away – I didn't need those anymore, anyway. And when I got home, Helen was shocked – I went overseas a teetotaler, had not even had a drop of beer in my life, and I came back smoking like a fiend with two footlockers of booze. She adjusted.

Leading troops in combat with all the horror was a great confidence builder. I was twenty-three years old when the war ended, and I made the following statement openly then and have repeated it many times since: "I don't care what kind of job or jobs I might hold in life; nothing could surpass the responsibility of leading two hundred men in combat." And this statement holds true to this day.

Chapter four
Joe Brownlee

Joe Brownlee was born in Knoxville, Tennessee, on April 12, 1922. He joined the Corps of Engineers in the Army in 1942. He was at Normandy on D-Day and also spent time in Austria. His final rank was second lieutenant, and his time in the war earned him many service medals and the Bronze Star.

I was at the Citadel, which is a military training school, for two years. My junior year, I was supposed to go into advanced ROTC, but I couldn't get into it because I am colorblind. That didn't keep me from going in the service, but it kept me from going in the Air Corps, like I wanted, and flying airplanes. It also kept me from being in the Navy and the Marine Corps. So the spring that I was at the Citadel, I was a sophomore, and they called all the sophomores and juniors into the gymnasium. A Marine Corps officer was there, and his purpose was talking us into leaving the Citadel and transferring into the Marine Corps and going to Paris Island, the Marine Corps training station, which is out there on the coast by the Citadel – it's just on the other side of Charleston. He was trying to talk us into going over there to officers training school and becoming second lieutenants in the Marine Corps. Well, this sounded like a good thing to me, and a bunch of us volunteered – thirty or forty of us. We went down to the front, and they lined us up and pulled a curtain back, where there were a bunch of Marine Corps enlisted men, and they gave us a

Marine Corps physical right there to make sure we didn't get
away while they had us signed up. And for the colorblind part
of it, they had a box with about a hundred pieces of yarn of
different colors, and they'd pick one or two and ask you what
color it is. They picked up a yellow one, and I could see that –
I'm not totally colorblind; I'm just green and brown colorblind.
So I passed the physical, and then I was in the Marine Corps.

Then they instructed us to go back to our barracks, pack
our gear, and be ready to leave at 0600 tomorrow morning,
when they'd pick us up. That was a great day; we were all so
excited that we were going to get in the war. Well, at about
eleven p.m., they called my name out on the public address
system to come over to one of the offices. I went over, and
there was the Marine Corps officer and an Army sergeant in
charge of records at the Citadel who knew I was colorblind. I
walked in, and this captain said, "This sergeant tells me you're
colorblind, mister." I said, "I've been known to be, but I'm not
bad. I got through your color test." And he said that wasn't
good enough, so they got out this book where each page has a
circle on it with a bunch of dots with different colors in it, and
it was designed so that if you are colorblind, you see an "X" or
something, and if you are not, you see an "O," or something
like that. I knew a guy who was in the Army later who got a
hold of one of those books, memorized it, and got into West
Point that way. But there was no way I could pass, so they
canceled me out of the Marine Corps. I found out that of the
group that I volunteered with that day, half of them were dead
in six months. They'd all gone to Guadalcanal in the South
Pacific, and they threw them out on the beach, and they were
slaughtered – several were good friends of mine. So being
colorblind saved my life there and probably some other places
as well. I don't know where I would have been if I hadn't been
colorblind.

So, even though I was a student at the Citadel, the fact
that I wasn't in ROTC made me subject to the draft. So that
summer I just went on into the service. I tried to get into
everything imaginable, but because I was colorblind and I wore

glasses, I couldn't, so I ended up in the Corps of Engineers. I'd taken civil engineering in college and had construction experience, so that was my interest.

We went to Bradley Field, Connecticut, which was just outside of Hartford, in July of 1942. In December of '42, we left there and went to England. In that unit, we built and worked on airports and runways and all kinds of construction connected with the Air Corps. We were in the aviation engineers, which was in the Air Corps, a part of the Army in those days – we didn't have the Air Force until '47 or '48, when it was changed to a separate branch of service. Until then, all you had was the Army and the Navy, and everybody was either in the Army, the Navy, the Naval Air Corps, or the Army Air Corps. All during WWII, that's how it was, and I was in the Army Air Corps as an aviation engineer. Then I got transferred to another engineering regiment, which was bigger.

I was in England for about a year and a half, and they bombed us there, and I was in London quite often, and there was bombings going on continually. They mostly bombed at night. I was in Cambridge for a good while, and then we moved into various other places, and, generally speaking, we never did get bombed in the camps where we were. If you were on leave in London, then there was evidence of it all the time. They had these balloons that were helium inflated and probably about fifty feet long on a cable about five thousand feet in the air, and you could see them all around everywhere. The purpose of them was to get in the way of airplanes flying around. The German bombers would come in at night, and they knew those things were there, and they were scared that they were going to run into one of them all the time. I never heard of one of them running into one, but there were enough of them around, and they tried to stay above them. I was going to London one time and met a fellow who was in the RAF, and we were on the train together. He lived in London and invited me to spend the weekend with him, so I went to his home and stayed with his mother and father. We wound up sleeping in the same bed, and during the night, they dropped one of these blockbusters close to us, and it threw the bed up and threw us out onto the floor. It was dark, with a little light, and I climbed back onto the bed. I remember looking over to the other side, and he said, "That was close, wasn't it?" Then we both went back to sleep. The Brits were used to it.

So I was in England from January 1943 until June of '44, when we went on to the invasion. In this second unit I was in, we formed an Army band – I played in a combo in high school and played at the university, but I didn't play at the Citadel. So we formed this Army band, and I was in that all seven or nine months before we went on the invasion. And when that happened, we packed up all the band instruments. Then they taught us all to be the regimental headquarters guards, and we went into Normandy late in the afternoon on D-Day.

Some went over there at six or six-thirty in the morning, and then we went in about seven or eight that night. At that latitude, it's still light until about ten-thirty at night. So they dumped us out in the surf. We waded ashore and through the dead bodies that died that morning – the tide had come in, and they were floating in the water, of course, as we waded to shore. I had the good fortune recently, on the sixtieth anniversary of D-Day, to have a meeting with four guys and their wives in Pennsylvania who had been in that same position as me. One of them was a short fellow, and when he started down the ramp, I was in the water up to my chin and was hollering at the boat captain to pull in a little closer. He did a little bit, but this guy came down the ramp and said, "I can't even swim." So I said, "It wouldn't do you any good if you could with all the weight you have on you. Just jump on my shoulders and hold on." That added weight helped keep my feet on the ground. So we waded on in, and all of us got out.

The fighting had pretty well moved over the rise, so we weren't in danger as we got out. But, actually, when we went to Omaha Beach, that was the first time I was exposed to any gunfire and anybody shooting at me and me shooting back at anybody. We stayed in Normandy and had a lot of interesting experiences there – and got shelled. We weren't infantry soldiers, so we weren't up at the front with the fighting. But we were right nearby. The actual line between the American soldiers and the German soldiers was not clear, and you never knew exactly where you were. One experience we had I have thought about through the years. I had about decided that I'd made it up, but the first time I got the chance, I asked one of these boys I was with in Pennsylvania if he remembered. See, I remembered that the two of us had found an American Army scout car, which is something like a tank but had rubber tires on it and ran really fast – it was used by the cavalry. Well, one was just sitting on the side of the road, nothing the matter with it. I had seen them, but I had never been in one before. But I got in it, figured out how to start it, and got it running while he got up on the turret. I said, "Let's take a ride," and we started down this little back road and drove along. We had no idea what we were doing or where we were going, which was crazy at the time, but we did it. All of a sudden, we came to a little village. We went in the village and saw a little village square. When I looked over in the village square, there were German soldiers standing around on the sidewalk – we'd gotten behind the line, apparently. Of course, we went around that little village square as fast as we could. Well, as soon as I started talking about it with this boy who was with me in Pennsylvania, he said he remembered it clearly, so apparently it did happen.

We stayed in Normandy until the Battle of St.-Lô, and we had two or three hair-raising experiences. One time, some of our construction equipment got intercepted by some Germans, and they had it surrounded. There were trailers, bulldozers, road graders, and all this heavy construction equipment. The Germans had a machine gun and mortars that they were firing up the road where it was. They asked for volunteers, and I, along with several other volunteers, went up, spent the whole day, and we finally got it out. We were fired upon all day, and we killed a number of German soldiers and finally captured all of them. I forget how many there were, but we were fired on that day. One of our soldiers was killed, and I was awarded a Bronze Star for that day.

When you captured soldiers, you would take them back to the rear and turn them over to people who set up camps and held them. Then they shipped them back to England just as quick as they could and got them out of there. But it might be a day or two before they could ship them back. As far as the ones we brought back that day, we just brought them back to our regiment, and I don't know what happened after that. Somebody else took them from there. But they were glad to surrender; they knew when you had them cornered.

I came back that night, and I remember it wasn't dark. We had foxholes dug, and a friend and I had been in a foxhole together. I just got in that foxhole and died – I was so tired and exhausted because I had been up so long and the tension all day. When I woke up the next morning, he was sitting up on the side of the foxhole cursing me. He said that I slept all night long and that they shelled our position all night long, and the foxhole was full of dirt, covering me, from the shells that had exploded close to us. But I didn't even wake up. So that sort of tells you how tiring it can be under that much tension.

After the Battle of St.-Lô, we left Normandy. We were attached to the 29th Division in Normandy, and we went on out and were attached to the 90th. We helped finish up the fighting and then left; we rode the first train to Paris. Paris had just fallen – it was probably late in July – and this was the first train that had gone over. They had a number of engineers who, starting way on ahead of us, would walk a piece of the track and wait until the train got there, and then the engineer on it would get off and the engineer who was walking would get on, and he'd drive the train across the tracks while the train engineer would just walk across. This was to make sure that the tracks were sound. You can't imagine how slow that was; it took us two or three days to get to Paris, which is probably a two- or three-hour trip at the most.

We went from there down to Marseilles. By then, the war was past Marseilles. We were rebuilding the shipyards there when we reactivated this Army band – we had great fun with that band. We would go around playing at various things like parades, and we would go to hospitals and play for people in there and for parties. We had a dance band, and we even played on the radio; we'd go down to Marseilles once a week at night and played on the radio. Then a colonel, who was the commanding officer of this engineers regiment, sent me to officers candidate school outside of Paris – as I understand it, this was the place where the French army officers were trained, similar to our West Point. But, when I was there, I saw little evidence of that. It was rather stark looking, as far as the barracks. But there I became a second lieutenant in the infantry.

At this point, I went to the 44th Infantry Division, which was in the Third Army sector, which was the southern part of the thrust into Germany. In fact, we went into Austria, which is south of Germany. By the time I got to them, it was probably May, or late April, and the war, for all intents and purposes, was essentially over. But in that section, they were still fighting. I was put in charge of a pioneer and ammunitions platoon. Each battalion in an infantry regiment had a battalion headquarters company, and each headquarters company had a pioneer and ammunitions platoon, and their responsibility was to pick up ammunition daily from the division ammo point and deliver it to the companies. Each time you went back to an ammo point, you got a ration of TNT, which is an explosive in little yellow blocks. You used it for various purposes – blowing up pillboxes and anything else you needed it for – but generally speaking, when the enemy was running, you didn't need it. But the division made you take it whether you wanted it or not, just to try and get rid of it.

When I came to this new platoon, the platoon leader that was there before me had been killed, or at least been injured badly. But we had all this TNT in these blocks; we had two or three six-by-six trucks that we delivered this ammo in, and one of them was full. Then the war ended, and we still had this TNT and other ammunition.

We were in the Bavarian Alps, in the western part of Austria, or the Tyrolean Alps, as they called them, and this was beautiful country – prettiest mountains I have ever seen, with snow and glaciers everywhere. They were more beautiful, I think, than our Rocky Mountains. I went a good way up and set up a rifle and pistol range for all these soldiers when the war was over. See, they didn't have anything to do, and the colonel was trying to keep them busy to keep them from getting into mischief, so that was a good thing. We'd take .45-caliber pistols up there with bushels of ammunition, and we stood there and shot at these targets. We'd have a gun in each hand, like cowboys. We used most of the pistol ammunition that way, but I still had this TNT, and the colonel told me to get rid of it and that I could not bury it.

I thought about this little bridge that had been blown out; it was a concrete bridge across a big creek above this little village where we were staying, and we needed that bridge back in so we could make patrols through that area. Because the war had just ended, we had to patrol that whole area to make sure there wasn't something going on that we'd disapprove of. This bridge was gone, and being in the Alps in June with all the snow melting, the creek that ran under where the bridge had been was flooding – it was so wide and so deep and so swift, and there was nothing to build this bridge out of. Well, this division engineering officer was in talking to our colonel and told him that they had a big engineering division and that they could do a lot of things, but they couldn't build a bridge right there. So I told the colonel that I would go and see if I could figure out a way to make it so we could use it. So, with my platoon sergeant with me, we went up there, and it looked nearly impossible. But right up the creek, just right above us, there was a bluff. This creek came out of a very steep bluff through a gash. So we got up there and looked around, and we found a cave back up that creek, a couple hundred feet back from the bridge. So we decided to pack all this TNT up there in this cave. Our plan was to explode it and blow the side of this mountain down into this creek, which would stop the water, and that way a bridge could be built. We had no idea what we were doing as far as the intensity of that much TNT being exploded at one time. This was before the atomic bomb had been dropped, and we never even heard of an atomic bomb ourselves at that time, but we created the first one I believe. For three days, we packed that stuff up and put it all down in that cave. Finally we got it ready, and a crowd of people had come around to see what was going on – they couldn't understand it, understandably.

Now, we had no idea of the intensity of this. I guess we had three or four tons of TNT down in that cave, way down in the ground. So we thought that we should stand back a safe distance, but we agreed that we didn't really know what a safe distance was. Well, the explosion blew a flame of fire out the end of the cave – this fire shot all the way across the river and set the mountain on fire. Rocks were blowing up in the air, and it blew up right over my head. Naturally, we ran and got out from under it. When, finally, the dust had all settled and we went back, there were rocks everywhere – huge rocks – and we pushed it with a bulldozer into the where the bridge was. Of course, the creek had stopped running then because all this mountain had dropped in there.

Years later, my wife and I were in New Zealand, and at a railroad station, we met this young boy traveling. He said he was from Germany, and I said, "Well, I was in Germany at the end of the war." And he said, "Actually, I am from Austria." I said, "Well, that's actually where I was, in a little town I'm sure you've never heard of." And I told him the name of it, and he said, "That's my hometown!" I said, "Well, there's a river that runs through it, and up that river about four or five miles on the left is a lake." And he said, "Yes, yes! The American Lake!" And I said, "Why do they call it the American Lake?" He said, "I have no idea. But it's a beautiful place, and you oughta go there sometime." I did, later, go up above and see the lake it had created.

We left shortly after that, came back through Germany, and caught a small boat into England. We stayed there two or three days and then caught the *Queen Elizabeth* to the United States. We arrived in New York, went to Fort McPherson in Atlanta, and then I got to go home for the first time since I'd been in the Army. I went in the Army in July of '42, and this was August of '45. I had a thirty-day leave, and while I was home, they dropped the atomic bomb. It was wonderful excitement. I realized, like everybody did as soon as they dropped the first one, that the war was over. The Japanese, of course, couldn't make up their mind what they were going to do – they were horrified. So they dropped the second one less than a week after the first, and that was pretty much it. The war ended. I was at home, and that was wonderful – VJ-Day. I was, of course, in Germany on VE-Day – Victory in Europe – and VJ-Day was Victory in Japan. VE-Day was May of '45, and VJ-Day was August of '45. I went out and celebrated with a good friend here who had been in France at Normandy but was injured and discharged. He was home when I got home, and he was the only person I knew at the time because everybody else was still in the service and hadn't come back. I would have stayed over there, but they were shipping us back quickly so we could go to Japan. People that I'd been in the service with in the Army band didn't come home until January or February of '46. But I came home earlier than I would have because of this division going to Japan. But when the atomic bomb stopped the war, we, fortunately, didn't have to go.

To give you an idea about Oak Ridge, I'm not sure the day that it started, but I think it was in late '42. When I went in the Army, I'd never heard of Oak Ridge – it had never been discussed, and I never heard of it. On the train coming to Fort McPherson in Atlanta in August of '45, just before the atomic bomb was dropped, a soldier came up to me and said, "I understand that you live in Knoxville, Tennessee." I said, "Yes, I live in Knoxville, Tennessee." He said, "We're from Ohio, but my parents have moved near Knoxville to a place called Oak Ridge." And I told him, "Well there's an Oakdale and there's a BlackOak Ridge, but there's no place around Knoxville called Oak Ridge that I'm aware of." He said, "Well, they built a town out there – it's somewhere near Knoxville – called Oak Ridge." I denied it, although at that time, it had already produced the atomic bomb, and they were getting ready to drop it. It was a big town by that time, and I had two younger girl cousins that worked out there. Of course, I got letters back and forth from my mother and my aunts, and they never said a word. I had no idea that Oak Ridge existed. That shows you how careful people were in those days to not say anything contrary to the interest of America and the American people. Today they are not that way. It sounds like half the news media, if not a bunch of the people, are against the country. They want to see things that harm the country instead of help to protect it. But, in those days, no one I knew had heard of Oak Ridge until I got home. Everyone in Knoxville knew about it, but they knew that they were doing something secret and they were not supposed to discuss it. That is something I've thought about a lot because of the different ways that people look at things today and the way they did in those days.

Before I went into the Army, if you met a friend, you didn't ask him if he was going into the service, but what branch of the service he was going into. You assumed that everyone was going in, that there wasn't any dispute about if you were going in. Nobody even considered that they wouldn't. Some people could not get in the service because they had physical problems or something that kept them from being eligible to go into the service – there were a few of them, and they were referred to as F-4s – but they were terribly embarrassed, and we felt sorry for them that they couldn't go in the service and serve the country.

But I finished and got home for good about the fifteenth of November. Adjusting back to civilian life never seemed to be a problem for me. After I got out in November, I didn't do anything until the following January. I just kind of let my hair down and did nothing, and then I went back to the university. I was in school, and I had classes where at least one class met once or twice a week at Ayres Hall. I had an automobile, and

I'd been to school there in 1939. So I drove my car right up to Ayres Hall to find a place to park, and there was a sign there that said "Faculty Only," but I parked anyway. And after the second or third time that happened, there was a ticket on my windshield. Well I ignored that, and a week or so later, it happened again. And I ignored that, too. This is probably because I'd been in the military, and I thought, "Just a year ago, I was on Omaha Beach. Why do I have to worry about where I park my car?" The third time it happened, a campus cop jumped out from behind some bushes and grabbed me. He took me down to the administration building, which was at the main entry down on Cumberland. This was in February, or maybe March, and I, remarkably, had been doing pretty good in school – I hadn't previously, but I was getting good grades then, taking business courses.

So he took me down to the administration building, and, I swear, the dean of students, the dean of men, and the dean of the business school all came in there, sat down, and started cross examining me about where I was parking my car. I just sat there, and then I said, "You mean to tell me that you three men have got nothing better to do running this university than fuss about where some veteran is parking his car? That doesn't seem important to me." Well, they thought it was real important. So I said, "I'll tell you what I'll do. I'll just pack my bags and start my own construction company." They all three followed me out to my car and begged me not to do it, and two or three of my teachers called me up a week or two after that and tried to talk me into coming back, saying, "You've got a 'B' in this course; don't quit now." But that was the end of my formal education. I never graduated from college, although I'd had one year at the university and two years at the Citadel and that short period after the war. And I've been a general contractor since 1947 – that's almost sixty years. My two sons run it now, but I'm there every day. I try to get away early in the afternoon, but I'm there every day, and I help a lot.

Being in the war changed me in every way. There is no way you can compare formal education to being in a war zone where people are being killed and you're subject to killing somebody in the war, and you are having to defend your life while shells are falling all around you and any one could fall on you and obliterate you. And you lived with other men under those circumstances, month after month after month, and year after year. That's the most wonderful education you could get. I can't think of anything that it changed my outlook on, but my war experience educated me tremendously. I learned a whole lot more there than I would have if I'd stayed back home in college.

You know, we were boys. When I was at Omaha Beach, I was twenty-two, and there were some a lot younger than me – nineteen or twenty. The first president Bush was flying a fighter plane in the south Pacific and was shot down when he was twenty years old. There were four or five of them – I recently read a book about them – and all of them were shot down and captured except him. He got far enough away from the island and went into the ocean, and there was a submarine out there waiting for him, and they picked him up. But the others were captured and slaughtered by the Japanese.

There was a bunch of young fellows. I was certainly not one of the youngest by any means. Most were a lot younger than me, but, on the other end, there were a lot twenty-five to forty as well. Living under those circumstances with people in a foreign country was a wonderful experience. It was horrible at times, but you learned, and a man matures quickly under those circumstances. I came back and almost immediately went into the construction business. I had a bunch of people working for me, and all of them had been in the service like I had. I had been managing while I was in the service – I was a sergeant until I went to OCS and became a second lieutenant – so I knew how to handle people and take care of them. But when I went in the service, I certainly didn't have those skills. Learning all those things was a great benefit to me, and I think most all of us benefited from the time we spent in the service.

The only bad thing that happened, I thought, is they gave us cigarettes at every opportunity. The K-rations had a

pack of cigarettes, and we were encouraged to smoke –
practically everybody smoked. I never got the habit myself; I
had a smoke, of course, but I never got the habit. Everybody
smoked, and so many of them became committed to it to the
point that they couldn't stop until later on in life. I have a
bunch of friends that smoked regularly for forty years. And the
Army really cemented that habit. Everybody smoked during
the '30s and '40s, and I guess they just thought, with a guy
under strain and pressure, that you needed a cigarette. I
remember when we'd capture these German prisoners, the first
thing they did when things calmed down is ask for a cigarette.
That was just standard procedure. When a guy got wounded or
shot, the first thing you did was give him a cigarette, and he
would lay there bleeding to death, smoking a cigarette. It's
strange to me; I don't understand it – not that I had anything
particularly against it at the time. I just had no interest in it. I
would occasionally smoke half a pack for some reason and
then not smoke again for a week or two.

My generation is called the "Greatest Generation," and,
well, there were twelve or thirteen million of us who were in
the service during that time. That's a lot of people who matured
quickly and then came back with the GI Bill, which helped
them get educated. I didn't take advantage of it, but most of my
friends finished college and became lawyers or doctors or
whatever. If they hadn't had that opportunity and if there
wasn't a war, our country wouldn't be what it is today. It
helped a lot of people become leaders of this country.

Chapter five
Fred Cagle

This chapter is unique because Fred Cagle wasn't alive to tell his story at the time of this project. He left a written account of his World War II experiences, however, and his wife provided further details. But first, below is a summary of his life taken from a memorial service held for him by First Presbyterian Church in Knoxville, Tennessee.

"Resolution of the session of First Presbyterian Church of Knoxville memorializing Fred H. Cagle, Jr."

Whereas, Fred H. Cagle, Jr., fellow elder and friend, died on December 4, 2003, we, the Session of the First Presbyterian Church of Knoxville, desire to express out gratitude to God for the life of Fred Cagle, for the example he set, and for the contribution he made to the life and work of this church, this community, and his family and friends.

Fred Cagle was always a Knoxvillian and always a Presbyterian. He was born on May 4, 1924, and baptized as an infant in Fifth Avenue Presbyterian Church. He grew up in the Park City area and graduated from Knoxville High School in 1942, receiving the highest scholastic award.

Entering The University of Tennessee in the midst of World War II, Fred finished only two quarters before enlisting in the Army Air Corps, where he trained to be a pilot on a B-

17 bomber. After graduation from flight school and before being sent overseas, he was chosen from his class to stay behind and learn to fly the new B-29 bomber. Several months later, he found himself on the island of Guam flying missions over Japan. He loved to tell the story of how his last mission over Japan helped end World War II. His B-29 story is included in an exhibit at the Oak Ridge Museum.

In the fall of 1946, Fred once again entered UT and became active in a number of organizations. As a Brother in Phi Gamma Delta Fraternity, he received the William Kreis Award. Always a thespian, Fred enjoyed his acting career with the UT theater group. Other activities included the Scarabbean Society, Phi Kappa Phi, Who's Who, and president of the Christian Association. As a senior, he was selected to be a Torchbearer.

Immediately after graduation from college and from The University of Tennessee Law School, he was called into the Army Air Force once again and served in the Korean War for another eighteen months. Shortly after returning to Knoxville, Fred became reacquainted with a friend from college days, Jean Johnson. Fred and Jean were married August 28, 1953. In August 2003, they celebrated fifty happy years of marriage with a trip to the mountains with their four children, their children's spouses, and the ten grandchildren. On Sunday, August 30, Fred, Jean, and thirty family members were present for the Sunday morning worship service at our church.

After their wedding at Magnolia Avenue Methodist Church, Jean changed her membership to Fifth Avenue Presbyterian Church. Four children later, the Cagle family joined First Presbyterian Church in 1965. At Fifth Avenue, Fred was a deacon, chairman of the Board of Deacons, and a Sunday School teacher. At First Presbyterian, he became a teacher in the James Park Bible Class as well as teaching the Singles Class. He was ordained an elder and served as Clerk of Session. Always active, he served on numerous committees and was always present for the Men of the Church breakfasts.

Fred was also active in several civic organizations, serving as president of both the Y Men's Club and the Knoxville Executive Club. He served on many committees of the Knoxville Bar Association and the Tennessee Bar Association and was elected president of the Knoxville Bar Association in 1970. He was elected as a fellow in the American college of Trial Lawyers, was a member of the International Association of Defense Attorneys, a Master of the Bench, Emeritus, in the American Inns of Court, and a fellow in the Knoxville Bar Foundation. Fred was a partner in the Frantz, McConnell, and Seymour law firm. He practiced law in Knoxville for more than fifty years.

Shortly before Fred died, the Knoxville Bar Association honored him with their highest award, the Governors' Award. This award is given to a lawyer thought by his peers to be exemplary and an excellent role model. It recognizes service as an attorney as well as service in the community. Fred did not live to know about or accept the award, which was presented posthumously to his family.

Fred served as a role model for us at First Presbyterian Church. We will miss him as life continues in our church, but we still have the example that he set for us as a dedicated Christian, loving husband, father and grandfather, fellow believer, and friend.

Be it resolved: That this resolution be entered in the records of First Presbyterian Church of Knoxville, that it be printed in the church bulletin, and that copies be mailed to his family.

Adopted unanimously by the Session of First Presbyterian Church of Knoxville on this 14th day of March, 2004.

"In the Hands of God"
by Fred H. Cagle, Jr.

During World War II, I was a B-29 pilot flying bombing missions on Japan from an air base on Guam. Our wing had been specifically trained in the use of new radar equipment, which enabled us to drop our bombs at night from an altitude of thirty thousand feet, too high for Japanese night fighters or guns to reach us. However, by the time we commenced our bombing missions in May 1945, Gen. LeMay had decided that we should fly at fifteen thousand feet for better bombing accuracy. Rumors were rampant about B-29s on earlier bombing missions having been shot down. Needless to say, we were all very apprehensive as we headed north toward Japan on our first bombing mission.

We left Guam in the late afternoon, taking off at thirty-second intervals, and arrived over the coast of Japan around midnight. Our radar navigation equipment enabled us to fly over only a short distance of land before reaching our target, which was an oil refinery. All our lights were off, and we were concerned that we might collide with another B-29 headed toward the same target. Earlier B-29s had successfully bombed the oil refinery so that the fires below lighted the sky ahead. Also ahead over the target area, we could see bursts of smoke indicating intense anti-aircraft gunfire, which we called flak. This flak appeared to be at our altitude and to cover the entire area of the fires from the oil refinery. Our course would take our airplane directly over the fires and into the flak. I cannot deny that my prior apprehension definitely turned into fear that will forever be etched in my memory.

This is not a testimonial of an emotional conversion experience or any act or decision on my part. My Presbyterian upbringing had instilled in me a faith in God and a strong belief that God has a plan and purpose for His creation, which includes me. I knew that this faith did not guarantee my safety, but I felt that God would not want my life to end at twenty-one years of age, with so little in accomplishments and so much potential for life.

As we continued on the course toward our target, our B-29 was directed with an automatic pilot system by the radar specialists and our bombardier. I suddenly realized that I would have no control over my life for the next few minutes and that my fate was strictly in the hands of God. I could pray and worry, I could curse the Japanese, or scream in fear, but nothing I could do would change the danger which confronted us. How wonderful it was to feel that God was in control. Even if I might die, His will would be accomplished, and I would have eternal life through His son.

As we neared the target, my thought turned to the Twenty-Third Psalm, and I began to say to myself the familiar words: "The Lord is my Shepherd." Never before had this psalm had so much meaning for me. To realize that God cares for me as a shepherd cares for his sheep, and that He leads, guides, and comforts me in my life's journey, even through the valley of the shadow of death which lay ahead of us, caused my fear to subside. Death was not such a fear if it meant dwelling in the house of the Lord.

I do not know how many minutes passed before we dropped our bombs and could commence evasive maneuvers with our airplane, but it seemed like an eternity. As I am reporting this incident forty-seven years later (at the time of his death, fifty-eight years later), you know that our airplane was not shot down on this occasion or on fifteen subsequent bombing missions. My fear tended to lessen with each succeeding safe mission, but when the flak was heavy, I continued with the Twenty-Third Psalm, mixed in with John 3:16.

I returned to college, became a lawyer, married, raised four children, and have six grandchildren (at the time of his death, ten grandchildren). I am now slowing down toward retirement after forty-two years of law practice (at the time of his death, fifty-three years). God has blessed me in this life. I would like to say that I have always completely put my life in

God's hands as I did on that first bombing mission, but life does not always present us with situations where we have no decisions to make which will affect our lives. God has given us the ability to reason and think, to know right from wrong, to evaluate good and bad, and to decide whom we shall serve – God or the world. It is not always easy or self-serving to put ourselves in the hands of God, and we often choose material things, personal pleasure, worldly recognition, brief happiness, and reliance on our own abilities to care for ourselves. It has frequently been necessary for me to be reminded that all our abilities and possessions come from God, and ultimately we must rely solely on Him.

Just as it calmed my fear on that first bombing mission forty-seven years ago (at the time of his death, fifty-eight years ago), it comforts me to know that our lives are in the hands of God. As Christians believing in the Word of God, we know those hands are caring and loving, that they are faithful and trustworthy, and that they are in complete control of all that may happen in this world and the next. It is for us to decide whether we will trust God and do His will.

All of you who may hear this account of my experience with God must make the same decisions and have the same temptations which have confronted me ... I hope and pray that together we can overcome our self-interest and with faith and trust, place our lives in the hands of God.

The memories of his wife, Jean:

Fred rarely ever talked about or relived his experiences during World War II. It was just as if that part of his life has been placed in a box and stored away. After the war, he was in a hurry to get back home, finish his education, and get on with his life. When our sons were in their early twenties, he could hardly believe he had really been flying an airplane over Japan dropping bombs when he was their age.

Many years later, a war memorial was being built in Washington and books were being written about the "Greatest Generation." The James Park Bible Class made a tape of the veterans in the class sharing their war experiences. The History Channel presented a very realistic program on the B-29 story, and World War II became a popular topic of conversation.

Someone gave Fred a book about the B-29 story that included the details of Japan's surrender. The story goes like this: The Japanese war leaders found out that the emperor was planning to speak over the radio that evening announcing his decision to surrender and end the war. The war leaders did not agree. Even though this was after the devastation of the atomic bombs, they wanted to continue fighting. They decided to take the emperor into protective custody in order to keep him from making the announcement.

Meanwhile, the Army air force had planned a massive air attack using every B-29 available, unless they received word that the Japanese had surrendered. When the planes flew over Tokyo, there was a complete blackout, which kept the war leaders from reaching the emperor to keep him from making the announcement. Therefore, Fred laughingly told the James Park Bible Class that he was on the mission that ended World War II.

He had taken his memories out of the box during a period of his life when he had time to read about and reflect on the war. He enjoyed sharing his memories of a time when our whole nation was patriotic and how we worked together to miraculously win a war for which we were in no way prepared.

Chapter six
Ed Coleman

Edwin T. Coleman was born in Plainview, Texas, on March 14, 1919. He joined the Naval Dental Corps in 1944 and was the dentist on board the *USS Pickaway* in the Pacific Theater. He earned three medals – the World War II medal and two for the American Campaign and the Asiatic Pacific – and one Battle Star for participating in the battle at Iwo Jima.

I went to Baylor Dental College in 1941 and graduated in '43. I had an ensign commission my senior year in dental school, which meant I would be going into the Navy. My first station was Great Lakes Naval Base in Illinois. I went into a dental clinic and served there for about six months. I was a lieutenant JG at that time, my first commission. Then I was assigned to a ship that was being built on Treasure Island in California, so after about six months in the Great Lakes, I was transferred to Treasure Island. While the ship was being completed, I took courses in firefighting, Naval regulations, and all the things a Navy officer would do, even though I was going to be a dentist on the ship.

You know, when I was in high school, I got an appointment to Annapolis. And I went to Dallas, took the tests, and they said, "You can't come into the Navy because you are colorblind." Well, I didn't know I was colorblind – actually, I'm not colorblind, but I am color-defective; I can't see certain shades of red. See, a Naval officer has to read flags, and signal flags are different colors. That's how they communicated without radio or anything else. Back in those days, they would run up a bunch of flags, and that would tell them something. I never did read flags because I didn't have to. But that was the reason you had to read colors. See, a colorblind sailor looking at the flags would only see grays or blacks or whatever, and that would be dangerous. So after I had been on the ship for six months or a year, the captain said, "I see you are not qualified to be in the Navy. How would you like to get out?" I said, "Fine, go ahead." But that didn't amount to anything because I had a waiver. So my colorblindness did not keep me out of the Navy.

On the ship, the *USS Pickaway*, there were three other medical officers. When the ship was commissioned, we set out on shakedown trial runs. Then our first assignment was to sail to Maui, Hawaii. We picked up fifteen hundred Marines and headed for Iwo Jima. We were in the second wave of the Iwo Jima assault, and our duties were to land these fifteen hundred Marines. The ship carried the landing craft similar to what they had in Normandy that we have seen all the pictures of recently. So we carried the landing craft and also large LCMs, which landed tanks. During the wave there, the Marines landed better than in Normandy, where they landed in the water and then were dropped off onto the ground. Our landing craft went in better, but I recall one of the ships there that had done this before, called *the Old Yellow*, which would not go in close enough. Evidently, they had done this on the first assault, and some of the men drowned, just like they did in Normandy. But we got all of ours ashore, and then we took the wounded and brought them back to Guam. All this time I was still a dentist on the ship.

When I first came on the ship, the executive officer had been retired and came back into the service, and our captain was also a retired captain who came back into the service. The first thing he said was, "You will serve a watch four hours on and four hours off." And I said, "No, sir." And he said, "What do you mean? You will serve four hours on and off. That's what you do in the Navy." I said, "No, sir. I'm under the command of the staff officer on the ship, who is the commander of the Medical Department, and I take my orders from him." See, I had had a course in Naval regulations and preparations, so I knew what my duties were, and this guy didn't apparently know. So that started me off just great – I had trouble with the executive officer throughout my whole career on the ship. And some amusing things happened.

Now, I did not wear khakis; I wore grays. They were converting all the uniforms to grays, but they never got it done. The people who had been in the Navy had khakis, so sometimes you could tell the new ones.

Well, when we took those Marines off, we then took the wounded back to Guam. Then we took some more Marines and moved them into other positions. And we went into Pearl Harbor again. Our captain, who was retired, didn't really know exactly what the protocol was, but he went by the book, so he ordered everybody in dress whites. When we sailed into Pearl Harbor and were all at attention, I remember a seagull landed on my cap. Anyhow, the harbor master got on the radio and said, "What are you doing with these men in dress whites?! Don't you know there is a war going on? Get 'em off there; they could be shot so easily all dressed in white!" After that, we were allowed to go ashore at Pearl Harbor, so we all got off with our cameras. And just as soon as we got to the gate, the Marine said, "OK, buddy, hand over your camera." I said, "Why?" And he said, "Well, you are not allowed to photograph anything in Pearl Harbor. This is a war, don't you know? These ships out there have been sunk." So they took about ten cameras away from us. We asked, "What are you going to do with the cameras?" And they said, "If you want them back, you can get your executive officer to sign an order." I thought, "Uh oh! I'm already at odds with him." So I went up to him anyhow and asked if he would please sign this order to get our cameras back. He said, "Huh! I'm not going to do that. You've lost them, and I don't care," or something to that effect. Well, then he went ashore, and the captain went ashore. And the officer of the deck, who was in charge of the ship at that point, was a friend of mine. So I went over and asked if he would sign the order so that we could get the cameras back. He said, "Sure!" So he signed it, and I went over and came back with cameras all over my shoulders. Then I was a hero to all these other corpsmen and sailors because I got their cameras back, including my own. Well, later on, when we were at sea, the captain and another executive officer called me in and said, "I see you got your cameras back." I said, "Yes, sir." He asked who signed the order. He said, "Who allowed you to do that?" And I said, "I can't remember; it just escapes me." So that was another checkmark against me. And that went on throughout my career in the Navy. But they let us take pictures when we were not in a combat zone – but not Honolulu or Pearl Harbor. Other places we went in, like New Zealand and Guam, we could take pictures.

We touched Iwo Jima, and we also went to New Zealand, Guam and, of course, Honolulu. We were in there back and forth, and we stayed at the Royal Hawaiian Hotel. They had Royal Hawaiian beach there, but it wasn't very interesting because there were no women in bathing suits – just men!

During battle time I had a battle station where I treated some of the wounded briefly. And the rest of the time I did dentistry for the ship's crew. We had five hundred on the ship as a crew, and then we had fifteen hundred Marines to accommodate. So I treated them for toothaches, fillings, replacements and so on. I had one sailor who wore a denture, and he wanted to get out of the Navy, so he broke his denture on purpose. He brought it in and said, "I guess, sir, I can't eat now. You will have to sign something so I can get out or be transferred off the ship." To his chagrin, I was able to fix it, so he never did like me very much after that.

One of my collateral duties on the ship was mess cater. The executive officer had all kinds of ideas, even though I was not supposed to do it. Well, after the war, the complaints about the food increased because we didn't have anything else to do, except carry passengers back and forth. One time I served him baked beans – Boston baked beans because he was from Boston – and nobody else got any. So then everybody else complained. "Why don't we get Boston baked beans?" "Why don't we get any beans?" Well, it's just one of those things.

I was issued a .45 revolver as a staff officer. You see, line officers were the executives – the captains and the people who ran the ship. I was a staff officer, which meant that I performed the duties of the staff, and in this case, that was the medical department. But I have one Battle Star for Iwo Jima because my ship participated in the second wave of the landing of Iwo Jima.

During that time, we were under an air attack while we were sitting out there. We went to our general quarters, and everybody got ready. But the planes never did appear because Halsey's fighters shot down one hundred forty-nine out of one hundred fifty of them. So the attack never did actually occur – we were never bombed or shot at. And we were a little bit protected; we had what you would call anti-aircraft guns on the ship. We had a five-inch cannon back on the fantail. I wasn't too concerned about us protecting ourselves because these guys used to practice while we were getting ready to enter the war – and they never could hit anything. They never hit the target at the time, but I shot my .45 several times, and I never could hit anything either. I wasn't supposed to have a .45 pistol, but they gave me one anyway.

One of the other medical officers had to make an inspection of the food – he got extra duties, too, just like I did. So he would go down and sample the ice cream-making machine every day, just to make sure it worked all right. He also had to inspect the chickens that we had on board. He came back and said, "I'm never eating any more chicken on this ship." I asked him why. And he said, "They froze 'em whole; they didn't clean 'em." So he didn't like the idea of what could happen while it was thawing, so he never ate another chicken. I ate it, though. I just figured that if they cooked it long enough, it would be safe.

When we crossed the equator, we had an equator ceremony. Everybody dressed up like King Neptune, and they dunked us in the pond and the tank they created. I took a lot of pictures, and I have a certificate saying that I am a qualified member of the King Neptune.

We went to the Philippines and Manilla. Japan started out conquering the whole Pacific, but we started fighting back and taking it back. But we had no VE-Day and no VJ-Day. The reason we didn't have the VE-Day is because, when we were crossing the international dateline, that day was skipped. So we didn't get to observe VE-Day. And then, again, on VJ-Day, we went across the international dateline and missed it again.

After the war was over, we came back to the U.S., to Portland, then Los Angeles and San Francisco, and then we would take people back or go back and pick up people. We were just a transport after the war was over. Those were my detachment orders. See, you had to collect a number of points before you could get out of the service, and I was still collecting points. So our duties were to carry these passengers into combat and to take off the wounded. We were supposed to go to Okinawa, but by that time, the bomb had been dropped, and we didn't have to go. That saved me from going to Okinawa. Truman was the guy who ordered that, and I was all for it because I might have been killed in Okinawa.

After the war was over, it was no big deal. Now, some of these men were actually shot at. Guys like Jim Talley and Bill Tate are the real heroes. They're the guys who flew the airplanes and were shot down – I mean it was really, really rough for them. I had it easy compared to many of these guys. But then, we could have been bombed and sunk, too, so who knows.

During the war, I wrote V-mail all the time. My family had a big collection of them. My sister saved them all, and I read them when I got back. But, of course, they were all censored. I have three medals, which were routine. I have them for the American Campaign, the Asiatic Pacific, and then the

World War II medal. And I got one Battle Star for being in the battle of Iwo Jima.

I stayed on that ship for three years, and then I got out of the service in '47. After the war, I was still a dentist, so I did dentistry from the time I graduated from dental school in the Navy. The main thing about going back to civilian life was that I had to find a place to practice. I grew up in Plainview, Texas, which was a town of about five thousand. And I wouldn't go back there to live if you paid me. We used to have dust storms, and my mother would get out and water the trees. We had a golf course that didn't have anything but sand – no grass. We didn't have any lakes or rivers or anything, and the whole community depended on crops like cotton and wheat. If we had a drought, everybody suffered. So it was not a good place to live, although there were good people there. My mother and father lived there all their lives almost. So when I went back to Plainview out of the Navy, I didn't know what I was going to do or where I was going to live.

But I had a sister who lived in Knoxville, and I had visited her before. In fact, I went to UT one year, back in 1937, so I was kind of familiar with Knoxville. So I came back when I was getting out of the Navy and visited her. I had on my Navy white uniform, so I looked pretty good. I went to some dances they had while I was here, and then I decided to come to Knoxville and practice. They started a clinic called Acuff Clinic here in Knoxville, and I was the dentist in the clinic starting in 1947. I met my wife at a wedding in this church, through a friend of hers, Rose Benedict, who was the one getting married. She was in her wedding, and that's where I met her. We were married in '49, and we have five children and ten grandchildren. I have been in Knoxville all this time and in this church since 1949, when I met all these other men. And as far as the Navy's concerned, I was on the retired list or the Reserve list for a while, and they finally dropped me, so I couldn't go back to any of the other wars, like Korea or Vietnam or any of the rest of them. I stayed at Acuff Clinic about five years. Then I moved into private practice on Hill

Avenue, and now I'm on Concord Street, where I moved my practice in 1967.

I went back to Pearl Harbor to see the *Arizona* about two years ago, and that was the only ship left there. Fifty years later, I couldn't picture how we sailed into Pearl Harbor. But there was an observation tower there, and my wife and I rode up to the top of that. I looked around and thought, "Well now, yes, this is where we came into Pearl Harbor during the war." Hawaii was also a very interesting place. I went back with my wife, and we had a wonderful time. We toured all the islands and saw all the things I didn't get to see during the war.

Being in the Navy was not bad – we had good meals and a dry place to sleep. It wasn't like being in the mud or with the tropical diseases or anything. It was a nice, clean place to be. And we used to have a little happy hour, where we would take some of the C-rations that the Marines had given us, and I used to make a Coca-Cola – I got a gallon jug of Coke syrup in San Francisco at one time, and I got one of those seltzer bottles. So we would make a Coca-Cola around four o'clock, and the medical officers would gather in my office, and we would just eat some crackers and drink Cokes. And that was fun.

My Navy career was very, very good. I didn't think about it being a career, but it was a good place. And I got to do what I was trained for – dentistry. I did my part in the war, and that's what I was supposed to do. I didn't get shot at or bombed. So, like I said, it was a lot easier than what these other guys went through – they suffered. I have a lot of respect for them and what they went through. And, of course, we are all grateful they are still here.

Well, we always say "war is hell," but we can't seem to put an end to it. The Bible is full of wars; they fought all the time. They killed ten thousand, and here we are all uptight about – I shouldn't say this – about two hundred men. On D-Day in Normandy, we lost thousands. We had friendly fire in War World II – we dropped bombs on the wrong people. But it doesn't upset me like these people who are ranting and raving about the people that are being killed over there in Iraq. I'm not saying that it is not regrettable, but it is just part of what happens when you have a war. But compared to World War II or anything else, the trouble now with the military is that not everybody in there knows why they are fighting. We were attacked – can't they remember that three thousand people were killed at the World Trade Center? Can't they remember that? We have already lost three thousand people, and they say we ought to quit killing over there and get out. It's really a burden on our leaders to know how to do it or what to do.

Chapter seven
E.B. Copeland

E.B. Copeland was born on November 30, 1919. He was drafted into the Army in 1941 under the Selective Service Act and during World War II served on Guadalcanal with the 244th Coast Artillery Corps in heavy combat. His time in the war earned him the World War II Victory Medal, Navy Presidential Unit Citation, American Defense Service Medal, and the American and Asiatic Pacific Theater Ribbon, with a Battle Star for the Guadalcanal Campaign.

Many historians feel that the turning point in the European Theater during World War II occurred with the defeat of the Germans at Stalingrad in 1942, and many historians believe the turning point in the South Pacific Theater occurred with the defeat of Japan at Guadalcanal in February 1943. In the South Pacific, for example, the Japanese had run roughshod since Pearl Harbor over the South Pacific islands in their ultimate mission to capture Australia. A gallant stand was made by the American forces to stop the Japanese advances on the small island of Guadalcanal in the Solomon Islands. A bloody battle starting on August 6, 1942, and ending in February 1943, successfully stopped the Japanese juggernaut, and from that point forward, the Japanese were in a retreat mode for the remainder of the war. I served on Guadalcanal with the 244th Coast Artillery Corps that was assigned to the 1st Marine Division and experienced the horrors of combat twenty-four hours per day for five long months.

I graduated from Birmingham Southern College, a private, liberal arts college in Birmingham, Alabama, with a degree in economics in June 1941. Shortly thereafter, I was drafted under the Selective Service Act into the Army in late October 1941. Draftees under that act were to serve one year in the military and then be discharged – but my service duty lasted for the next four and a half years. As a private, I was sent to Fort Eustis, Virginia, for my scheduled ninety days of basic training. My training started in early November 1941 but was interrupted a few weeks later when the Japanese bombed Pearl Harbor on December 7, 1941. With only six weeks of basic training at Fort Eustis, I, along with other draftees, was soon assigned to the 244th Coast Artillery Corps (CAC), a New York National Guard outfit.

In January 1942, the members of the 244th CAC boarded a ship and left the Brooklyn Navy Yards as part of a large convoy headed for the Philippines to reinforce our beleaguered troops there. Of course, we were not told of our destination until we were out at sea. After passing through the Panama Canal and into the Pacific Ocean, it was learned that the Philippines were at the point of surrendering to the Japanese. Our convey was then rerouted to Melbourne, Australia. We were onboard the ship for fifty-two straight days, with many young soldiers becoming violently sea sick due to turbulent waters and daily storms in the South Pacific. Many of these soldiers – really boys, some no older than eighteen – had never seen an ocean, had never been on board a ship, or for that matter, like me, had never been outside of their home state.

After arriving in Australia, we stayed for only two weeks, during which time we were billeted in private homes in the small gold-mining town of Bendigo, about fifty miles north of Melbourne. Being of Welsh descent, I was delighted that I was assigned with two of my buddies to a Welsh family named Williams who treated us as if we were part of their family.

After two weeks in Australia, we boarded our troop ship with the destination of New Caledonia, at the time a French possession located north of Australia. We went about deploying our 155 mm howitzer cannons on the coast of New Caledonia to protect the shoreline against a Japanese attack that was expected to come within a short period of time.

On August 6, 1941, we learned that the First Marine Division had invaded the small island of Guadalcanal in the Solomon Islands held by the Japanese. The mission of the Marines was to establish a beachhead and capture an airstrip along the beach areas where our fighter planes could land. This would give us a base and put us in a position to help stop the advance of the Japanese to Australia. The Japanese had a significant force of soldiers on Guadalcanal, and the fighting was fierce and bloody. When the Marines captured the airstrip for the first time, they named it Henderson Field after a downed pilot. The U.S. possession of the field was short-lived, however, and over a period of weeks, the Japanese retook possession at times, while the Marines held possession at times.

When the Marines held Henderson Field, they would put down metal runners on the runway to give our planes a firm footing since the sandy beaches were too soft for landing and takeoff. The Japanese had large artillery guns on rail tracks in the hills behind the airstrip and would lob shells on the runway, blasting large holes in the metal runners and preventing our planes from landing. After firing their shells, the Japanese would quickly retreat the guns on the rail tracks back into dugout caves in the hills.

The Marines who were already on Guadalcanal were not equipped with artillery having sufficient range to reach the Japanese positions in the hills; hence, my outfit was hurriedly sent there in late October 1942. We were attached to the First Marine Division, and our mission was to blast out the Japanese artillery in the caves up in the hills.

As we landed and waded ashore at Guadalcanal, the Japanese air force was ready for us and immediately commenced bombing and strafing the beach time and time again. Our only protection was the foxholes we had hurriedly dug on the sandy beaches. It gave you an eerie feeling to be fired on for the first time in your life – a feeling that would be experienced almost daily during the months ahead. When the strafing finally stopped, we were able to unload our 155 mm howitzers. As we pulled the massive guns through the rough jungle trails, young, hollow-eyed, battle-weary Marines began applauding us because they saw some hope and help for the first time since they arrived on Guadalcanal in August some two months before us.

All in the 244th CAC Battalion felt we were well prepared, well trained, and ready to put our preparedness into action. During the fifty-two days on the ship from the Brooklyn Navy Yards to Australia, there was ample time to thoroughly train all of us newly drafted recruits.

Once on Guadalcanal, we found that we would be firing at a stationary target in the hills behind Henderson airstrip, rather than at moving ships as we had been trained. We quickly determined the change in technique needed and focused our howitzers on the targets in the hills that contained the Japanese artillery. We were proud of the success we had in our first combat engagement in scoring ninety-two hits out of ninety-three firings. That success resulted in the complete obliteration of the Japanese artillery in the hills. From that point forward, there was never another interruption of service on Henderson Field, and we retained permanent possession of the field for the rest of the battle of Guadalcanal. But the fighting, bombing, and strafing were not over – not by a long shot.

Around this time, the Japanese made a determination that they could not afford to lose Guadalcanal and put together a convoy of thirteen thousand troops with naval and air force protection headed for Guadalcanal. Their mission was to send in an overwhelming force to wipe out the American soldiers on the small island. We were told the Japanese were on the way and to prepare for the fight of our lives.

Fortunately, our Navy and air force were alerted to intercept the convoy at an area between the tip of Guadalcanal and Savo Island. That area later became known as the Battle of Iron Bottom Bay. Our naval and air forces sunk scores of Japanese ships, but we also lost many of our ships and planes. Iron Bottom Bay got its name from the huge number of both Japanese and American war ships and planes that sunk to the bottom during that historic battle.

During the Iron Bottom Bay battle, all of our planes and ships engaged in combat, leaving Henderson Field unprotected. Two Japanese cruisers made their way a few hundred yards off shore from our position and began firing heavy artillery with the goal of putting Henderson Field out of commission. The Japanese cruisers systematically tried to bomb every square inch around Henderson Field, including an area where the 244th CAC Battalion was located. Our only protection, again, were our foxholes. If you could hear the projectiles whistle above, you knew that you would not be hit. Therefore, any extended silence without hearing a whistle was terrifying. When the firing finally ceased some hours later, tragically, we found a number of our comrades killed or seriously wounded. The Iron Bottom Bay battle depleted the Japanese navy to such an extent that they gave up trying to get large expeditions of troops onto Guadalcanal. Instead, from time to time, they ran ships with troop replacements and supplies, but with no naval or air protection.

In one instance, the Japanese tried to sneak in an unprotected troop ship without any accompanying support. By this date, I had been promoted to instrument sergeant, with duty in the command tower beside the executive officer during periods of firing our 155 mm howitzers. As the unprotected Japanese troop ship approached shore, my executive officer got down on his knees and prayed that the ship would come within our range. The unprotected ship did come within our range, and we opened fire full blast. We literally blew the ship apart. From my position in the command tower, I had an unobstructed view and witnessed the slaughter of hundreds of helpless, terrified

Japanese soldiers during that daylong onslaught. The panicked soldiers were running around the deck of the ship, jumping overboard – anything to escape the relentless shelling of our heavy artillery. The end result was the transport finally being beached. The few Japanese soldiers who survived were able to reach shore and disappeared in the dense jungle to later die of starvation or dreaded malaria.

As horrible as our shelling of the unprotected enemy troop ship was, we had ourselves experienced similar shelling by the Japanese in the previous weeks. From the first day we arrived on Guadalcanal, we were bombed incessantly – night and day – by the Japanese battleships and planes. There was never a night that "Condition Red" – a signal to hit the foxholes – was not sounded. Usually at night it was a lone Japanese bomber that flew over to attack and harass us. We called the bomber "Maytag Charlie" because the droning engine sounded like an old-fashioned wringer washing machine. We wondered at the time if we would ever in our lives get a full night's sleep again.

Until one has been though the horror of war, they cannot fully understand why it is paramount before going to war that every means possible be exhausted to prevent this battle carnage. Not only are the troops in harm's way twenty-four hours a day, the mental anguish of the families back home is equally torturous. For those who have been in combat from the Revolutionary War through all wars up to our present conflict in Iraq, the images of seeing your fellow soldiers as well as enemy soldiers being slaughtered leaves an indelible imprint that will never go away. War is truly hell for both sides involved.

After Guadalcanal was secured in February 1943, because of the heavy loss of life on the island, many of us were offered field commissions or the option to return to the States and attend officers candidate school – OCS. Several of my battalion and I chose to attend OCS. After returning to the States, the malaria that many of us contracted on the island despite preventative measurers began to take its toll. The post's hospital wards were lined with beds of sick soldiers with raging fevers, soaking sweats and shaking – called the rigors – so violent that the beds literally vibrated across the floors. Fortunately, modern 1940-era medical treatment spared most of our lives, and we continued our assigned duties. The reoccurring malaria, however, stayed with us for many years.

All of the soldiers selected to attend my OCS class at Fort Monroe, Virginia, were combat veterans either in the South Pacific or in Europe. The Army set high standards for those selected for OCS, and only about 50 percent who started actually graduated and received a commission. The greatest honor of my life was to be chosen by my combat-hardened OCS classmates to be the honorary commander of our graduating class.

After receiving my commission as a second lieutenant, I was assigned to remain at the officers candidate school as an instructor. My tour of duty at Fort Monroe led me to meet Betty Stephenson, of Hampton, Virginia, who was working as a civilian on the post. Her father, MSG Paul Stephenson, who had retired here, his last post during his military career, was also a civilian working at Fort Monroe. Betty agreed to become my wife, and we were married on the post four months later at the Church of the Centurion on February 3, 1945. I received an honorable discharge from active duty in March 1946 as a first lieutenant, Coast Artillery Unit commander, but remained in the Army Reserves until 1952. I earned the World War II Victory Medal, Navy Presidential Unit Citation, American Defense Service Medal, and the American and Asiatic Pacific Theater Ribbon, with a Battle Star for the Guadalcanal Campaign.

Betty and I, along with our first baby daughter, returned to my hometown of Birmingham in 1946, and after a few years and a few moves, wound up in Knoxville in 1953. We have three daughters, Catherine Copeland, Sarah Pennington and husband Charlie, and Cynthia Hughs and husband Carswell, and grandsons Chip and James Pennington. Betty was the love of my life for fifty-eight years and is truly missed every hour and every day since her passing on June 9, 2003.

Readjusting to civilian life wasn't too difficult. I didn't have any trauma; the only thing I had was a bad case of malaria after I got back to the States, but that was typical of anyone on those islands. Emotionally and mentally, I didn't have any problems. Being in the war did change my outlook on a lot of things. The main thing I learned was that you never wanted to go to war unless it was absolutely the last resort. Like when I mentioned the unescorted Japanese ship that we fired on – the vision of seeing literally thousands of troops on the deck panic, run and jump off while we're shelling them, just seeing them slaughtered like that, was a vision you just don't want to think about. That's the thing that most men in combat come away with – the vision of something like that. That just tells you to never, never go to war unless it is the last resort. We made a foolish error in going into Iraq, and it's been nothing but chaos since. And it's not only the soldiers going through that kind of trauma, but it's also the people back home who have a loved one there that at any moment could be killed. It's very stressful to everybody.

Just like today, we have one hundred twenty thousand or one hundred thirty thousand troops over in Iraq, and there are many families back here in the States worrying twenty-four hours a day if that loved one is going to get back home. And that is tough to deal with. You just never, never want to put anybody in that position unless it's the last resort. If it's an option you have, don't take that option, but if it's the last resort, do it – you got to – but not when you have other options. I think most anyone who's been in combat will have the same feeling.

Chapter eight
Tom Dempster

Tom Dempster was born in Warrior, Alabama, on July 6, 1917. He joined
the Navy in 1941. In November 1943, he was injured in flight and spent
thirty-four months in the hospital, which was the remainder of his time in
the service. When he got out, he was a lieutenant commander and had
earned a Purple Heart, an Air Medal, and, with his squadron, the
Presidential Unit Citation.

I'd been out of the university with a degree in mechanical
engineering for about one year when I joined the service in
August 1941. I didn't take ROTC in school and I knew the
war was coming along, and I thought I'd better do something.
So I joined the Navy and went to Navy flight school. It took
about nine to ten months, and I finished in July 1942.

After flight school, I had orders to report to San Diego
for transitional training school. When I got there, I checked in
and they didn't have time, so they sent me across the hall to the
pilot's replacement squadron. The man there said, "You're
gonna go to New Caledonia," but he didn't tell me where it
was. He said, "You're gonna go to VP-71," which is a
squadron, and he gave me a train ticket to San Francisco to get
a ship to find this VP-71. Well I got up there, reported to Naval
headquarters, and stayed there about two weeks. One day they
called me – I was staying in a hotel, about to run out of money
– and they said to be at the pier to catch a ship to go to VP-71.
So I went down and caught that ship – the *SS Wisconsin*, a

merchant marine vessel. We were twenty-six days at sea and ended up at Auckland, New Zealand. And when I got to Auckland, they said, "Go to New Caledonia," which was eight hundred or one thousand miles up the ocean. So they put me on another ship, and when I got up there, they said VP-71 had been relieved and that they had gone back to Kanehoe Bay in Hawaii. So they hitched me a ride on a Marine Corps plane to go back to Honolulu. To go there, we had to go to the Fiji Islands, then to Samoa, then to Canton Island, and then Midway. So, I got a whole tour of the South Pacific. But anyway, I hadn't drawn any pay, and the pilot, Lt. Carlson, said, "Do you need to get paid?" I said, "Yes," so he said, "Let me put your name down as a crew on my airplane." So I got my flight pay because he certified that I was there in New Caledonia, to Samoa, to Canton, to Johnston, to Midway.

I really had two tours of duty in the Pacific – one in the central Pacific with the old Navy PBY squadron in late 1942 and the early part of '43, and then they split our group up into two groups and put us in B-24s, which the Navy called PB4Ys. And we went back into the South Pacific, and it was down there that I got hit and spent the rest of the time in the hospital.

Our job was patrolling the ocean in twelve-hour patrols, flying sectors looking for enemy ships, mostly. The Japanese had all these little islands – what seemed like thousands of them – and they had these garrisons on each of them to maintain shipping around them; it was our job to keep them isolated. We'd go out about four hundred miles out left by fifteen degrees, and then you'd go another four hundred miles, then come crosswise – making a "Y" – and you could patrol a whole lot of water. Somebody figured each sector would cover fifty thousand square miles of area, which was mostly water – you might see a little island, but mostly water. We had twelve planes and fifteen flight crews, and we'd make these patrols about every third day or every other day. There wasn't anything else to do anyway.

On this particular day, in November 1943, we were out at the very end of our sector – eight hundred miles out – and we saw a little ship, a little freighter later identified as *Minato-Maru*, and we decided we would bomb it. We went over it about three times and dropped bombs at low altitude – we weren't over one hundred fifty feet above the water. We dropped a bomb on it, missed, and then dropped another one. The last time, the ship blew up underneath us. I got hurt, and another crew member named Bob Griffith, who was the belly gunner, got hurt. See, when the ship blew up underneath us, it just exploded, and we got shrapnel that came through the bottom of the airplane. We got back all right, but it took a little over five hours to get back. We had to throw everything over the side that we could – we had some pretty good damage to our airplane, but we got back. When we got back, they already knew we had some trouble, and they met us at the airstrip with an ambulance and took us to the hospital. Then I left that group at the end and stayed in the hospital for thirty-four months. Sounds bad, but it really wasn't. I had a fractured mandible – the jawbone – which didn't heal, and they had to do bone grafting, and that just takes time. The first bone graft didn't take, and I had to wait four months to do it again, and that didn't take, so you have to wait all the time.

The Navy had a mobile hospital, which were tents, in Guadalcanal, and from there they would send you to another one that was more advanced – Espiritu Santo in the New Hebrides Islands. That one was in a building – Quonset huts – and from there they brought me back to the States, to California, and I was there about two years. From there they transferred me to Bethesda, Maryland, near Washington, D.C., and that is where I finished up.

Most of the patients in the hospital were Marines, mostly amputees. I had my mouth wired shut – when they do the grafting, they have to keep it immobilized, so they wired it shut. I had it wired together for about fourteen months. That wasn't fourteen months at one time – it was three months one time, then another three months, then four months, and then another four months, a total of fourteen months. I could only drink out of a straw, just liquids. So it wasn't too bad; you could spend a lot of time boozing it up. If you were married, you could bring the family out there.

When I heard about the atomic bomb, I thought it was good that they dropped it. It didn't surprise me; the scuttlebutt was that there was something big being produced in Oak Ridge – nobody knew what it was, but they knew something real big was going to happen. I don't think anybody expected a bomb; they probably expected some sort of high-class or high-pressure missile or cannon or something. When it was dropped, I guess I was in the Naval hospital out in California.

During the war, I got about a weekly letter from my family. They would send me a little newsletter or something. The company that I went with had a newsletter – a local thing – and they would send that out. I got the Air Medal just for being in the war, and we had a presentation ceremony at the hospital. My unit got the Presidential Unit Citation, so each person in that unit was awarded that. I was a lieutenant commander when I got out – not for pay purposes; they gave me an honorary rank. I was a lieutenant, and when I got out, they advanced me one rank just for "hanging up on the wall." Then they gave me a medical retirement.

After I got home, I went to work for Dempster Brothers, Inc. – that was the old family business, but I hadn't been with them before – just went to work for them when I got back. I didn't have any problem readjusting; some said they did, but I didn't. Probably, if the war did anything to me, it sort of broadened me out a little bit – and especially some of these kids who were just fresh from home, just out of high school, got a fast education, and when they got back took advantage of the GI Bill. A lot would not have had that opportunity if they hadn't gone in the service.

Our group gets together every two years for a reunion. Last time we were in Oakland, California, and this year, we will be in Washington, D.C. Usually we go every two years, but this time it will be just after one year because everyone is getting too old. We've been to San Diego two or three times and Portland, San Antonio, Pensacola, St. Louis, Norfolk –

we've been pretty much all over. But we're losing so many of them, it's not enough to put on a party. Last time it was sixty-nine, and that counted women, children and everybody else. There were originally about three hundred – well actually there were one hundred fifty, but the squadron went back with another one hundred fifty, so there were about three hundred total.

Chapter nine
Bill Dickey

William Dickey was born in Knoxville, Tennessee, on October 18, 1923. He entered the Army Air Corps in 1943 and was part of the 3rd Cargo Resupply Squadron. He helped resupply troops in the European Theater and saw the invasion of Normandy and the Battle of the Bulge from the air. His time in the war earned him an Air Medal.

I was inducted into the service at Fort Oglethorpe, Georgia, in April of 1943. I was drafted; at the time I went in, they had quit taking volunteers. So just as soon as your name came up, you were in. But all of my friends were in the same boat – they were all doing the same thing. If I hadn't been in there, I would have felt left out. Actually, I was kind of looking forward to it. At that age, you are not old enough to have sense enough to be afraid of anything.

After a week or so at Oglethorpe, I was transferred to Miami Beach for basic training, and I spent about two or three months there. Then I was transferred to Scott Field, Illinois, for radio operators school. From there, I was sent to Madison, Wisconsin, for radio mechanics school, which I didn't care for much, and I understood that if you washed out of there, you would be sent overseas. That's all I needed to know because I was anxious to get overseas, so I washed myself out more or less. I didn't tell them that because when they saw my grades, I went almost immediately to POE in New Jersey and headed for England. I spent about eighteen months in England and France.

I was a member of an air cargo resupply squadron, and we dropped supplies either by parachute or we landed and unloaded if we were in friendly territory. We dropped supplies to paratroopers who had landed in Normandy about twenty miles inland on D-Day. We just flew over there, and I saw it all from the air. You could look down and see it, and hopefully you didn't get shot down. And when we had completed our mission, we just turned around and went back to England. Then later on, during the Battle of the Bulge, we dropped supplies to the surrounding troops. We would usually throw out supplies that were shackled onto the bottom of the plane, and the pilot would release them. We had some stacked up beside the door of the plane, and when we got the signal, we would just start throwing them out. So I just helped load the plane and throw out the supplies over wherever they were supposed to be, usually when troops were encircled, like the Battle of the Bulge.

We would get fired at, but, of course, they were not as anxious to shoot our planes down as they were the bombers. We were just dropping supplies. The plane was hit by flak, but it wasn't ever damaged enough to go down; the flak just went through the ceiling. Sometimes it would miss me by two or three feet but didn't get me – it was a near miss, I guess you would say. But we had some who were shot down and some taken prisoner. I missed that, thankfully.

Later on in 1944, we dropped supplies again to troops that had outrun their supply lines. I spent the remainder of that time in England, and we were scheduled to be deployed directly from Europe to the Pacific. We were on our way to Marseilles, France, to be deployed to the Philippines when, as fortune would have it, the atomic bomb was dropped and brought the war to a quick end. So, instead of going directly to the Philippines, we went directly to the United States.

When we heard that the bomb had been dropped, the ship that everyone was going on almost exploded with cheers and enthusiasm. And then we were deployed right on to the United States. Fortunately, I got there in time to be discharged in roughly a month. I went back to Atlanta to Fort McPherson, where I was discharged in November of 1945.

I didn't get home from the time I went in until I got out, which was about thirty months. So when I got back, I entered the university and finally graduated with a BS in business administration after about four years over there.

I've never been back overseas. I might have wanted to, but when I had a chance, I was getting old and a little bit infirm, so to speak. But when I was in the war, I got to go to London a time or two and Paris. I saw a lot of sights that would have cost many dollars as a tourist paying to be there. About ten years ago, I received a visit from a man I was in the service with who was passing through town. We had dinner together, and that is the last contact I have had with anyone I was in there with.

Chapter ten
Tom Evans

Tom Evans was born in Knoxville, Tennessee, on December 15, 1922. He joined the Army Air Corps in June 1942 and was a pilot in the China-Burma-India Theater. Although he saw combat, he was never injured by enemy fire. His time in the war earned him an Air Medal.

My dad was the principal of Knoxville High School, which, along with Austin High, were the only high schools in Knoxville from about 1910 until they built three new high schools after the war. He had four sons – I had two older brothers and a younger brother – and he was well known, of course, because most of the people that went to high school in Knoxville knew him. All four of us joined the air force over a period of time. My brother Dick joined first, long before Pearl Harbor, before we got into the war – he just wanted to fly airplanes. So he was an instructor pilot in what was called the Army Air Corps at that time. My brother Stewart went in later. Dick flew combat missions against the Germans over Africa and Italy, then came home and got married, and then went to the South Pacific and flew some combat missions against the Japanese. So he had a long time of service.

I graduated from Knoxville High School in January of '41, and the Japanese bombed Pearl Harbor in December of '41. And, like a lot of people, I was eager to get into it in those days because of the bombing of Pearl Harbor. So I joined the Army Air Corps in June of 1942. By that time, I was a sophomore at The University of Tennessee and was in a program called the Aviation Cadet Candidate Program as a reservist, or a private in the Army Reserves. In that program, I was deferred from active duty until I graduated from school, as long as I maintained my grades and stayed in school or until the president called a national emergency and called the reservists up, which he did in January of '43. So I was called into service with the first crowd of reservists, went through training, got my wings and my commission in 1944, and got my overseas training at a base in South Carolina. This was the same base where Jimmy Doolittle picked up his crews to fly his famous mission – in March of '42, he flew sixteen twin-engine medium air force bombers off the aircraft carrier *Hornet* and bombed Japan. That was the first offensive action we were able to take.

Our group, the 12th Bomb Group, had four squadrons in it. The 81st was the one I was in. Our group could put thirty-six planes into the air at one time. So I went from that base in South Carolina to India, and I was based in India in an area that was on the edge of the jungles and the mountains – they called them hills over there – of the Chin Hills. Our missions were flown from this base in India across from the other side of the mountains and the valley in Burma — the Irrawaddi Valley, the road to Mandalay. In the campaign, I was bombing bridges and working with troop concentrations, supplies, railroad yards, and that type of thing. While we – mainly the English, the Indians, and the Chinese together – were driving the Japanese out of Burma, I was involved in the campaign to bomb the Japanese ahead of their advances. During that period of time, we drove them all the way out of Burma down through the valley and out of Rangoon.

I had twenty-eight combat missions. Well, I say combat, but there wasn't a lot of combat to it, except that we were the ones making the noise and they were trying to get out by that time. I was late getting into the action. This was now late in the war after the Japanese left Burma. So my unit then moved to a bigger city in India on another field where we had transitioned into a new airplane called the A-26, which was a new medium bomber, a twin-engine airplane and the very latest thing. While we were doing that in August and September of 1945, the atom bombs were being dropped. So we never got to use that airplane in actual combat. But I flew it quite a few hours, and we became proficient in it and were ready to go into the war in China or in Mongolia. We thought we were going to be sent to Mongolia to fight the Japanese there when the atom bomb was dropped. Then it was all over with.

While I was over there, the mail was pretty good. It would take anywhere from two weeks to a month, and if it was a package, it took longer. We ate pretty well over there; I didn't have any complaints about the food. We had plenty of chicken and eggs. We didn't have much red meat like beef, but sometimes we would get something they called "bully beef," which was Australian beef, but it didn't compare with American beef. We never got any American beef over there, but I'm not complaining about the food. The only people in the service that ate better than we did were the Navy guys on ships; they really fed them good. I came back home on a ship from Shanghai on what is called an attack transport, which was a type of ship that was made to transport troops to islands. Well, we would line up and go through the same chow line that the Navy boys did, except the Navy guys would go first. Then the air force guys, who were just passengers, would line up behind. And it was unbelievable because the word getting around was, "We're having pork chops today," but by the time we got up there for our turn, they would say, "We're sorry, we are out of pork chops. We don't have any more pork chops." Now, we might have pork chops two days later, but they were out of pork chops that day, and we would get Spam or whatever. I complained to one of the Navy officers one day. I said, "Hey, how come that just as soon as the air force boys get up there in the chow line getting ready to be served, you all run out of the good stuff, like fillet steaks and pork chops?" And he said,

"Well, the only way I can explain it is that if you don't like the food, maybe you can just walk home." Of course, we were out in the middle of the Pacific Ocean at that time, so that was a big joke. I said, "OK, I get the point, no more complaints. Just get us to Seattle; that's all we ask for."

On a little side story, one day we were on a mission, and we had made our bomb run and were returning home when we broke out lunch, which was what was called a C-ration, a little box with some dry food in it. One of the things in there was a piece of chewing gum. So after I had finished eating all this dried stuff that they had furnished for a bite of lunch, I popped that piece of chewing gum in my mouth, chewed it up, and it just fell apart – crumbled like sand in my mouth. And I said, "This is horrible! They call this chewing gum?!" So I picked up the wrapper and looked at it, and it said Walla-Walla Gum Company, Knoxville, Tennessee. Here I was flying over Burma chewing this gum, and it was awful.

I was injured during the war, but not through enemy action. I cut the end of my thumb off with a machete one day – I just sliced it at an angle, but it grew back. It's funny, but it still shows. I joke about that because it was the only time I had anything happen that brought blood. I didn't see a lot of enemy action. Our job was to interrupt the Japanese retreat out of Burma, to try to kill as many of them as we could, and to blow up their supplies. We bombed bridges so they couldn't retreat. We bombed railroad yards so they couldn't get their supplies through. We bombed roads so that trucks couldn't travel over roads easily. Of course, they could repair them, but it interrupted their movements, and that was our job. As far as enemy aircraft was concerned, I didn't actually see a Japanese airplane in the air until after they surrendered, and then I saw a lot of them flying around. But by that time, all they were doing was getting ready to go home and trying to get out. They were just like we were – they wanted to get home after it was all over with.

I did run into anti-aircraft fire quite a bit, where they were shooting at us with big guns while we were flying over the targets. They had protection around the critical targets, like bridges. You can't build a bridge overnight that carries trains and big trucks across it, so they wanted to protect them. They had these great big guns and surrounded them so that when you fly over to bomb the bridge, they shot at you. We got shot at a lot, but I never got a hole in an airplane, never got hit. I think maybe the good Lord was looking after me at the time because you are sitting there in the airplane and flying it, doing what you are supposed to do, and you see little black puffs of smoke here and here and up here and over here, and you know that they know you are there because they are shooting at you, and they know what your altitude is because these bomb bursts are all around you. Of course, the sky is a pretty big place and an airplane is a comparatively small thing. But we just never did get hit. It was more than luck — it was luck all right, but it was more than luck — but it certainly wasn't skill, because when we got on a bomb run, we were a sitting duck. See, you would come to what they call an IP, which is an initial point like a building or a bridge, and then you take a heading, turn on that IP, and you fly so long and then drop your bomb. After you line up on that target and you are on your bomb run, you don't deviate from that, and they know that. The guys just shoot at you — it's like shooting ducks out there. They knew where we were going to go, but they weren't very good shots.

　　　After the atom bomb was dropped, I was transferred into a troop carrier squadron for a while, flying another twin-engine airplane that was not designed to carry bombs but to carry troops. Now in China, there were Nationalists and Communists, and we were in favor of the Nationalists. So we moved a couple of Nationalist armies from the interior of China to confront the Communist armies of China. We had no sooner gotten through with the Japanese than we were involved in the fight between the Chinese Nationalists and the Communists. Unfortunately, the Communists won, and it has taken about fifty years for them to recover in China, but now they are a major force in progress in the world.

A sideline to my war experience is of some interest to local people, particularly at Oak Ridge. The workers at Oak Ridge did not know what they were doing; they didn't know they were building an atom bomb that was going to end the war. It was the biggest secret in the world. There were just thousands of people out there working in this great big complex that was built overnight, but they didn't know what they were accomplishing. So they decided they wanted to do something for the war effort, and the workers at K-25 chipped in their earnings from a couple of Sundays they worked overtime and bought an airplane to send off to help the war effort. That brand-new airplane was brought into Knoxville and dedicated here. And because the workers had worked on Sundays, they named it *Sunday Punch*. So they dedicated it and sent it off to the war but didn't know what had happened to it for a while. Well, it ended up in my squadron, and I flew it. You see, the airplane came into our unit, and I heard about it through the newspaper clippings that had been sent to me. Nobody here knew that it was in our squadron, and nobody over there knew that it came from Knoxville until I got this clipping. So I went to my commanding officer, Col. Dalton, and told him about it. "Oh, that's great," he said. "We will just assign that airplane to you, and we will get some publicity out of it." And he did. The air force thought it was good to get the news back home, and I've got pictures and newspaper articles and stuff about it.

Since that time, the story was almost dormant for fifty years – nobody seemed to be interested. By then, we were all working, raising families, and doing other things and had almost forgotten World War II. But somebody at Oak Ridge decided they wanted to know whatever happened to the *Sunday Punch*. And they found out that a local guy had flown the airplane, so they called me up one day and this fellow said, "Is this Lt. Tom Evans?" And I said, "Well, I used to be a lieutenant, but right now it is just Tom Evans." And he said, "Well, do you happen to be the fellow who flew an airplane that the Oak Ridge K-25 workers bought and sent overseas named *Sunday Punch?*" I said, "Yes, I did." He said, "We need to get together." He happened to be a curator at the World War II museum in Oak Ridge, and he wanted to build a story around this airplane called "Whatever Happened to the *Sunday Punch?*" and put it in the museum. So he and I got together to talk about it several times. He elaborated a little on it and almost made it look like I was a hero, but all I did was "drive a truck," so to speak. I learned to "drive a truck" pretty good, and other people would load it up and I would take the load over and dump it out in Burma, and then I would fly back. That is what I did in the war, just piloting this airplane.

When we heard that the atomic bomb had been dropped, we didn't know anything about it – nobody knew that the United States had developed the atomic bomb. There wasn't a word mentioned in the news. If anybody knew, it was the best-kept secret in the world because I don't think it got out from the people who were supposed to know and were testing it out in the desert of New Mexico. I don't think they even were positive it would work when they dropped the first one. At that time, I understand we only had two of them. The Japanese hesitated to surrender after the first one, although it wiped out Hiroshima. But they thought the United States didn't have any more of them, that there was just that one. When we got Nagasaki later, they said, "Oh my goodness, they are going to knock down every city in Japan." So that is when they surrendered. But it took the only two atom bombs that were actually functional at that time. But there wasn't a word mentioned. Nobody knew it except the people who were involved in building it.

When we heard about it, well, it was kind of funny. I hate to admit this, but we were having a good time. It was all new – we were flying around in a foreign country that was very different from here. I got to see things that I didn't think I would ever see in my life. I've got pictures of me at the Taj Mahal, which is a great mausoleum that was built in India. I've seen the Great Wall of China. I've been to Peking, which is now Beijing, the capital of China. I was in there before any

Americans or anybody other than the Japanese and Chinese. I was privileged to be able to help fly the Chinese army from Hankow, China, into Peking. And when we got into Peking, we went around in rickshaws downtown, the only Americans. Crowds would gather around us, look at us, and pat us on the back. We didn't know what they were saying, but it was an exciting time. So, I guess I would have to say that I took it sort of nonchalantly. I thought, well, OK, the war is over. That's great. We are going to go home and resume our lives, but this has been a wonderful experience. And another thing was that we loved this new airplane. It had about twelve .50-caliber machine guns on it. It would almost blow a boat out of the water. And it carried a good load of bombs, so we knew we could knock down bridges with it and even dams. As a matter of fact, it was later used in Korea.

The worst things I saw in the war was one day when one of our airplanes drifted off line and ran through a bunch of Chinese laborers who were working out on the runway; the props just cut them up into pieces. I ran out there to see what was going on because the tents we were living in were right off the edge of the runway, and that was a gory sight. I saw a lot of dead Japanese because while we were supporting the British and the Indians and the Chinese in Burma, we captured an airfield – or the British captured an airfield and surrounded it and protected it in such a way that we could fly our airplanes in there, refuel, and then fly short missions, maybe two or three missions in a day. We would fly out and do certain things and then come back to this field and fill up with gasoline again. The Japanese would come in at night and try to infiltrate – they were never able to do that, but they tried. They left their dead out there in the field. The British and the Indians that protected the field would kill them as they were trying to come through at night, and so the next day, those of us who were there on the base were curious and would go out there and roam around and look at them. But as far as being involved in hand-to-hand or personal combat where they are shooting at you and killing people around you, I didn't see any of that.

You know, I got home on about the second of January, and it was either the third or fourth day of January when I went over and checked into school. It was good to come home – I'm a homeboy. But adjusting back was almost instantaneous; it was almost like I had been on a vacation. I didn't have any psychological problems with going back. The only thing that did make a difference was that I had been out of school at that time for over three years, and I was in the middle of taking engineering courses like calculus and physics and chemistry. I remember those three because they were the hardest courses I took. Even though I made pretty good grades when I was a freshman and a sophomore, it was continuous — everything was based on something you had already learned. But I had forgotten so much of calculus and physics and chemistry in those three years that when I came back, I frankly was about ready to flunk out of school. Besides, you know, I was about twenty-three years old at that time and single — girls looked pretty nice and I was dating a lot. I had a car, and I wasn't really interested in getting an education. I was more interested in getting a degree, getting a piece of paper saying that I am a college graduate. And I was ready to put in the time to do that, but I was really anxious to get out of school. One of the hardest things for me to fit back in was the fact that my girl had another boyfriend by the time I got home, and I didn't know that until I got home. I went to see her the first night I got home, sat in her living room, and talked with her and her mother. Her brother suggested we go out for a while, and she said she didn't think she would. So that was the end of that. So I didn't have the problems that some guys had because some of them had it awfully rough. I'm sure you've seen the movie *Saving Private Ryan*. Those guys were the heroes of the war. Coming out of those landing boats under fire like that and going through the water, and some of them were dumped out in water so deep that they went straight to the bottom. They had all that heavy stuff on them, and some of them were killed before they could get out of the water. Those guys had it rough. I imagine those who survived had a time getting over that.

When I came back home, I elected to stay in the Reserves, rather than be separated from the service completely. And I was in my second year at UT when I had an opportunity to go back for a short period to active duty for three to four months at a time to schools in what was called the Air University. I went to a school called the Air Tactical School, which teaches tactical flying – going in behind the enemy lines and bombing strategic targets as well as tactical targets. I also went to a school called the Air Inspector School that was something like the FBI; a group of people would go around and inspect to see that the rules are carried out in the various Air Force bases. For instance, this thing that got so much publicity that happened in Iraq in the prisons there, if that had happened on an Air Force base, the air inspectors would be expected to know about it because it is their job to know everything that is going on and that all the rules are being abided by. I did go to school and qualify in that after the war ended, and at the same time, I stayed current in flying.

As an air officer, you could get out of flying if you didn't want to do it anymore, but most air officers wanted to continue with their flying. So I stayed current. I flew all sorts of different airplanes around the United States. An interesting thing about the Reserves back in those days, and I guess it is pretty much the same today, is that if I wanted to go someplace and I had a week off from school, I could drive down to Marietta, Georgia, go into operations, sign out an airplane, and fly anywhere I wanted to. I will have to admit that it helped my love life a little bit to be able to fly around because I had lady friends in Miami and in Ohio and in Memphis, and I could always get an airplane and fly around. But they encouraged that because the experience keeps you current in flying. It's sort of like learning to ride a bicycle. You know, once you learn to ride a bicycle, you can always ride one, but if you are going to be good at it, you need to keep current at it. So they let us fly about as much as we wanted to.

We had to put in two weeks every summer of active duty. I usually went to Memphis to the air base down there to do that. Of course, we flew during that period and maintained our proficiency in instrument flying, which is flying in conditions when you can't even see out of the airplane. When you are flying in storms and the ceiling of visibility is pretty low but you have to land, you've got to come down through that "soup," as we call it, and hopefully break clear before you are ready to land. Sometimes it is so thick that you can't see anything until you get right on top of it, and that's really tricky.

But when the Korean War broke out and they were recalling Reservists who had experience in flying A-26 airplanes in 1953, by that time I had a wife and two babies. They gave me a choice of either getting more active in the Reserve or getting out. Well, that meant if I wanted to get more active in the Reserve, I had to go on active duty and go to Korea and fly in combat again. But by that time, I wasn't particularly interested in doing that. So from the time I joined in '42, I was in about twelve years, including my active time and my Reserve time.

I kept in touch with some of the men I met during the war for a while, but to my knowledge, there is only one of the fellows that I actually flew with in the same airplane who is still living. He is a Chinese boy from San Francisco, and I talked with him on the phone a couple of times, but we don't have anything in common other than the fact that we flew in the *Sunday Punch* together. But my co-pilot and close buddy, a fellow by the name of Paul Duquette, died about three years ago. He lived in Pharr, Texas, and we were going to have a squadron reunion in San Antonio, which is where we were when we graduated from flying school and got our commission and our wings – it was the first time they had had a reunion there. So I called him up and said, "How about getting together, and we will meet and share a room and go to the reunion," which we did. But by that time, he had Parkinson's, and he was having problems getting around, so I had to watch him closely. He died a year after that. So I don't have any

contact with any of those fellows anymore. I have gone to one
reunion since then, in Nashville, and I ran into a couple of
fellows from my squadron. One fellow named Hill who lived
in California was there with his son and his wife, and they
practically had to carry him around he was in such bad shape.
He had Alzheimer's and Parkinson's. He shouldn't have been
there, but he had enough sense in him that he wanted to go to
the last reunion. He died shortly after that.

I haven't been back overseas since the war. Frankly, the
only place I would be interested in going back to would be
Kashmir, which is a beautiful part of northern India. It's very
different; the way people live is like going back five hundred
years. But it is clean and in the mountains – it's on the edge of
the Himalayas. I took a rest leave for two weeks while I was in
India, took a car, and went up into the mountains – it was kind
of like getting in a car and going up in the Smokies. We went
up into the mountains, rented horses, and took trails up in the
snow in the middle of the summer in India, where below it was
over one hundred degrees all day long, but we were up there
throwing snowballs at each other.

I never did, but I also wouldn't have minded going back
to China, which is a very interesting place to go and visit. I
haven't actually been out to the Great Wall of China, but I have
flown over it and taken a few pictures out the window of an
airplane. So I've seen the Great Wall, and I've roamed around
in the Emperor's Palace – that was an interesting thing. After
the war, the Japanese didn't do anything to what is called "The
Forbidden City" — the walled city in the middle of Peking
where the emperors lived. They just let all the big buildings
stand there. When we were moving the Chinese army in, we
went there, and I decided I wanted to go over there to see it.
The gates were wide open, and there was nobody saying, "You
can't go in here," or anything, so we just got out and roamed
around. There were very few people there at that time. I
remember when President Nixon went over there to sort of
break down the barrier between the Chinese Communists and
the United States – it was a big deal on television. As they

showed it on television, I would laugh and say, "I was there. I stood right there on that very spot." Nixon was supposed to have been the very first American to go in there after World War II, more or less. But there were Americans who went in, and I think I was ahead of all of them.

I was very privileged because of the things I got to witness, like downtown in Nanking. Nanking was a walled city on one of the main rivers in China, and it was the provisional capital of the Nationalist army for a while, until the Japanese bombed them out. You may have heard of the "Rape of Nanking," when the Japanese went in and slaughtered people. They treated everybody terribly and it was a horrible thing. But I have been right in downtown of that city and out to the tomb of Dr. Sun Yat-Sen, which is a great big mausoleum on a hill. Those things would be interesting to go back and see because when I was there, we were always in a hurry.

When I was at that field where the dead Japanese were in Burma, a buddy of mine named Tom Perryman, who is still living, and I decided we wanted to see Mandalay. There was a fort named Fort Dufferin in the middle of the city of Mandalay, and we wanted to see that because we bombed it when the Japanese had it. So we bargained with a fellow at a British motor pool; we gave him a carton of cigarettes (they couldn't get American cigarettes, but we could), which was like gold to him, and he gave us a Jeep. So we had the Jeep and then got a couple of cans of gasoline and took off up the road — the road to Mandalay. We saw a lot of the places we had bombed, and we saw the conditions the people were living in. We went up into the hills — it took us about a week to do that, and we almost ran out of gasoline, but the Lord was looking after us. We were near an abandoned Japanese airfield northwest of Mandalay, and there were no telephones, radios, or communication, except by foot, and we began to get concerned because we were on our last tank of gasoline. Then we came on this airfield. So we started looking around, and we found a bunch of big fifty-five-gallon barrels sitting out near one of the buildings. There wasn't anybody there, so we opened up one of the fifty-five-gallon drums. We stuck our fingers down in there, and it was gasoline. So we were able to fill up our two tanks that we carried on the Jeep, and we never ran out.

Burma is also a place that I wouldn't mind going back to, but it is a closed nation. It was taken over by a militant dictator after World War II, and it has been almost a closed nation to tourists. But it's a beautiful country. I would say that the living conditions in Burma could be ideal because they have plenty of water; they have those rivers that run out of the Himalayas.

I'm sure being in the war has had a lasting effect on my life. I was born and raised in a Christian family; we were members of the First Methodist Church. People would say, "Are you a Christian?" And I would say, "Yeah, I'm a Christian." But I really didn't know what it was to be a Christian until later in life. I think probably the war had something to do with it. I had a close call one day, and there was a difference of twelve hours in where I was in India from home – the middle of the day in India was the middle of the night at home – and I knew my mother was praying for me every day. And it just flashed through my mind that she must be praying for me right now because I came that close to crashing an airplane. No telling what would have happened. But things like that make you think that life can be ended overnight, and then what? As I look out there at night and see those stars and think that there is never a beginning and will never be an end and the heavenly bodies are beyond even counting, there has to be a God that created all of this and has control. The war had something to do with my thinking about things like that because I can see how fast things can change.

I had a friend by the name of Karnash when we were in training down in San Antonio, Texas. He went up one day, and they were practicing stalls – that is when an airplane gets to a point where it is no longer at flying speed, and it becomes just a big hunk of metal up there and begins to fall. Well you practice that because you need to know how to recover if that ever happens to you. And it happens on occasion when you are in thunderstorms or when you are coming in for a landing or you flair out too high. So they were practicing, and they went into what is called a flat spin, where the airplane, instead of going straight down, starts to spin around like a Frisbee might – a Frisbee spins flat. Well, they never did pull out of it, and he didn't get out of the airplane. And just like that, there is this guy, just one of us, and all of a sudden he is dead. It makes you think about the future life and eternity. But I escaped the real bad part of it.

WeWere
There

PHOTOGRAPH
SECTION

Fred Baumann

Wallace Baumann

John Bolinger

Joe Brownlee

Fred Cagle

Ed Coleman

Tom Evans

Al Holmes

John McAmis

John McDow

Frank Moore

Kay Ogden

Rob Schmid

Warren Sylvester

Jim Talley

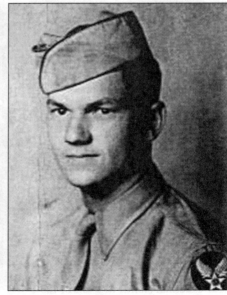

Bill Tate

Vince Torbett

Ed Coleman stands in front of the *USS Pickaway* on January 20, 1946.

Tom Dempster receives the Air Medal from commanding officer Capt. John P. Owen at the U.S. Naval Hospital in Mare Island, California.

John Moore, left, poses for a photograph with a friend.

Frank Moore is pictured at center.

Tom Evans is pictured inside "The Forbidden City," the walled city in the middle of Peking, China, where the emperors lived.

Rob Schmid, far left, enjoys the beach with his bombardier, co-pilot and navigator in Okinawa after the war.

E.B. Copeland, pictured in front of a chapel, said of this photograph: "How do you like the couple in the rear? You don't often see a girl up here, so it was by accident that I got this couple in the background."

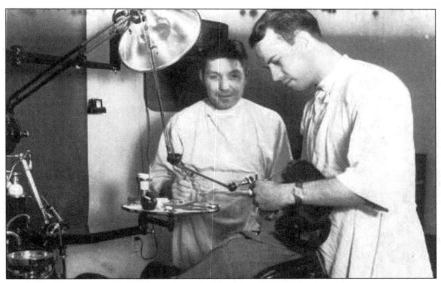

Ed Coleman, right, assisted by Harry Morris, works on a patient at the "2309 Dental Clinic" in Green Bay USNTC – Great Lakes, Illinois, on May 2, 1944.

Rob Schmid tries out the slopes in Sun Valley, Idaho, about 60 miles from his base, on April 1, 1945.

Three P-51 Mustangs are pictured in the air.

Fred Baumann poses
for a photograph in
Marsailles, France, in
February 1945.

Bob Hansard, right, poses for a photograph with a friend.

Bill Hunt poses for a photograph in uniform.

Photo courtesy Tom Evans

A train falls off a bridge that spanned the Irrawaddy River in Burma after being bombed by U.S. Army Air Corps bombers.

The four Allied flags hang from the the Arc de Triomphe two days after V-E Day. Wallace Baumann photographed the Arc on May 10, 1945, from the Champs Elysee during a four-day pass to Paris, France.

Photo courtesy Wallace Baumann

A bridge that spanned the Irrawaddy River in Burma collapsed after being bombed by U.S. Army Air Corps bombers.

An unknown soldier's memorial is shown under the Arc de Triomphe two days after V-E Day in Paris, France.

German soldiers surrender in Italy.

The inside of an A-26 cockpit is shown. "This is why a pilot gets base pay plus fifty percent for flying," said Tom Evans.

Photo courtesy Fred Baumann

Seven P-51 Mustangs are pictured in a line after the war in Piagiolino, Italy.

Photo courtesy John Moore

Italians greet U.S. service members as they arrive in Rome. The Coliseum is shown in the background.

Bill Dickey, bottom left, is pictured at Welford Park Army Air Force Base near Newbury, England, in June 1945.

Vince Torbett, top left, poses with fellow band members.

Chapter eleven
Gordon Ford

Gordon Ford was born in Knoxville, Tennessee, on March 11, 1927. He joined the Navy in 1945, but by the time he was finished with his training, the war was over. He spent most of his time in the San Francisco Bay area, transporting soldiers coming back from the Pacific and their replacements heading out. He attained the rank of seaman first class.

I was in high school in the library one day and found this book titled *Dive Bombing*. I read the book, and one of my ambitions was to be a Navy pilot dive-bomber. I was a lot younger when the war broke out than my peers. I remember in December 1941, I came home from church, turned on the radio, and learned then that Pearl Harbor had been attacked. They were going one by one into the service, getting drafted, while I was left behind. But, while I was in high school as a junior and senior, the Army Air Corps and the Navy were coming in and giving exams for the young men who might have the capability of becoming pilots and getting into the V-12 or V-5 programs. This was my ambition, and since I was there, they allowed me to take the test, which I passed with flying colors. But I was too young, and by the time I became old enough to go into the service, the schools were closed. At that time, I was one and a half quarters into The University of Tennessee. I did not want to be drafted, so before my eighteenth birthday, I decided to volunteer so I could be sure to get into the Navy. So I went down and volunteered, and the recruiting officer told me he thought I'd be a good candidate to be a radio technician. I told him that I did not want to be a radio technician and that I wanted to be a pilot, but if I couldn't be a pilot, I wanted to be on a PT boat. When I look back now, that was somewhat stupid. A PT boat was a torpedo boat; it's a small boat that cruises and goes into the enemy fleet and drops torpedoes. That is what John Kennedy was assigned to, and that's where he became a hero. I wasn't looking to be a hero, but I guess at the time, being adventuresome, I felt like if I was a dive-bomber or on a PT boat that I would be right in the middle of it. But I didn't even get close.

So in February of 1945, I enlisted. I was not called until April 1945, at which time I went to Great Lakes to train. I was interviewed by the officer who would determine where I would end up in the Navy, and he suggested that I take the examinations to qualify for some kind of special training. After the test, I went back and told him that I would like to be a quartermaster or a motor machinist on a PT boat. He advised me that it didn't make any difference where I wanted to go, I'd passed the test and would be going to radio technician school. Now, the deal was that if I had enlisted as a potential radio technician, I would be a seaman first class when I got out of boot camp. But since I did not do that, if I went to radio school, I would be a seaman second class when I got out. Nonetheless, I was sent to a high school in Chicago that had been converted to a pre-radio school. I did not make the top 10 percent in the first four weeks, so I was allowed to repeat. But I did not made the top 10 percent in the second week, so I was sent back to Great Lakes.

Before all this, VE-Day had come and passed while I was in boot camp, so the conflict in Europe was over and my destiny then was none other than the Pacific front. But then VJ-Day happened, and the war was over before I ever got into any type of school. I remember when we heard about the atomic bomb, I was in the outgoing unit at Great Lakes, and I think the feeling for most of us was that we didn't realize the full ramification of the bomb. We knew it was a big explosive –

enough to bring the Japanese to their knees and surrender. But, at that time, we didn't realize the full potential. Tests were still going on, and they were asking for volunteers to go over and participate in these tests. I put my name in to volunteer, but it never materialized.

So, since I washed out of the radio school, I was sent to an outgoing unit at Great Lakes. One morning, I was put on a train, which was an old cattle car arrangement that was going to California. I'd been there a few days when they announced that the next morning at 0600, the seamen first class would be on the tarmac and that they should go to supplies to get their jungle gear. All seamen second class were told to be on the tarmac at 0600 with their sea bags to leave for transport in San Francisco. I was not yet a seaman first; I was still a seaman second. Those guys who went through radio tech school and got their seaman first were now bound for Guam, but I was bound for the frontier at San Francisco.

I ended up in what was called the small craft unit. You may be aware of the *Delta Queen*, a steamboat on the Mississippi River. Well, the *Delta Queen* at that time was in possession of the Navy and was tied up at Pier 40 in San Francisco. I was on the sister ship – if you could call it a sister ship – the *Delta King*. We tied up at Treasure Island, and our job was to carry the troops from Treasure Island to the Embarcadero, and from the Embarcadero back to Treasure Island. The ones coming on the Embarcadero to Treasure Island were the soldiers coming back from the Pacific, and the ones going from Treasure Island to the Embarcadero were the replacements. They weren't injured; they were all mobile. The interesting thing is that on the ship coming back, I met a lot of men from Knoxville. They were happy to see someone from home so early, and at the same time, it was rewarding to get their stories.

One time, we got into sort of a windstorm. The waves were pretty high, and we were on the steam boat going not too far from the Golden Gate Bridge when we got caught in this windstorm and steered off course because of the boulders and the winds. We rode the waves, but we did finally gain control of the boat and got it back.

On the LCT, we got some leave time through the week after hours, and we could apply for weekends. But there were only eight people on the ship, and we had four Liberty cards. So we would try to toss coins to see who got the Liberty cards. We had to have half a crew aboard ship at all times.

The interesting thing was that the boat was propelled by three engines and was manipulated pretty much by varying the speed of the three engines for backing in and turning in close quarters. We had a motor machinist who operated the throttles, a quartermaster who operated the wheel, and the captain who would be up on the bridge to give the orders to change the speed or back down, right engine forward, that type of thing. Well, he got transferred, and his replacement was a captain off of a one-propeller ship – the operation and docking was quite different, and we had quite a few collisions. Finally, the motor machinist and quartermaster decided to do the job themselves. So the captain would give the order, and they would say, "Aye Aye," and then do what needed to be done to get the boat in. We made many, many beautiful landings at the dock. The captain then would strut off very pleased with how he had handled the ship coming in.

I was on the *Delta King* for several months assigned to the waters of the San Francisco Bay. Eventually, the transfer was diminished to the point that our ship was put out of commission. I was then assigned to an LCT. Our job was to provide supplies from the San Francisco/Oakland Navy Depot, a supply depot, to the third fleet and other ships in San Francisco Bay. We not only transferred food and supplies, but also personnel. So my duty was primarily in the San Francisco Bay area and Mission Street in San Francisco. When I finally got settled in San Francisco Bay, I applied, took a test, and got my seaman first class.

Basically the war was over before I got into it. I did keep a map on my wall before I went in the service, keeping track of the progress as it moved across Europe. I was not able to do that with the Pacific because it was moving around so much day by day that I couldn't keep track of it. But in Europe, I'd listen to the radio day by day and find out where the troops were. Of course, at that time, the news was a lot different than it is today – we had to rely on the newsreels at the theaters and the radio news to determine what was really going on. People would go to the movies just about every week to see a new movie, a comedy, and you'd get the newsreel. The reporters would have a camera in the field, and you'd see a little of the war. It would also tell where the troops were, how many had been injured, and so forth. The newsreel was a very important part – it was like today's television. But it's not like today – if something like Pearl Harbor were to happen today, CNN would probably be right there filming and reporting the whole thing. They would go on to tell what happened and why we were not ready and where everyone was. Today, you actually see it on TV as it is happening, and I'm not sure this is all that great. I think it, for one thing, gives the enemy our position and what our equipment is. We were very careful during the Second World War to guard where our positions were, what the equipment was, and who was going where, but now it's all on TV for all the world and the enemy to see. I don't think this is the way to go about it.

I sometimes think that I did not have much to offer for the service, but at the same time, I was able to transport the older troops coming back and the troops going over. Someone had to do it, and that fell to my responsibility. So one day, I realized that what I was doing was, let's say, not contributing a lot to the cause. I managed to get an interview with my base commanding officer and told him that I had dropped out of UT to go in the service and that I didn't feel I was contributing an awful lot now, so I asked him for a discharge so I could go back to UT in the fall. Strangely enough, he granted me this wish, so I got my discharge in July of 1946 and returned to The University of Tennessee to complete my engineering degree. I got some GI Bill, such as it was. I wasn't in any length of time to get much of the GI Bill, but, of course, it helped. Sometimes

I sort of regret that I didn't see more of the world than I did, but again, since the war was over, I was more interested in getting back home and getting the past behind me.

During the war, I wasn't a real good writer, myself, but I got lots of letters from home. When I went back into school, all my old buddies were still there. It wasn't too difficult to readjust. I think probably just being in the service itself helped me mature significantly – it was the first time away from home and on my own. I was disappointed that I never got on a PT boat, but the war was over. I probably would have gotten there if the war was still on. I do feel that the good Lord is taking care of me in all ways because there have been several incidents that I know his hand has kept me out of harm's way.

Chapter twelve
Bob Fulton

Bob Fulton was born on July 3, 1918, in Knoxville, Tennessee. He entered the Army in 1943 at Fort Devons, Massachusetts, after participating in an ROTC program and graduating with a Master of Business Administration from Harvard University.

W e had a colonel who was in charge of the ROTC, and when the war was declared, he had a nervous breakdown; I never saw him again. He had a nice, easy thing there in the ROTC at the university, and he just never expected to be called to active duty.

As far as what I did during the war, well, this will explain it all. I went over there, and they put me in the 464th Laundry Company – we did laundry. Everybody on the island was delighted.

There were fourteen semi-trailers; each one was a complete laundry, with hot water heaters, dryers, spin dryers, washing machines. That's what we did. People were quite delighted. In fact, there were some people there on the same island – Fiji Island – and they kept bringing their laundry too.

I saw some combat, but I wasn't in it. The 24th Infantry Division had secured the island as they drove the Japs up in the hills. But I saw a lot of dead bodies out there that were Japanese – kind of gruesome. It rained every day – sunshine every day, too, but it rained. And everything just grew prolifically, and a dead body in two or three days has all the grass and everything growing up through it, so I saw a lot of those.

I thought dropping the atomic bomb was a good way to end the war – it ended it. And some of our friends who were getting ready to be shipped on up to take Japan sure sighed with relief. I mean, that stopped all of that. But the morality of it? I can't see the difference between dropping a bomb on somebody and shooting them in the head or in the back or anything else. If the object is to kill the enemy, they certainly stopped the war with it.

I was only in there three years. There was a field officer over there who said I had cancer, and he sent me home after three years. The Army sent me up to a hospital in Kentucky, but I wasn't in there very long. And then on to rest and rehabilitation, which I really didn't want; I was tired of sitting around. They sent me to Miami. They already took over all the resort hotels in Miami, and that's where I stayed. Just fun and games.

But one of my classmates – I have forgotten his name now – he left from over there in the West Coast. I was with him out there in San Francisco when his ship came in and he left. He was shot somewhere over there before a boat came to take me overseas. So it was risky business for everybody.

It wasn't like some of the stuff now, where you can get out of it – you just went. It was a nice experience since I didn't get shot. There were a lot more of them shot over there on Solomon Island.

Chapter thirteen
Conway Garlington

Conway Garlington was born in Knoxville, Tennessee, on June 10, 1923. He was in the middle of his studies at The University of Tennessee when he decided to join the Naval Air Corps in 1943. He made it to ensign, which is the equivalent of a second lieutenant in the Army. Conway spent most of his time in flight training, and the war ended before he saw any combat.

I can remember in December of 1941, I was a freshman at The University of Tennessee, and I was working part time at a filling station right on Cumberland Avenue. I worked on Saturday and Sunday, pumping gas. I remember I had a radio, and I was listening to music when all of a sudden they said, "We interrupt this program to announce that Pearl Harbor has been attacked by the Japanese." I was a student at UT, and that was the beginning of the war. I was just nineteen, and I wouldn't be drafted until the following fall.

So in the fall of 1942, I was going to be drafted. I had started UT and I wanted to finish the year, so I went down to the Army Air Corps recruiting office, told them I was over at UT and would like to finish the calendar year, and asked if they would defer me until then. They said, "No, we couldn't promise you that." Of course, we were right in the middle of a war, so I said, "OK, thank you." So I moved on over to the Naval Air Corps, and at that time they had a group of prominent people in Knoxville who were recruiting for the

Navy officers training – V5 was the Naval Air Corps training officers. I went to a prominent lawyer here and told him that I wanted to finish this calendar year, and he said, "Let's see what we can do." So he picked up the phone, called Atlanta, and told them that he had a young man there who wanted to join the V5 program but wanted to wait until the spring. They said that was fine, so I joined.

Another fellow who was a friend of mine did the same thing, but in the spring – April of '43 – there were a lot of Army Reserve candidates at UT who all got called up to the Army. So here we were, my friend and me at UT in April and May with nothing but girls and 4Fs – guys who were not eligible for the Army. My friend said, "I'm not going to wait around here for another six weeks; I'm going to go on in." So he quit school and joined, but I waited until my year ended.

In June I went in the Naval Air Corps training program. It was excellent, but long. It seemed that every time we were finished with one practice or one area, they would add on something else. But I went to the University of South Carolina in Columbia, where we just marched, had calisthenics, and studied aerodynamics and math. I was there from June until August of '43, and then I was sent to the University of Georgia for preflight training. It was an excellent school, but again, it was just calisthenics and taking classes, but no flying. Then, after I finished that, I went to the Naval air station in Millington, just north of Memphis, and we started flight training there. After six months or so, I was sent to Corpus Christi in Texas for basic training, and that's where we starting upgrading the planes we would be flying. I didn't get my commission and wings until February of '45, which was almost twenty months.

From there, I went up to the Great Lakes, where they had converted a coal burner ship with a flat top on it. We had to land and take off six times to qualify for carrier-based flying. They had carriers in the Pacific, but this was a training ship – it was the Glenview Naval Air Station out of Chicago. It took three weeks to qualify because they were backed up. After I finished that, we were going down to Fort Lauderdale to pick up our squadron and start flying the planes we would be in, which were torpedo bombers. They were carrier-based single engine – the biggest single-engine plane there was. There was a pilot and a radio operator who sat right behind me with a .50-caliber machine gun and a torpedoman who sat in the bay of the plane. We took these training exercises and learned how we would go out on target practice.

We were carrier-based, but I didn't go out to the Pacific fleet; I flew off the Atlantic coast. See, the Army Air Corps flew mostly land-based, and the Navy flew off of carriers. We had some amphibious planes, like the PBY, which was a big plane that could land on the water. The real difference was that there was no comparison between the Naval Air Corps and the Army – we were so much better. Just teasing. I think the Army had more multi-engines; we didn't have any big bombers – that was all Army. We were primarily single engines, except for those seaplanes, which were used to rescue people who went down.

After I finished that training, a lot of these fellows went out to the west coast and then out to Hawaii to join the fleet, which means they were going to be placed on carriers and fight the Japanese in the Pacific. They picked about half a dozen of us and sent us down to Texas to train for a night torpedo squadron. What we would be doing is flying at night, including taking off and landing at night. I was down there when the war ended. We were killing so many people in that training program that they stopped all flight training. I didn't fly any more.

After the war, they wanted to ferry all those planes in Texas to what they called the graveyard in Miami, Florida. They picked a bunch of us to fly these planes. We came up from Texas, flew around the Gulf Coast, and had to land in Mobile at an air base there. We then spent the night and gassed up so we could go on to Florida.

That was about it; I was in training the whole time. Well, I got my commission in February, and I think the

Japanese surrendered in the fall of '45, and the Germans in the spring of '45. I was commissioned just a few months. One thing they criticized was that we had too many pilots in the program, so they would start "washing out." We couldn't all stay in the program, so they started "washing out" a lot of good men, good pilots. The next thing we knew, they would say we need more pilots, so they'd start pushing everybody through.

I was never in any combat. The only thing I was involved in was anti-sub when we flew some patrol out in the Atlantic for submarines. I didn't get to do what I was trained to do. The war stopped and I got out.

I came back in December of 1945. The war was over in the fall, but it took some time to get discharged. I was discharged in Memphis; you usually were discharged the closest stop to your home. I came back, entered the university with the GI Bill in January, and started my junior year. Back then you could take three years of business administration and the fourth year you could go to law school. In the fall of '46, I went to law school and got my Bachelor of Science.

But I had all this time on the GI Bill left. I didn't want to go to work, I didn't want to go to another school, and I didn't have anything else to do, so I just stayed in the law school. I went for two more years at the law school and got a Bachelor's of Law – since then it has become a doctorate of law, so I paid fifty dollars and they gave me a doctorate. I was living at home, making seventy-five dollars per month, and had all my books and tuition paid. The GI Bill was the best thing that ever happened. I would never have gone to law school without it. I got a job with a local firm after I graduated. Although I wasn't going to practice, I didn't have anything else to do, so I stayed with them.

I later married a girl who grew up in this church – I grew up in this church, too – and we were married here. We had four children and a very nice life.

I really didn't want to travel once I got home because I spent that time in the service. But, I think back when we were in the '40s, even though there was a war, it was a good period.

My mother never worked, she stayed at home, and I just think the family was more stable and it was a better time. During the war, I wrote home pretty regularly. I sent money out of my paycheck back for savings bonds.

When I was stationed in Corpus Christi, Texas, I had a friend who was also a cadet. We had a pass, so he and I went to a Presbyterian church one Sunday, and a car nearly ran over us as we were walking across the street. We were in uniform and we went on into the church. There was this girl and her mother in church sitting behind us who had been in the car. We got up and were sort of laughing about it, but they asked us to come home with them for lunch. So we went to lunch. The girl – a rather attractive girl – said that she and a friend were going to go to a movie that afternoon and asked if we would like to play bridge. I played bridge, so I said yes. We played bridge that afternoon, and I started dating her. They had an apartment over a garage, and I would stay up there when I came from base, even drive her mother's car. I wrote my mother and told her that I hoped she didn't mind that we played bridge on Sunday. But we didn't gamble – that's the difference between then and now.

Also, when we were still cadets in Columbia, we'd get off on a weekend and go to church. Then we would come outside and sort of stand around waiting for someone to ask us to go home for dinner. We got a lot of invitations – people wanted to help these young men in the service. I did that every time I went to church.

I told my friends who were in the Army – most of them were in France for D-Day – that I slept every night between clean sheets. The Navy was good. I think there was one place to be that was better than the Navy, and that was the Marines.

Chapter fourteen
Bob Hansard

Bob Hansard was born in Knoxville, Tennessee, on August 4, 1925. He joined the Navy in November 1943. He was there for the invasion of Normandy and participated in the invasion of southern France. After the war ended, he stayed with the Navy as an instructor for midshipmen in the officers training school at Annapolis until he was discharged.

After leaving high school, I joined the Navy before I became eighteen because I wanted to get in the Navy instead of the Army. They called me back in November of '43, and I did my basic training in San Diego, California. Then I was sent to service school at Great Lakes. I spent several months there. After that, I was assigned to the *USS Marblehead* — cruisers are named after cities, and there is a Marblehead, Massachusetts. It was an old four-stacker, and it was in New York Navy Yard being repaired. The ship was pretty well torn up during the first part of the war; in fact, they made a movie about the ship – "The Story of Dr. Wassell" – about it supposedly being sunk and guys being trapped below deck. The *Marblehead* was in the China Sea when Japan declared war, and they supposedly sunk it. One of the guys telling the story said one side of the ship was a foot under water, but they made it back to the Philippines and got some repairs. Then they went to Hawaii and then San Francisco and in time got it repaired. Next, they went through the canal and came back to the States. But they were still working on it when

I went aboard. The first thing I noticed was when I went down the ladder to the main deck and saw that the water faucet was hanging upside down. Another thing they do, of course, is paint the sides yellow for rust prevention before they paint the color of the ship, but I thought they were gun holes. Looking at the ship, I wasn't sure if I should go aboard or not – it looked like it was torn all to pieces. But they got it going; I guess I was in Brooklyn for a month before we shipped out.

From there, we were in North Atlantic convoy duty for a couple of trips. From Brooklyn, we went to Boston, and at Boston, we picked up the convoy. I think one of our convoys had a hundred or more ships in it, but your speed is determined by the slowest ship in the convoy – if they can only go eight knots, that's your speed. So while others were shooting for subs, we were trying to get in to help the merchant ships. So we had our destroyers circle all the time around the big convoy in case a sub got in the center, which we had to deal with one time. If you're the last ship and you can't keep up, you fall back. But usually they tried to give them some protection.

The last trip we went on with a convoy, we were the flagship, meaning we were the ship supposedly keeping track of all the convoys. We went from Boston Harbor to Belfast, Ireland, and from Belfast, we went into Plymouth, England. We pulled into Plymouth on June 5, and at that point, we knew something big was going on because the whole harbor was full of ships. And all the soldiers were topside – everybody knew that something big was going to happen. Well, we were doing the invasion of Normandy. There were many ships that had gone in and bombarded the coast, but when we were there, the bombardment had just about completed. We really didn't have anything to do, so they pulled us out. I do remember that it was quite a show and we were all excited about what was going on and wanted to see more of it.

So on June 6, about three-thirty in the morning, we left the bay, pulled out into the channel, and I remember at that particular time I was impressed with all the ships – as far as I could see were ships. Leaving, we went through Gibraltar back into the Mediterranean and into Palermo, Sicily, to get ready for the invasion of southern France. So we played around there until August 6 – I remember it was two days after my birthday that we went into southern France for the invasion, and we were in there about four days and five nights. But we did bombard the heck out of them. During the invasion, the rudder of the ship was hit, so after the invasion was over, we pulled out. They didn't have room to take us in the States, so they sent us to Rio de Janeiro for repairs.

After we got the ship repaired, we were patrolling Argentina because the South American country was shipping arms to Germany. We were down there for about a year, which to us seemed like a vacation – with the beach, good food, and everything. There was our ship and the *Omaha*. After the *Omaha* would go out for two weeks patrolling, they would come in and we would go out. I was one of seven guys chosen to board ships that we caught and sent back into port, and the whole time we only took one ship back – it was loaded with guns and ammunition. Germany didn't occupy Argentina; they just had a lot of Germans down there and were sympathetic towards Germany. We knew they were shipping arms and things to Germany, and we were keeping them from doing that.

I was never injured during the war. But off the coast of Cuba, we had one guy wash overboard; a big wave came over our ship, and he was less than five feet from me. I grabbed hold of a covering, and he grabbed hold of the lifeline – the only thing between you and the ocean is this cable, and it has a little strip that you can grab hold of – but he disappeared and we didn't go back for him. We had two observation planes, and the motor mechanic would get out there in the morning and turn the props and loosen the engine up, but one time, one of the guys left the switch on. Well, I was standing and talking to a guy who was slicing tomatoes into a big tub, and one guy was over where the plane was. He gave the prop on the plane a flip, and the engine started and it hit him. I saw blood come right across that tub of tomatoes, so we didn't eat any tomatoes that night. I saw the guy who went down, and we circled, but there wasn't anything left of him. During the invasion of southern France, we had an officer who died from being hit by shrapnel. Airplanes made a run on us every night at about fifteen to eleven, and you could almost time it. So the Germans would fly over, and sometimes the plane would make a dive, and one made a dive on us. It hit the ship one time, ricocheted, and sounded like a hundred bullets, and one of the commanding officers got hit.

While we were in and near the States, we had good food. But over there in the Mediterranean, it got pretty low – watermelons, cantaloupes, whatever you could get. Gibraltar was the nearest place that we could get supplies, but that's a pretty good trip from around Sicily.

After Germany surrendered, we went back to Panama, where we were ready to go to the Pacific. I'll never forget – we were aboard topside watching a movie when we got word that Japan had surrendered, so we didn't have to go through the canal. When we heard about the bomb, I said, "Gee whiz, this thing was made in Oak Ridge, and we had no idea what was going on with all that traffic and everything when I was in high school back in '41, '42 and '43." So it was a big surprise, and, of course, we laughed because we knew we were going to get to go home.

Chapter fifteen
Al Holmes

Al Holmes was born in Columbus, Ohio, on January 31, 1917, and died on March 17, 2006. He graduated from Ohio State University, worked for a while, and then attended Harvard University to pursue a Master of Business Administration. At Harvard, he enrolled in the school's ROTC program, and after graduation, he joined the Army. Al headed a bakery unit in New Guinea and the Philippines during World War II and was never in any combat. He worked his way up from second lieutenant to first lieutenant and finally to captain. His service earned him a Bronze Star.

When I graduated from Harvard Business School in April of 1943, I went into active duty in the Army. I went to Camp Lee, Virginia, for OCS and was commissioned. Shortly thereafter, I was shipped overseas to the southwest Pacific, and the first place I went was New Guinea. This place was supposedly the second-wettest place in the world – I believe it because it would pour down rain, then the sun would come out, and two hours later the trucks would roll down the road in a cloud of dust. Then it would rain again.

It was so damp that all your leather and everything else would mildew. I had a GI haircut when I was in OCS, and then I let my hair grow when I got to New Guinea. Well, I discovered long hair was not the thing to have because it would mildew – everything would mildew. And so I cut it off again.

And from there on, I was in a couple of places in New Guinea. And in the Army's wisdom, they sent me to command a bakery unit on Owi Island. Owi Island was an island off New Guinea, and it was just a coral strip about two miles long and half a mile wide – solid coral. The 5th Air Force headquarters was there, and they had two airstrips the entire length of the island. The interesting thing there were the B-24s – the longest range bomber we had at the time – would take off from there for bombing missions to Borneo, and it was such a long trip that they didn't always get back. They would run out of fuel. So, (Charles) Lindbergh came over there to teach them how to extend the range by conserving fuel and how to fly the airplanes to get the most economical fuel consumption so they could get back. It was all top-secret news in those days, but Lindbergh was out there trying to train these pilots. I never met him – nobody met him – it was just rumors then. But later on it was confirmed that he had been out there.

Now, I had never been in a bakery in my life, but there I was, commander of a bakery unit. Fortunately, I had good men who knew what to do.

There at Owi, every unit had a volleyball court as a place for the men to get exercise. We had a volleyball court that was coral, except one point in the court had a high spot where there was a little bit of mud due to decomposition of the coral. But getting down in it would mess up the volleyball court. Right next to me was another division that had a bulldozer. So I went over there, saw the captain one day, and said to him, "I have a couple men that know how to bake a really delicious pie, and from Australia, we can get some pretty good fruit – peaches and cherries." Most of our rations from Australia were not fit to eat. But, anyway, I said, "I've got a baker that can make a delicious pie, and if you have somebody over here that can run a bulldozer and do a little bit of cleaning up of that area to keep that mud from coming down on my volleyball court, I'm sure I can get a couple of my men to bake a couple of delicious pies for you." He said he'd do what he could do, so I went back to my quarters – my camp – which was close by, and it wasn't very long before I was awakened by the chug of a bulldozer. There was a bulldozer out there working and doing what I asked for. And guess who was driving the bulldozer? The captain. Well, that was the way we did things over there during the war – we helped each other do things.

After that, we went to several places on the way to the Philippines. We came in for the operation going on at Zamboanga. As the story goes, Zamboanga is where the monkeys have no tails. Have you ever heard that song? They're bitten off by whales. All I can say is a lot of monkeys lost their tails on account of that song. Anyway, at that time I was attached to the 41st Infantry. We came in and went to make a landing on an LCI – a Landing Craft Infantry – and we got stuck on a coral reef and had to spend the night on the reef waiting for the tide to come in so we could get the ship off the reef. So we landed the next day and our men located all of our equipment.

Twenty-four hours after we landed, we were able to produce bread and send it up to the front lines for the troops. Bread was one of the good things to eat in those days. And for the next couple of months, our little bakery unit was putting out more than two and a half times the volume of bread that the organizational tables said we were capable of doing. And the nice thing about that is some colonel or general was impressed enough that he thought it was worth me getting a Bronze Star medal for what I had done. So I appreciated that.

I got a call from the hospital one time, and the commanding officer of the hospital was mad as hops. He said, "This bread you sent us is crawling with weevil." Well, I said we'd look into it. So I went over to the hospital and we cut a loaf of bread, and sure enough, it had pepper all over it – live pepper! It was crawling around. So I said, "Well let me go get you another shipment of bread." The trouble was, at that point, we were getting our flour from Australia – we couldn't get any American flour, which we had previously – and our rations were rather sparse.

So I went back to the bakery and had the men make some more bread and cut loaves of it – no weevil. So I told them to send that over to the hospital. They did, and the next day the commanding officer called and was still mad as hops. He said, "This is no better than the bread you sent before! It's full of live pepper!" What we had to discover was that the baking process was the right amount of time for the weevil larva in the bread to incubate and come alive. So if you ate the bread right after it came out of the ovens, you were all right, but if you waited a day, you got a lot of "meat" with your bread. And there was nothing we could do about it. So, those were little things you ran into – unexpected things.

I came home from the Philippines. I was in Zamboanga longer than any American GI over there. But the war ended and I got to come home. I was overseas about twenty-eight months in the southwest Pacific area, New Guinea, and the Philippines.

I was right happy when I heard about the atomic bomb because our unit was attached at that time to the 41st Infantry Division, and they were making preparations to go to Japan. We were sitting out one night on a coconut log trying to watch a movie in the rain and the news came in. Of course, we forgot about the movie. All of the men were so excited. I had to make sure that the supply room was locked up securely because all of the men wanted to get guns and start shooting. When we got things calmed down, two other officers and I had our own little party in a Philippine house we commandeered, and we were right happy. Of course, we didn't know what an atomic bomb was or anything else – we hadn't gotten any news about that – we heard it was just so many tons of TNT.

When I got home, I went to work for a dairy company that my father was interested in down in Tennessee – that's what brought me to Tennessee. It was a milk and ice cream business – these were some companies my father was interested in. The trouble was, when anyone saw me, all they saw was my father. So I decided to get out on my own.

I got into the frozen-food business. That's what brought me to Knoxville. I used to say if I left the business I was in, I would leave Knoxville the same day. But after nine years with the company, I left that business and decided I liked Knoxville – and I'm still here.

I grew up in Broad Street Presbyterian Church in Columbus, Ohio. When I came down here, I joined First Presbyterian Church in Knoxville. One time I went to Florida on a business trip, and I called on some former neighbors of mine in Columbus, Ohio, who had to moved to Florida in retirement years. While I was in their living room visiting, this pretty little girl walked in – she was the daughter of their neighbors. Right then and there, I decided I needed to really work on that Florida territory. So we were married in St. Petersburg, Florida, at the First Presbyterian Church of St. Petersburg, where she was a member. So we're solidly Presbyterian – my background is Presbyterian and hers is too.

After getting out of the Army, I had the GI Bill available to me. I did not want to go back to school anymore – I didn't want to take art classes or something like that. But I was attached to the air force so much overseas – I didn't pilot anything, but I rode in a lot of planes – I got interested in aviation. So, I used my GI Bill to learn to fly – nicest thing I ever did. I had my own plane for 25 years. My three children didn't even know what it was like to take an automobile trip because we used the airplane for family transportation. We were real fortunate to be able to go places all over the United States. I've landed, I think, in 46 states, practically every province in Canada, a few places in Mexico, and quite a bit in the Caribbean. So, we've really used that airplane. It's been the greatest joy of my life, being able to use that and see things.

I probably wouldn't have been able to do that if I hadn't been in the Army. My GI Bill paid for my flying lessons. That was the nicest thing the government ever did for me. But it sort of rubbed off on my family. My daughter Missy got her private flying license. She doesn't fly much any more, but my son Albert, who is a doctor, flew a lot with me. He now has his own plane and uses it in his work. He goes every place he can by air, and every other week, he flies up to Middlesboro,

Kentucky, to see patients right by the airport. So he's addicted too.

The war disrupted my life for quite a while. One of the results is I didn't get married until a later age. But Norma, my wife, says they put me in hot storage to keep me from getting married. I came back and finally found her, and we've been married now 51 years – happy 51 years and still going strong. We have three children and nine grandchildren. We figure we are tremendously blessed.

Chapter sixteen
Bill Hunt

Bill Hunt was born in Knoxville, Tennessee, on July 19, 1921. He entered the Army in 1942 and joined the Corps of Engineers. He spent four years in the Army and twenty-one years in the Army Reserves. During World War II, he spent a lot of time in Okinawa, Korea, and Leyte, P.I. After the war, he graduated from The University of Tennessee with a degree in industrial management.

A t the time, I had been at The University of Tennessee for two years, but I couldn't keep my mind too much on studying because everybody I knew was volunteering to go into the air force. So I went up to the post office with my father to see about the Air Corps. There was a long line of people around the corner and around the next corner, and I thought, "This is a heck of a way to treat an older person like my father, to have to wait through all this. I'm going to come back later."

They had an ordnance inspector course over at UT, so I went over the next day to see about that and signed up. It was a three-month course, at the end of which they would send you to an ordnance school – mine was Wolf Creek Ordnance Department in Milan, Tennessee. So, with the training we had, we could fit in with very little instruction in several different lines. They had shell loading for 155 mm and 37 mm shell where we were. I started off in one and ended up in the other for about three months. Then they found my location in the draft, and they had room for another.

After that six-month period, I was more than ready since I'd been doing something for the Army anyway. So I came back to Knoxville, and they had five buses going down to Fort Oglethorpe, Georgia. We got on those buses and went down there on November 11, 1942.

They really had too many people, so after we went through a physical examination and got uniforms, they sent us back home for two weeks. After that, we went back down to Oglethorpe and waited until our name was called from a list. We didn't know where we were going; we just knew it was time for us to go. So we got on the train and started north.

Seeing as I'd been in the Ordnance Department, I thought maybe I'd go to an ordnance plant – that had something to do with what I'd been doing. It was nighttime when the train stopped. I said, "Is this the ordnance department?" They said, "No, you're in the Corps of Engineers. This is Fort Belvoir, Virginia."

Then I had a three-month basic training course, at the end of which, if you had an AGTC score of a certain amount – one hundred ten, I think – you were eligible to go on to OCS (that's Officers Candidate School). Those of us who did have that score were given a week of pre-OCS, where they would treat you just like you were at OCS just to see your reaction. Two of them got on either side and started hollering at you usually.

Our class started out as T-32 – that was the name of our class – and forty-five were in there. Three months later, nine of us graduated. The rest of them were sent back, all the way back home, because they were not suitable at that time with their restrictions. Some of them were master sergeants and had been in the service; it just tore us up to think that we, who had no experience whatsoever, had to see all of these guys who had experience in the Army get sent back a week or two weeks or a month before they could continue the course. But the course ended for me in June of 1943.

My first assignment was Camp Claiborne, Louisiana, and they had three posts there. When we got down there, our orders were to report directly – do not stop, do not pass "go," like in some of our games. We got there on Friday afternoon, and I went into the office of this unit. They said, "What are you doing here Friday afternoon?" I said, "Well, they said report directly, so here I am, a new second lieutenant." He told me that everybody had gone into town and to come back on Monday morning. So I went back into town and spent the weekend sightseeing. I came back Monday morning, and then they were ready for me.

The first job I had was out on the rifle range as a range officer. We had to teach the men how to shoot the guns and how not to, all the safety rules and things of that type. I liked guns because I'd been a collector for a long time and they were of interest to me.

Then from Camp Claiborne, Louisiana, I was sent to Camp Swift, Texas – that's the best spot in Texas. There I was, a member of the 1320th Engineer General Service Regiment. They had quite an extensive area there, and we trained with that unit for three months to go overseas. At the end of that time, we boarded a troop train and went across the country. I know we went through Salt Lake City because we could see the mountain and everything, then to San Francisco and Camp Stoneman – but we were only there long enough to get everybody two pairs of combat boots. No one was let out of camp because if they were let out, some of them might not get back.

We went down to where the boats were docked right there by the Golden Gate Bridge. I saw the great big "General Class" ships, and I said, "Look there, that's our ship." Then someone said, "No, that's not your ship; it's behind it." We went on a little farther, and there was this little ship, a converted Baltimore mail liner. They were still converting it, and they hammered on it all the way across to Oahu.

It took about five days to get to Oahu, and we went to a place called Fort Hasey. That's beyond Diamond Head over near Kaneohe Naval Air Station. It was dark, it was rainy, and we had to put up tents. Basically, we had the craziest arrangements of tents hooked to telephone poles, to wires, to other buildings, to each other. The next morning, when they came out to inspect what we had, they told us to tear it all down. Then they lined them all up uniformly like they should be and had some semblance of a training camp.

Half of our regiment was Fort Bellows Field and half was Fort Hasey. So we had our training there. We built construction facilities like corps houses on Hickam Field, which was the air force base there, worked on the roads, and did things of that type for about three months. Then we went to Maui – that's another one of the five islands.

We were there for three months and built a concrete radar installation on top of Mt. Haleakala, which was ten thousand feet up. That was quite a job to do, but there was beautiful scenery. When you're up there, you come down through the clouds. We were there for three months and then went back to Oahu for one more month, so that makes seven in all.

Then some of us were called out to cadre, which means going to another unit that has some vacancies and needs some people in a hurry. Three of us, who still correspond with each other, went that day from different units. We went to the 110th Engineer Combat Battalion – that was a white outfit. They had been up to Kiska and came down to Oahu for training in sea landing and small boats and things of that type. I went into the big recreation hall, and all the troops were lined up around the wall, sitting, and had their duffle bags. I said, "You all are new folks; did you just get here?" They said, "New nothing; we're going tomorrow morning. You got a gun?" I said, "No," and they said, "Better go get one." So I was in the unit for one day there, and then we went down and boarded the boats.

They changed our destination at sea. First we were going to Yap, which was a strongly held Japanese post, with a concrete fortification and everything. But they decided that we should bypass Yap and go to the Hawaiian Islands because they had not seen very much aviation activity in that area. So, we went to Eniwetok and Manus, which was about one thousand miles and took thirty-one days aboard the boat before we were to leave there to go to Leyte.

We arrived at Leyte on October 20. We were in the harbor at two in the morning, and everybody was told to get out on deck, that if there were any mines to be located, they'd be here, coming into Leyte Gulf. So we put on our Mae Wests and went into the Dinagat-Homonhon Islands. When it got light enough to see it, there was the old fleet in that bay. It took quite a while to get the first line of infantry in far enough so that we could come in behind them. We were an engineer unit supporting those front-line troops. They had engineer troops with them, but we were backing them up, doing more stable work like bridges and roads.

After making big figure eights in our landing craft for about three or four hours, we went in about noon. Behind us were a cruiser and a couple of destroyers, which were firing over our heads all day long. To hear that and going in circles makes you a little bit seasick, too. And the operators of those Higgins boats said, "Don't drink your water in your canteens; use some of ours because you should save yours – you'll need it." Well, those canteens of theirs were five-gallon cans that were just recently painted and smelled of banana oil. And all the water tasted like banana oil. We were glad to get ashore when the ramps went down to get just a little bit of water and try to find where our unit was.

After a while, we located the unit and found out where we were supposed to go. They didn't take too long to get started, but in that five-day period, the Japanese decided that they would come over and drop some bombs. So they came over and dropped a bomb on the 50th Engineers – that was our sister engineer battalion, which was right next door to us. They dropped one bomb in the middle of their supply area, and it set off everything else into an ammunition dump that exploded all night long. And we were there, right next door to them. You could see these shells go out across the water – it was just like

Fourth of July. Then they told me, "Hunt, you get your group together to go fight the fire." I thought, "Firefight – we'll take shovels and picks and things of that type." So when we got up the beach to that area, they said, "No, we meant bring your rifles to fight the Japs."

Incidentally, our troops, without orders, took their bulldozers and went into that area that was exploding, took hold of those sleds that ammunition was loaded on (like pallets), pulled out the wire cables, hooked their dozer onto it, and pulled it out. Some of it was burning and some was hot, and they took it out of there so it wouldn't blow up. They did that on their own and got a lot of medals for it.

We spent the next few days trying to pick up everything and reform those areas called dumps. We would operate those dumps and set everything that was coming in for other ships out farther in the bay.

There was a catmon hill right next to our unit that had a perimeter of tents. Each night, the lights on that catmon hill would go up a little farther, which meant that our troops were pushing the Japs up towards the top. They were smoking cigarettes, and we could see those lights. Each night, a sniper would shoot down at the beach. Well, the beach was all lit up like nobody's business – just a perfect target – but the Japs were just leaving it for the air force to try to defend that island. Of course, our troops were pushing their troops back away from the beaches, and they'd gone in about two hundred yards.

Since they had done that, we were moved up from the beach to a place called Tolosa, which is right on the beach. A little farther inland is Tanawan to Dagami, and that was our stretch of road, sixteen miles altogether. We worked on completing that road. The Japanese road was fourteen feet wide, and the standard military road for our Army was twenty-two feet, so we had to bring in material and widen everything they had. Their roads were six feet up off of the rice paddies, which was very narrow, and when our traffic started hitting them, and with the rain, we'd just flatten all that out in the rice paddies. So we'd have to build the road up again. We spent half our time just building the roads and things of that type.

After a while, they decided we would go on to Okinawa. On Easter Day, April 1, we landed there, and it was a beautiful day – sunshine and everything. We landed at a point where all the troops came in. We had the corps under John Hodges, a major general, and we had the Marines under Geiger, and all of them came right in the same area. The place called Orange 1 and Orange 2 were the beaches that we were to come in on. We were supposed to land on Orange 2 but landed on Orange 1. There was a creek that ran down between the two areas, so we had to go across that creek to be in our correct area.

On the first night of our unit's landing on Okinawa, I took nine members of the 110th Engineers, two light .30-caliber machine guns, and one heavier .50-caliber machine gun to an area about half a mile northeast of Orange Beach 2. This spot was designated for us by our battalion commanding officer. These security weapons were set up and ranged in at about thirty feet from each other, with the .50-caliber machine gun in the middle, covering a road that came our way. Three men of our security force were assigned to each gun and given directions that one of the three was to be awake at all times, or on duty for two hours and off duty for four hours. I took a position thirty feet behind them and dug a slit trench about two and a half feet by six feet by fifteen inches deep so as to be relatively safe from enemy fire. My instructions were: "Don't all of you go to sleep at the same time." Then I went to sleep. It so happened that they did also, tired from handling these extra weapons and ammunition. About three hours later, I was awakened by a rifle shot, followed by people running. Then seven more shots, and there, about two feet away, was a big Jap marine in blue uniform shot eight times. I'm glad one of our 110th Engineers woke up in time.

Then on the next night, April 2, 1945, I was down on the beach overseeing an LST being unloaded onto the shore. It was dark, but the whole beach landing area was lit up to facilitate the off-loading of supplies. All of a sudden, there was a big swoosh of a shell on the way, and then a big explosion next to our LST in the water. This was followed by shell number two as it hit the beach. Then shell number three came over and landed about half a mile inland. The enemy had missed their target and quit firing. This amazed the second lieutenant, and he asked a ship crewman what our boatload was. He smiled and said, "Explosives." It seems that a Jap sub had surfaced on the other side of the coral reef that surrounded Okinawa island and aimed its deck gun at our LST.

We were there at Kadena Air Strip when they said, "Hunt, you go up here on security." So, they picked out a certain spot, and I was to take a machine gun section up there for perimeter defense because the Marines were up that way and the Japs had pulled away from the beaches up into the hills. That night we set up our machine guns there, and the next day another lieutenant and I went up and inspected the airfield. There were a lot of old, shot-up Japanese planes all around. They had an ohka bomb, which was also called a dumb bomb – it was a glider that had a rocket in the end of it and a 2,000-pound bomb in the nose. They'd take those things on bombers, go out over the fleet, release them, and they'd have a little guidance with those rockets on the end. They could guide it right into a ship and blow the whole thing up.

So we would work on roads and bridges from Kadena down through Futema, which is a little bit farther south. We were there for the rest of the engagement and were slowly pushing them back. They had quite an extensive fortification that had all their guns inside caves – they put them in there in the daytime and pulled them out at night to shoot back over the ridges. The island of Okinawa is one set of ridges after another, and when we were coming up there, they would be fortifying the next ridge so they had something to get behind, and our troops didn't. But we had tanks and air power and so forth. Our planes would come around and launch rockets into those caves, which helped a lot.

Our general was killed in the lower end of Okinawa. The gun that was used was hidden and hadn't been fired all day. Our general was out posing for some photographers next to a big boulder when they fired one shot, hit that boulder, and killed him, just like that. Gen. Stillwell came in to replace him, and he was the one who was over in India and the Burma Road and places like that. He was sixty-two at that time. But Simon Bolivar Buckner was the man in charge of all of our troops. His grandfather was the Buckner who was in the Civil War. He was the only general who surrendered twice.

After a while, the airplanes were coming from Honshu – that's the end of the Japanese islands – to bomb our ships around the island, fly on over to China, load up, and come back. It was just four hundred miles, just like a milk run. I was standing there one time and saw a Jap plane come out of the clouds right above us. He picked out a battle ship, went back in the clouds, and came down right into the side of that ship – I think it was the *Tennessee* – put it out of commission for about two weeks.

We had things like that going on all the time. Two of our planes were coming in that had lost their communications. Our people thought they were Japanese and got both of them. One of them landed in the cemetery up on the hill behind us and turned over. We had a bulldozer and turned him back over so he could get out – it didn't kill him. The other one circled around and crashed into a barge loaded with fuel. All of our single engines looked like the Japanese to our gunners. It made you sick to see some of them being shot down right in front of you. But this kind of thing happened until P-38s came in – they had twin guns and twin engines, so they could tell it was an American plane because the Japanese didn't have things like that.

Before Japan surrendered, it was determined that we would go into the Japanese mainland and be decoys with our line of ships. We were to load into the landing craft and go in towards shore. Then a destroyer would come by with a smoke screen, turn around, and go back out. That was to make the

Japs think we were landing on that coast, when we'd be landing on the other side instead. MacArthur had a lot of good ideas; everybody thought he was great. Many people who didn't know him – especially Harry Truman, our president – didn't care for him because he didn't take orders. But the Japanese revered MacArthur when he came over there because he was such an even-tempered and fair person to deal with.

We left a little bit later and went up to Korea on an LST, which is a smaller boat than what we'd come up on, but those bow-door-opening LSTs would come right onto the beach. The ramp would go down and be right there on the shore. At Okinawa, they couldn't do that because there was a big reef out there before you got to the shore, about ten miles out.

So we went up to Seoul, Korea, landed at Inchon, which was the port, and were on occupation duty there for six more months. When it came time for the unit to disband, I was in the S4 section – that's supply – and we had to turn in all of our equipment and account for everything that we didn't have, but we had a lot more than we started with that belonged to other people, that we had borrowed from them. When we were out on the road in Leyte and saw a blue bus or some sort of military vehicle the Navy had that ran out of gas there, we'd go out when it got dark, bring it into our motor pool, and paint it olive color – it was in our motor pool then. We had a big time doing all those things.

We weren't right in the front lines, but once in a while, we did get closer than we wanted. I know that at Okinawa, we were on a hilltop; there was a gap in between and mountains on each side. We were in the middle on top of a plateau, and the hill in front of us had a low place where all of our motor pool was. The Japs would fire their guns all night long at those artillery pieces of ours, and we fired at theirs all day long. So our camp was right in the middle of this for about thirty days straight.

Then a group of planes came in after our motor pool had sent trucks out to work on the roads. The Japs spotted all these headlights coming into the motor pool area right below our camp, and they put a string of bombs right across there. It blew up all of them. One bomb was delayed action, and we determined that it was still there, about twenty feet from our tent. They told us we would have to move, so we moved down about one hundred yards into the valley, and sure enough, twelve hours later that bomb blew. Part of coral went way up and came down through the tents. When one went off before that, I'd just gotten out of the tent for breakfast, looked at this little depression, and thought a shell must have hit last night. Actually, there was a delayed-action bomb right below it. When I went back in the tent, it exploded and everybody in the tent dived under things, but old East Tennessee just stood there saying, "What's happening?" Then chunks of coral came through the tent, and I just happened to move back before it just brushed me on the back. If it had hit me, it would have hit me just square in the head. It killed some of our troops in that area, and when they set that motor pool on fire, we lost one or two troops there. But, on a whole, we didn't lose on Leyte, and I thought that was great.

One thing I remember is that at one point, the Japs dropped some leaflets over our place that said something like, "You're a long way from home boys, in hostile territory, but don't worry boys, your lives are not in immediate danger. Why? Because we will not bother with you small fry; it's much simpler cutting off your lifeline. So fire away boys to your hearts' content." Well, we fired away.

In Korea, our job was working on roads again, building a Quonset hut for the Russian embassy and putting a flagpole up for it. Then, according to a person's total points, they would be going to the repo-depo, which is where they would ship out. When you were there, you'd ship out after one or two days only. I went over on the *General Leroy Eltinge* and went for two weeks on the northern route, around Alaska and into Seattle, Washington. I was hoping to come back under the Golden Gate Bridge, but Seattle looked awfully good. When we saw the lights of the coast, which we hadn't seen for a couple of years, we got off the ship, and the Red Cross gave everybody a hot dog and one of those pasteboard cartons of sweet milk. I thought well of the Red Cross for that.

From the Fort Lawton staging area, we got on a troop train, and it was five whole days going back across the country down to Fort Smith, Arkansas. Every time another train would come through, we pulled off on the side and let them go by because all we were doing was going home, but they were going somewhere, maybe overseas. We were glad to get to Fort Smith, Arkansas, and from there, we boarded a train and a bus to get back to Knoxville.

I got in at about two in the morning, and it was nice to see home again. I had started out at one hundred thirty-five pounds and came back one hundred sixty-five pounds –being aboard that boat for two weeks doing nothing but eating and looking at the scenery will put a little bit of weight on you.

When I got out, they had things for me to sign to continue insurance and to stay in the Reserves. I signed everything they put in front of me; I didn't want anything to interfere with being back at UT and finishing up. I just sort of buckled down, started studying better, and changed my goal from engineering to industrial management. That worked fine – I started getting an "A" once in a while.

So I got in the Reserves the next month after getting out, in the 110th Engineer Combat Battalion. We went to summer camp together for twenty-one years at different places. We enjoyed that quite a bit, and then our unit would go for reunions at other places.

So we got to travel each year, two weeks for summer camp and maybe four days out of the year for reunions. There are two other engineers I kept in contact with; one is in Charlotte, North Carolina, and one is in Harrison, Michigan. We send cards each Christmas, and this past month, I went over to see the one in Charlotte.

Being in the war changed my outlook on life one hundred percent. People in high school or at UT now don't really know what they will end up doing or really what to prepare for. If you are first starting off at the university, you have some sort of goal. When they come out of high school, they, especially the men, should have universal military training because they don't know. That would be the best thing in the world to spend a year doing that – being prepared and the country being prepared.

Chapter seventeen
John McAmis

John McAmis was born in Knoxville and was a member of First Presbyterian Church his entire life. He died on April 18, 2005. He graduated from The University of Tennessee in 1943 with a degree in mechanical engineering. He first spent about a year in Detroit helping assemble B-29 airplanes and then went to K-25 in Oak Ridge to work on the Manhattan Project.

My buddy Jim Maloney and I both graduated from Knoxville High School in 1938 and from UT in 1943 in mechanical engineering. We drove from Knoxville to Detroit together in his car, a 1933 Plymouth. We were employed by the Chrysler Corporation, and they had a school that was called the Chrysler Institute of Engineering. We attended this school while the war was going on. This school met in the morning from about eight to ten, and we went to work shortly after and worked all day, six days a week.

We were employed to build a B-29 airplane, which was the largest airplane in the world at the time. It had a wingspan of about fifty yards, it was a propeller-driven plane, and each of the motors was twenty-two hundred horsepower. The part that was actually manufactured in Detroit was the nose section, which is where the pilot and the co-pilot are. We also built some of the leading edges for the wings. Other parts of the airplane were built elsewhere. We shipped our part of the plane on the train to Omaha, Nebraska, where the plane was assembled. There were about fifteen hundred of these planes built. About eight or ten years ago, I saw one assembled, and that was the first one I ever saw.

My buddy and I were part of a class of forty men. The other fellows were from colleges mostly in the eastern United States. We were in the plant where these parts were manufactured, and our job was to coordinate the manufacture of this plane with the designer of the plane, which was Boeing in Seattle, Washington. They had a man in Detroit, and we worked with him. We kept up with all of the changes in the aircraft. The plans called for a certain design, and then there were modifications. For example, to fly to Alaska in cold weather, there are numerous modifications required in the plane, and we kept up with the modifications so they could be incorporated in the plane. That was our job.

Personally, my contribution to this airplane was the pilot's window. The part for the pilot's window came in, and it was supposed to pull out on a track on each side of the window and open, but it didn't work. It was my job to fix it so it did work. If you know anything about the manufacture of an airplane, you will know about something called lofts. Lofts are big sheets of aluminum – huge – and all of the pieces of the airplane are drawn on these lofts to full size. They call it a loft because the original drawings were made in a loft. The lofts were sent to the manufacturers of the parts, and the parts were made to these drawings at the exact size shown. Then they shipped all these parts out to be put together. But the pilot's window was the one that didn't work, and Jim and I were given the job to fix it. They gave us a blank loft, and we made the drawings of the window. To the best of my knowledge, it worked – we never heard from them again.

We were there a little over a year, and then we moved to Tennessee – they took the whole class of forty men. We weren't in the Army, but the Army was telling us what to do. They moved that whole class to K-25 in Oak Ridge. In 1945, K-25 was the largest building in the world. It was built in the shape of a "U," and it took forty-five minutes to an hour to walk around it. Around the perimeter on both sides were compressors, each driven by fifty-horsepower motors. They separated uranium 235 from uranium 238; the isotope that was used in the atom bomb was separated in this plant. There was some kind of formula – instead of pure 235, it was combined with something. I'm not sure what it was, but it was gaseous. They called us a gaseous diffusion plant. There's a little bit of difference between the weight of the U-235 and the U-238 – not much difference, but a difference. There was a barrier that separated the mixture that had U-235 and U-238 together, and they used compressors to force the gas through the barrier. One of those isotopes went through more easily than the other one, so you got an enrichment each time it went through this barrier. It had to go through the barrier time after time after time, and when that was done, there was this cascade – one riser pumped through the barrier to the next compressor, through the barrier into the next compressor, and so on, all around the "U" in two streams. Finally, it was more or less pure U-238, which was used in the atom bomb.

Actually, we did know what we were working on – we figured it out. We weren't supposed to know. It was called by a code name, but we had drawings to show how this thing worked and what we'd be doing there. It was obvious to us that whatever it was, it wasn't being made in large quantities. There was just one railroad coming to it, and you just never saw the railroad move. So, whatever it was, it was being made in small quantities. From that, we deduced that it must be part of the atom bomb. But we never told anybody.

When you checked into the Wheat School here from a point in Oak Ridge, you were indoctrinated by the FBI or somebody and were told not to say a word about what you were doing in the plant. I don't think we signed any papers or anything like that, but we were classified with a "Q" clearance, which allowed us to read whatever they had. We didn't read anything about uranium. We were not supposed to talk about where we were working. If people asked you about it, you were to be evasive about it. We were told to say we were working on blackout britches for lightning bugs. That was our excuse. I remember trying that on my eye doctor. He was very much interested in what I was doing out there – I was courting his daughter at the time. I doubt he bought it, but he knew something was going on.

We were there a little less than a year. When the atom bomb was dropped on Japan, everybody left. Jim and I came back to Knoxville, and we were graduate students at UT and started teaching engineering there. I taught thermal dynamics. The students we had were soldiers coming back from the war, and they were all business. It was a delightful time to teach at UT. I had a method of teaching where I sat them down by the alphabet, row by row by row. Each one had a number. I had four different classes during the week, so I couldn't keep up with them any other way. You could depend on them sitting in their assigned chair for that class each time. Those guys were there to learn; they wanted to be engineers.

The best thing that happened to me was in 1946. I met a girl in 1941 in Wrightsville Beach, North Carolina, and in 1946, about the end of the year, she decided it would be OK for us to get married, which we did. She's the light of my life.

Chapter eighteen
John McDow

John Jett McDow was born in Covington, Tenn., on January 6, 1925. He joined the Navy in 1942 at age seventeen. He spent most of the war training in shipboard duties such as anti-submarine warfare on destroyer-type ships. When he went overseas, he spent time in China and Japan. After the war, he earned a doctorate and enjoyed a career in academia, while remaining in the Naval Reserve until 1977.

I was born on January 6, 1925, in Covington, a rural West Tennessee town with a population of thirty-two hundred, the youngest of eight children of Robert Simpson and Lucy Cocke McDow. There was an equal number of boys and girls in the family. As war in Europe was appearing on the horizon, Nazi Germany invaded Poland on September 1, 1939. There existed a foregone conclusion that the United States must take steps to be prepared for hostile involvement. The military draft implemented in 1940, and, of course, the attack on Pearl Harbor on December 7, 1941, by Japan sealed the fact of the United States being fully engaged in the war.

Evidence of the war in our community soon became very apparent just within twenty to twenty-five miles of the city. A gunpowder plant, a Naval air training station, a B-17 bomber training base, an emergency airplane landing field, and an influx of small fabricators of small-machine parts in the area all brought the war effort close to home. A strict rationing plan for critical goods and foods was implemented for gasoline, automobile and other machinery tires, meats, sugar, coffee, canned goods, shoes, some other apparel, new equipment of all kinds, and other items. Policies were implemented, like no new trousers could have cuffs, a change that remained after the war and has continued to an extent today. Failure to report to the County Rationing Board the butchering of three head of cattle for local use ended in a local butcher spending time in a federal penitentiary. Military service personnel could obtain extra family ration coupons on certain items when on official leave at home. I never asked for extra coupons, as my family always had a garden, chickens, and cows, like many people did even within the city limits of Covington. Everyone was encouraged to have a "Victory Garden."

I graduated from high school in May 1942 at the age of seventeen and enrolled at the University of Tennessee Junior College at Martin two weeks later, trying to complete as much college as possible before entering military service. The military draft started at age eighteen. A Navy representative came on campus offering the opportunity to enlist in the Navy and sign a contract that would allow us to stay enrolled at the university until called to active duty, which would most likely be at the end of that academic year. We then would be sent to another college or university to continue pursuing college work, be on active duty, and be a part of the Naval Officer Training Program.

Since I was just seventeen, I had to get my parents' permission. My mother said, "I'm not going to do it." You see, I was the youngest of eight children. There were four boys, and she said that they would not require me to go because they would not require all four boys to go. But they did require it, and I got my father to sign so I could go. See, I would be eighteen in January, and they would draft me into the Army then. That is what I could not seem to explain to my mother — she thought I would not have to go at all. I always wanted to go into the Navy.

I enlisted in this program and was sworn into the Navy on December 11, 1942. Even though I was the youngest in my family, I was the first to be sworn into service and the last to be released from active duty in 1946. The other three were married, which gave them a considerable number of points toward being released from active duty.

The Navy kept tabs on us while we were still enrolled in college. They required colleges and universities to report our enrollment and certify that we were obtaining intense physical training. The latter was no problem since the University of Tennessee, at that time, required physical education for the first two years in all undergraduate academic programs. The physical education coaches required somewhat more activities of those of us who had been sworn into the military service. The U.S. Army had a similar program.

The United States population in 1940 was 132,164,569, as compared to being almost three hundred million in 2006. The total number of Americans who served in the military services during World War II was 16,353,659. Twelve and a half percent of Americans who would normally be in the work force were in military service. This placed a heavier workload on those at home to produce additional agricultural and manufactured products for our own military service personnel, home people, and our allies, England and the Soviet Union. More women went to work in agriculture and in the manufacturing industries. Many women also joined the military services.

I received orders to report for active duty on September 29, 1943, at the University of South Carolina, Columbia, and began training in communications, navigation, Morse code, meteorology, and physical training. In December, I was transferred to the University of Miami, Coral Gables, Florida, continuing in more advanced courses. In March 1944, I was issued orders to report to the Navy V-12 Program at Franklin and Marshall College, Lancaster, Pennsylvania. We enrolled in regular college courses and were given some latitude in choosing courses that we wanted to take. I endeavored to enroll in courses that would apply to engineering programs. In February 1945, I received orders to go to the United States

Naval Reserve Midshipman School in Fort Schulyer, New York City.

Several impressive situations and activities took place while at Fort Schulyer. First, a sizable number of those who prepared and served our food were Italian prisoners of war. Second, a very impressive memorial service was held on the school's parade ground in memory of Franklin Delano Roosevelt, U.S. president and the commander and chief of the Armed Services, who died April 12, 1945.

The other activities involved some special field trips. First, in conjunction with instruction in nautical navigation, we went in small groups to the Hayden Planetarium at the American Museum of Natural History in New York City to receive special instruction in celestial navigation. This was very beneficial in our navigational training. The second field trip in April was going aboard the *USS Franklin* (CV 13), an aircraft carrier that had just returned from the Pacific. The *Franklin* had been in a sea battle near Kobe, Japan, on March 19, 1945, after which only seven hundred six of the thirty-four hundred ship's crew survived or were not seriously wounded. This was considered to be one of the worst losses to the U.S. Navy in World War II. After arriving at the Brooklyn Navy Yard, more bodies had to be removed from the burned and damaged area of twisted metal and other debris.

Our class of twelve hundred midshipmen graduated and was commissioned ensign on July 3, 1945. These exercises were held at the Cathedral of St. John the Divine in New York City.

The next step was to obtain additional shipboard training, although some had been given at Fort Schulyer on ships operating in Long Island Sound. My orders were again to the Miami area for both dockside and shipboard instruction — navigation, seamanship, damage control, firefighting, abandoning-ship drills, gunnery, combat information center instruction, using the latest radar at the time, and ship handling at sea were the major areas of training. Toward the end of our assignment, the atomic bombs were dropped on Hiroshima and Nagasaki.

You know, I'd go through Knoxville because I was stationed up East a lot. I'd ride the trains and would run across some guys that said, "There's something going on out at Oak Ridge, but nobody knows what they're doing." It was very secure out there. People didn't know too much about the atomic bombs until they started reading about it when they were dropped. I picked up a newspaper, and I'm sorry I didn't save that newspaper — it would have been historical. They just didn't know much about it, not what we know now. I was surprised.

So, the bombings did not interrupt our training, but a hurricane did when it hit the Miami and Homestead areas a short time later. That was the first hurricane I was ever in, but I was in another one aboard ship.

This was in 1945, and the Soviets were our allies and England was our ally, but the French and all the others were taken by the Nazis. We furnished the Soviets and England with ships and food. When we were in Miami, there was a substantial number of Soviet officers and enlisted personnel also being trained there. Some spoke English, some didn't. We were told, even though they were allies, not to discuss any military plans with them. We were constantly reminded not to discuss any military information with the Soviet personnel. It was felt that the Soviets could turn against us. See, they didn't come into the war with Japan until after the bomb. They wanted to get their territory, and that is the reason they came in as an ally – they didn't particularly care whether they helped us over there or not.

At the time, we all thought that we would all go to smaller ships. We were supposed to be in the next invasion. So, when the bomb happened, it cut our orders to a cruiser instead of small ships. Eight of us received orders to report to the *USS St. Paul* (CA-73), a relatively new heavy cruiser. We were given a short leave period and then reported to Naval Operations in San Francisco Harbor for transportation to the

Far East. The *SS Azalea City*, a merchant marine transport, took us to Tokyo Bay, Japan, where over one thousand allied ships had been prior to peace signing on the *USS Missouri* on September 2, 1945. This fleet of ships was a tremendous sight. By coincidence, the *SS Azalea City* anchored within sight of the *St. Paul*. However, early the next morning, the *St. Paul* was seen steaming toward the Tokyo Bay entrance. We found out later that she was headed to Shanghai, China. The eight of us transferred to shore at Yokohama, where we stayed for about a week, which gave us time to tour the area. There had been a great deal of damage done to the shipyards and factories by the U.S. bombers. Japanese children would stand along the side of the road holding out their hands and asking for candy. We were able to catch a Navy seaplane that was going to Okinawa. This flight enabled us the opportunity to see a substantial part of the southern islands of Japan from the air.

Okinawa had just experienced being hit by a very severe typhoon shortly before we arrived. Also, there was a great deal of damage from the invasion by U.S. troops along the coastline, as well as on the island, still in place. Japanese holdouts were still hidden in the surrounding mountains and were periodically firing on the Americans moving across the island. A number of them stayed up there for several years before coming down to surrender. This was in the papers in the United States – some of those guys didn't give up until about 1950.

We stayed in a Navy Seabee camp while waiting for transportation to Shanghai. Fortunately, we soon obtained a ride on a C-3 airplane that was taking a Jeep to Shanghai. I was never in combat. The only danger I was ever in is when we ran into some floating mines. A sharpshooter on the ship would shoot and blow them up before we got too near to them. Other times, I heard some of the shooting, but I never got shot at.

I had a friend who was in New York, and we kept up with each other. I went to see him one time, just before I was commissioned. After I got on the ship, he wrote me at my home in Covington, and by that time, I was in China on a ship.

He sent it to my home and addressed it "Adm. John J. McDow." My mother didn't pay attention to that and forwarded it to me. When I got my mail aboard ship, I was so embarrassed. But he was just kidding around.

Shanghai was still "old China," like we had studied in school. The ladies dressed in kimonos. There were very few motorized vehicles, even in the city of Shanghai. The streets were crowded with rickshaws and pedicabs. At midnight on December 31, 1945, China changed its travel system from driving on the left side of the highways and streets to driving on the right. The change went very smoothly with no accidents, since men powered most of the modes of transportation. I thought that the drivers of the rickshaws might not be literate enough to know of the change, but they did. (My wife, Dot, and I had a lot of Chinese students in our home later, and I asked one of them, "Do you remember when China used to drive on the left side of the road?" He said, "Oh no, we never did." I told them to ask their parents.)

When moving about downtown Shanghai's streets and alleys and in the outskirts of the city, many different aromas from the cooking of food and smoking materials in unusual pipes filled the air. No doubt, some of the smoke came from substances that would have been illegal in the U.S. Pickpockets and beggars were in considerable numbers on the streets. Later, while walking in the city, I felt a quick brush against my jacket side pocket. When I reached in the pocket, it was completely empty. Fortunately, there was nothing of great value in that pocket. One in our group was a victim of a pickpocket when we were on the way to the ship, and he lost his wallet.

Upon reporting aboard, I was assigned duties of an assistant division officer of a 45 mm gunnery division. Of course, I had other duties, including standing watch on the quarterdeck and on the bridge at sea as junior officer of the deck. Later in the tour of duty, I was transferred to the Combat Information Center, which handled all radar equipment operation on the ship.

The *St. Paul* was anchored in the middle of the Whangpoo River, which empties into the Yangtze River fourteen miles downstream and then onto the Pacific Ocean. To the portside of the *St. Paul* was downtown Shanghai, where a major street, the Bund, ran parallel to the Whangpoo River. On the open land on the starboard side of the *St. Paul* was a Japanese prisoner of war camp. The prisoners could be seen from the *St. Paul* and appeared to be quiet and docile. When Chinese ships would come in, they had to go with the current and didn't have good steering, so we would have to watch for collisions. Well, one time, a ship came in and there was a collision and it made a big hole in the bow of our ship. The Japanese POWs in the camp were very jubilant, jumping up and down, laughing, and rolling on the ground. Our own ship crew welded a large metal patch over the hole, which worked out fine to keep the ship afloat. This was replaced when we later went into the San Pedro California Shipyard upon returning to the States for a scheduled maintenance job in March.

In December 1945, Communist demonstrations were staged on the streets of Shanghai. At that time, Chiang Kai-shek was the Nationalist leader and was supported by the United States. Mao Tse-tung was one of the top Communist leaders operating in other sections of China near the Soviet border. All American military personnel were ordered to stay clear of the areas of these demonstrations. As history has it, the Communists took over China on October 1, 1949.

The *USS St. Paul* (CA-73) served as the flagship for Vice Adm. C. Turner Joy, who was the Naval officer in charge of all Naval operations in China. He became a very competent specialist in handling matters in the Far East and seven years later was the top U.S. representative to broker the cease-fire operations of the Korean War. He was a very competent Naval commander who expected the best of performance from all personnel in carrying out their duties. And, on the other hand, he was a very compassionate commander toward all personnel. There was a constant stream of dignitaries from other parts of

China and from Washington coming to visit Adm. Joy on the *St. Paul*.

Adm. Joy was really good to us junior officers — he would invite us to his parties, and there were always dignitaries coming aboard ship. At the parties, there were champagne, Cokes and things like that. It was just sort of a get-together with some of the Chinese dignitaries and their families from Shanghai. A Naval destroyer ship was named for Adm. Joy several years later. I think it was after he died because back then, they didn't usually name something after someone while they were still living. President Reagan was one of the first ones that I know about who had a ship named after him while still living.

In Shanghai, I would often go ashore. I bought things for my family — I enjoyed shopping in Shanghai. I also went to see movies. The ones in Chinese had English on the side of the screen, and on the American movies, they had Chinese on the side. I tried to get as much of the culture as I could while I was there. We had a very good friendship with the Chinese.

When we departed from Shanghai in February 1946, Adm. Joy and staff were transferred to the new Shanghai arrival, the *USS Los Angeles*. When we stopped on the way back at Pearl Harbor, Hawaii, all personnel had to go through customs and declare all our purchases, just like tourists. Then we sailed directly into the San Pedro, California, shipyards for repair and upgrading for a period of about three months.

While in the San Pedro Naval Shipyard, there were a number of other ships there being prepared for the well-known atomic bombing experiment of dropping two separate bombs on older, retired Naval ships. This took place in the Bikini Atoll in the Marshall Islands in July 1946. This group of ships included the *USS Nevada*, a battleship painted a bright orange and to be the center of the blast, an aircraft carrier, and a number of other ships. The *USS St. Paul* was selected to escort this fleet of ships as far as Hawaii. After a short stay in Pearl Harbor, we returned to Long Beach, California.

In early July, the *USS St. Paul* was selected to represent the U.S. Navy at the celebration of the one hundredth anniversary of the U.S. troops' first occupation of California, which became the thirty-first state fours years later. Gov. Earl Warren, his wife, and twin daughters attended the festivities and the ball that were held for this occasion. Of course, Gov. Warren became chief justice of the U.S. Supreme Court in 1953.

You know, there was a book I found that said they predicted there would have been one million American causalities to take Japan – either killed, wounded, or prisoners of war. There are some who say we should never have dropped the bombs, but there were less people killed as a result of them. I don't know if that justified it, but it was the best thing to shorten the war.

I was released to inactive duty on August 16, 1946, and returned to my home in Covington to prepare for re-entering college at The University of Tennessee in Knoxville in September, like many other veterans. Most veterans were discharged from the military service upon release from active duty. However, some of us did not have that option, as we had spent a substantial time in training. I do not recall precisely when we had the option of resigning our commission, but it was several years after the treaty of the Korean War was signed. By that time, I was active in the Naval Reserve Program and chose to continue to remain in that status. The United States and the Soviet Union were having very strained relations, until the Soviet split into fifteen different independent states in 1991.

So I got out in August and went to UT in September to continue my engineering degree. I finished that, and then I received an assistantship at Michigan State. So I received my master's and later went back and received my doctorate at Michigan State, where I did research and teaching. Back then, you could get on the faculty with a master's, and I got on the faculty at Michigan State. I was offered a job in Oklahoma, so I went out there, and then to Louisiana, and then back here to UT. I was gone from UT about thirteen years after I graduated.

We carried orders that we were subject to being called back. I thought I was going to be called back during the Korean War – some of my classmates were called. I figured out the reason: They weren't in the Reserve and I was. The Navy said, "We got you, so we're going to call some of these others that we don't have." That's the way they operate sometimes. But Dot and I planned what she would do if I were ever called in.

My military obligations in the Naval Reserve were to meet weekly, which was later changed to a monthly weekend, at a Naval Reserve Training Center and to go on active duty for a full two weeks of training at some Naval station aboard a Naval vessel for more-concentrated training. I was assigned for several years to specialize in anti-submarine warfare, which involved training and operating at sea on destroyers, submarines, a submarine tender, and aircraft carriers that had anti-submarine capabilities. My most memorable occasions in this extended duty were being aboard a submarine submerged at sea when a fire occurred, catapulting from the *USS Bennington* (CV 20), flying into California and then returning to the ship and landing by tail hook on the flight desk, and spending a day of instruction in port on a nuclear submarine.

My final training duty was with the Military Sealift Command at Cape Canaveral, where we worked with the space program in recovering falling objects from liftoffs and with nuclear submarines when they practiced firing dummy nuclear missiles in a restricted area.

My family — Dorothy, Ronald and Jane — was able to go with me on a number of two-week training duty periods, having the opportunity to enjoy a lot of activities on the Naval station or in the community area. Once, Ronald, at age fifteen, was able to spend a day at sea with me on the *USS Lexington*, an aircraft carrier, while the ship was in full operation.

During the time that I was training in the Reserve, there were periods that the Navy issued us standing orders of where to report within three days for mobilization when there was a public announcement to do so. Although that never had to be done, it was on the verge of so doing several times when there were very strained relations with the Soviet Union.

I retired from the U.S. Naval Reserve on June 30, 1977, at the rank of commander, USNR, after thirty-four and a half years of active duty and Reserve service in the United States Navy.

Chapter nineteen
Frank Moore

Frank Moore was born in South Carolina on July 25, 1915, but his family moved to Alcoa, Tennessee, when he was three years old. He joined the Army Air Corps in 1942 and became a pilot. Although he had some training on four-engine planes, he flew exclusively C-47s during the war. He came out of the war a captain and then reached lieutenant colonel while in the Reserves. Frank died on December 26, 2005.

I joined the air force in '42. To get into that you couldn't be beyond 27, so I signed up about seven days before I was 27. Then I waited about six months to be called up to active duty and went to Maxwell Air Force Base in Montgomery, Alabama, for preflight training. From there, I went to primary flight training. I was training to be a pilot.

So I went from there to basic training in Greenville, Mississippi, and I got through that all right. Then I went for advanced twin-engine training in Columbus, Mississippi, and then to Sedalia, Missouri, to troop carrier training – for C-47s, gliders, paratroopers and things like that. Then I went by train and boat to Italy. Margaret Bourke-White, who was a photographer for *Time Life* magazine, was on the boat. She had blue hair – I sure remember seeing her, a woman with blue hair.

Frank is talking about the famous Margaret Bourke-White, who
was born June 14, 1904, in Bronx, New York, graduated from
Cornell University in 1927, and went to Cleveland, Ohio, to start a
career in photography. In 1929, she became an associate editor at
Fortune magazine, and in 1930, was sent to the Soviet Union on
assignment, according to many reports, becoming the first Western
photographer allowed into the country. In the mid-thirties, she
accepted a job at the newly created *Life* magazine. She was in
Moscow when the Germans attacked and sent photographs of the
invasion to *Life* magazine. Reports show that she was the only
foreign photographer in the Soviet Union at the time. During the
war, she also photographed events in North Africa and in Italy and
became the first woman accredited by the U.S. Army as a war
correspondent. She crossed the German border with Gen. George
Patton's troops and was one of the first to photograph the
concentration camps there. She also photographed the Korean War
and life in South Africa under apartheid. Bourke-White died in
Connecticut in 1971.

It took twelve days to get over to Italy, and when we
got there, we dropped supplies and troops. We did get fired on,
but we had air coverage – fighter pilots. From Italy, we flew
some of the patients that were hurt, but basically they had a
hospital ship that took care of the injured and transported them
by boat. But we had some of the "walking injured" that we
flew back.

We stayed in Italy until the Germans quit. I remember
when the Germans quit – they came out of the woods with their
gray uniforms on, and they were happy to be over with the war.
Lots of people in the air force could speak German, so they
talked to them, but I didn't speak German. After they quit, I
didn't come home straight away. They flew the troops back in
stages, so I went to Puerto Rico first.

While I was in Italy, I went to midnight Mass on New
Year's Eve and got to see the pope. I wrote to my family a lot –
postage was free, so we wrote quite often. I had a twin brother
who worked out there in Oak Ridge, but, of course, he didn't
know what was going on either.

After the war, I stayed in the Reserve and flew as long
as they would let me because I liked it. When I was called to

go to Korea, I asked for time to close my business, but they never called me back, so I didn't go.

Chapter twenty
John Moore

John Moore was born in Brooklyn, New York, on August 21, 1918. He joined the Army in 1942 and was a member of the Corps of Engineers. During the war, he served mostly in Italy and was on his way to the Pacific when the atomic bomb was dropped. His final rank was captain.

I took advanced ROTC and was in the engineers, and in June of 1942, I was commissioned as a second lieutenant in the Corps of Engineers. They told me I was going to have at least two weeks before starting, so I took my fiancée up to see my folks in New Jersey, and just as soon as we got there, I got a telegram to report to Fort McPherson, Georgia. So we had to turn around and come back immediately.

I got to Fort McPherson, which was a regular Army unit, and they were ready to go overseas. Well, I was just out of school and as green as could be as an officer and in engineering experience. The only thing we had done was at a summer camp where we built a pontoon bridge across a little steam – that's the only experience I had; I had no experience with explosives. They quickly saw that and transferred me out. And I'm glad they did because they went overseas within a week after that. I would have been so green I couldn't have helped much.

Then I was assigned to Fort Knox for nine months, and all the time we were there, we were on alert. My fiancée, Mary Lea, and I were trying to be married, so we planned the

wedding for September and she made all the big plans. I could
have been gone, but luckily I didn't get sent overseas. See, they
didn't think Sicily was going to be a problem, so they didn't
take people overseas as quickly. I asked the captain for a week
off starting one week after the wedding, which was September
12, and he said to me, "You can have three days off this
weekend and be back here." So we got married and went to
Gatlinburg for one night. I had an old, beat-up car that we
drove back to Fort Knox. It was so sudden that I hadn't made
any arrangements for housing. Of course, Fort Knox was
overcrowded with eighty-eight thousand troops when it
normally had about a quarter of that. The first night back there,
we stayed in the officers quarters, which had just single beds,
but we managed. Then we found a room with a lady who
would not let Mary Lea use the kitchen, so we got out of there,
and we finally found a house between Louisville and Fort
Knox with three other couples. Some of the couples left, but
we stayed there until I went overseas in the first part of '43.

All the troops in my outfit got on a troop ship and went
across in five or six days, but I went on a convoy, and I was the
only Army officer aboard that ship. We landed in Africa,
bypassed Sicily, and shortly thereafter, we landed in Salerno.
On invasion day, we lost the ship behind us, and somehow two
ships were sunk in our little convoy, and all my supplies and all
my personal things were lost. I only had what was on my back
and two concentrated chocolate bars, which we had to live on
for a day or two until we could get food. But the Italians were
very happy to see us, and they gave us oranges and things like
that. We began to settle down, but it was touch-and-go for a
while there.

We lived in very tough conditions the first year we
went into Italy. It was muddy and rainy, and I slept in a pup
tent. The snow was deep, and I didn't take my shoes off for
days because, if I did, I couldn't get them back on again. It's a
wonder that we didn't get sicker than we did. The only place
where we had any heat was in the mess tent, where we went to
eat, but the rest of the place was ice cold. The first winter in

Italy, when I went to bed at night on my cot, I never took my clothes off. And everything I owned I put on top of myself to try and keep warm, whether it was another uniform, a blanket – anything I had I put on top of myself to keep warm so I could sleep.

Then we had an order from higher up that said, "Prepare to evacuate." The Germans threw everything at us, and we had a small force landing in Salerno. But, fortunately, we were able to make a foothold in Italy and went on in. As far as the war was concerned, the purpose of the Italian Campaign, in my understanding, was to keep the German army busy. So the Italians surrendered very quickly – they didn't want any part of the war. They claimed to be "lovers," rather than "fighters." So we were sort of a holding action to keep the Germans busy because they knew that eventually the U.S. and allied forces were going to invade on the coast – but the Germans didn't know that. During the Italian Campaign in '44, we were in the southern part of Italy, which is the poor part of Italy and is very hilly. We had one campaign after another, taking one hill, lost a lot of men, then take another hill, and there'd be another one. We finally decided in Italy that we'd do an end run and go around the lower part of Italy and go in on Anzio, which was parallel to Rome. That was a very intense campaign, and we lost a lot of men – there's a big cemetery right next to where we were camped.

The Germans had a huge railroad gun that they brought out at night. There was a beachhead and we were unloading on the shore, and the Germans were shooting this railroad gun. At that time, it was the biggest gun; it shot five miles, which was unheard of, and at night it would fire on ships in the harbor. It had what they called a booster, and from our camp, which was an ammunition camp, you could hear the booster go off as it went out to the coast, which was only about a half-mile away, as they tried to hit some of those ships. Well, they got smart pretty quick, and they would unload during the day and go back out to sea at night. But it wasn't too effective. Although, a couple of those boosters failed, dropped in our ammunition dump, and set our ammunition on fire. We had a tank with a bulldozer blade on the front of it, and when they hit one of our dumps, they were all surrounded by dirt and everything. One night we got out of the tank and thought we had it covered up, and one exploded. That was the closest I came to getting killed in the war at that point. It blew my helmet off, and one boy got hurt, but there was enough covering on it. But, anyway, we stayed there for months and had to live underground because of the explosions at night.

Once I went into Rome with a Naval officer I met on a ship. I saw him on the ship, and he asked if I had any wheels. I told him I had a little Jeep, and he asked if we could ride up to Rome. I said we could try, so we rode up to Rome. I give the Germans credit – they did not destroy a thing in Rome. There was a little bit of fighting on the south side – you could see where they did a little fighting – but Rome itself was perfectly fine. The Coliseum, the hotels, all the historical things were still intact. I still have many pictures that I took. See, the troops went through Rome while they were pursuing the Germans – there weren't any American troops there. So when the Naval officer and I went into Rome, we were just swamped by the people and the children.

The only good part of the war that I remember is when the Army took over the Excelcio Hotel in Rome, which is like the Waldorf Astoria, and they used it as a rest camp for the armed forces. I went back there twice, and that was delightful – first hot bath I'd had in months and the first meal we had. It was a delightful place.

So the Germans left Rome and went north, and by then, the campaign was winding down. In other words, the northern part of Italy was the fine part with all the nice cities, but it's flat, and the Germans knew they would have a hard time defending it, so they withdrew pretty quickly. We kept many Germans busy because they were afraid we would swing around and go into France. Actually, our mission was pretty well accomplished. We thought we might go into southern France, and as it was, they did take a contingency in the south of France just in case we did invade from the south. But they knew the main invasion was going to be on the Normandy side on the beaches there. So I stayed in Italy. I was in Anzio, which was a place where we lost a lot of men. Then we went on because there were some problems with Yugoslavia. We went all the way up to Trieste, which was at the very top corner of Italy. Then we came back to the staging area, and I was in a specialized ammunition outfit planning to go to Okinawa.

At that time, I had been overseas two and half years, and it was very depressing. We were going to go to war with the Japanese, which was very disappointing. We set sail from the west coast of Italy, and they dropped the atomic bomb just about at that time. Then we thought surely we would not have to go, but the captain wired whoever he was supposed to wire, and his orders were to proceed as directed. That was devastating to us, but when we were going by the Rock of Gibraltar at around midnight, we got a wire to proceed to New York. We were very happy. We were sort of laughed at when we left Italy; some of the guys who were only there a year said they would be home in six months. They said, "We'll be home and you guys will still be over there." But we were a specialized outfit – I know of two field hospitals and several other specialized outfits on that ship, and we were supposed to go through the Panama Canal to Okinawa.

We got into New York in late August 1945, and the Red Cross met us at about eleven o'clock at night. They had milk there, and I drank down three little cartons of milk, but I hadn't had milk in so long that it made me sick. They, of course, were going to feed us at night, but I couldn't eat anything. We stayed there for a short time, and then we were sent to a camp in Georgia. I was able to call Mary Lea there, and then we were on a freight train. Now, back then, the steam engines used coal, and we had no air conditioning. It took almost twenty hours to get from New York to Atlanta. Mary Lea had stayed in a hotel, and she left there to stay with her aunt, but I called and she came back. And I said, "Don't touch me until I get in the bathroom and get this grime off me." If you've ever been on a steam engine, all these soot particles of coal came out. And we were on that thing for two days, sitting up, with very little water, and I was just happy to get home.

When I went to Anzio, I was a detachment from our ordnance company – the whole company did not go there. I was in charge in Anzio, and that's why, when we left there, I was made captain. Since I was captain of the outfit that was going to Okinawa, I was ordered to Camp Rucker, Alabama, to deactivate. Mary Lea went with me, and I was criticized for bringing her in a Jeep. But we had no other transportation. We went up to the mess hall and a guy said that I couldn't ride a civilian in the Jeep, but that was the only criticism I had. So I deactivated the unit, and then we came on home.

I didn't get hurt during the war, thank goodness. But we had several chances. Our ammunition company was sometimes on the front lines. And in Anzio, we were ahead of the troops where our ammunition dump was – that was the worse part of my experience in the war. We had to live underground – there was a tent above it, but we had to live underground – because of the explosions. There was also the time I almost got killed on a motorcycle. I was riding along, and the roads were narrow. But there was a little ledge along a path on the edge of a road that I rode on because trucks were going back and forth. There was a certain place where the ledge disappeared down the hill, but I didn't know that. So when I got to that point – luckily, it was a big, heavy Army motorcycle – I jumped off. The motorcycle hit me on the side of the leg and left a black mark, but another second or inch and I would have been underneath that heavy motorcycle, gone down the hill with it, and would have been crushed and maybe killed.

During the war, we'd write letters, and the officers were supposed to get all of the letters – and there were hundreds of them. The soldiers wrote just about every day. And I confess that I didn't read them all – they were all personal. What we were looking for was information about where we were, which they weren't supposed to write. The officers were supposed to read every letter, but a lot of them just got passed by. Really, we didn't have time.

When I got home, I really didn't have any trouble readjusting. Mary Lea met me in Atlanta, and we stayed a day there. Then we came back and stopped somewhere in the Carolinas, and we stayed a night there. Then we came on home. I stayed in the Reserve for three or four years. Then the Korean War started, and they started sending me letters. But we had just built a new house, we had a new baby, I just got a new job, and I wasn't ready to leave home. So I didn't go. I resigned my commission in the Reserves. I knew a lot of fellows who did that, but some were called up anyway because they were needed so badly.

One thing I still remember is if you have ever smelled a dead body that is three or four days old, you'll never smell anything worse in your life. I have a picture of a dead German soldier – he'd been dead for maybe a day or two. His helmet was there, and I got his helmet – I have it down in the basement. I don't know why I took it, but I put it in an old footlocker that I had. I showed that picture of the dead soldier to my grandson. I said, "Now this was a young fellow. He was just like you, eighteen or nineteen years old. He belonged to some family who loved him, and, of course, he was German. And he was killed. This family was without a son." That's the horror of war, and that's what touched me. Young people are still being killed – they are doing that all over.

Chapter twenty-one
Kay Ogden

Harry Kay Ogden was born in Murfreesboro, Tennessee, on December 13, 1922. He joined the Army in 1943 and spent most of the war as a medical student, but he spent some time at a psychiatric unit treating traumatized soldiers. His time in the war earned him three medals – Good Conduct, American Theatre of War, and World War II Victory.

I was a student at The University of Tennessee starting in 1941 in the College of Agriculture, following in the footsteps of my father who was an agronomist there. I remember very well where I was when Pearl Harbor got attacked – I was working on the poultry farm at UT. It was a Sunday morning, and I was out there cleaning out the chicken houses when the man in charge of the poultry department – Dr. Parker was his name – came out to inform me that Pearl Harbor had been attacked. It's funny how you remember these very eventful moments. Most of the time you don't remember what you do – if you asked me what I was doing yesterday, I couldn't begin to tell you – but I remember those days very well.

Well, a colonel came through UT in the latter part of '41 and said, "I know you fellows want to finish school, so all of you need to join the Reserves and you'll be able to finish school before they call you up." So everybody signed up. And then, about six months later, they drafted all of us at one time – that made it very simple for them. So I was drafted in November of '42 and called up to active duty in April '43. I did my basic training at Fort McClellan, Alabama, in heavy weapons company. I was in basic training with Ed Boling, who was president of the university; Charles Brakebill, who was Boling's right-hand man; and Doug Matthews, who started Brown Squirrel (furniture store). We all went through Fort McClellan in the heat of the summer in Alabama.

While we were down there, we took a bunch of examinations – not military examinations; these were academic examinations. After that, they let a bunch of us go into what they called the ASTP – the Army Specialized Training Program. I took a bunch of tests, and they said I should be an engineer, which was the last thing on earth I wanted to do – I didn't like mathematics in the first place. They sent me to Brooklyn, New York, to a tech school for engineering, and I was there from September '43 to March '44. Well, militarily things were going bad for the United States during that time, and the engineering program that I was in was discontinued. Most of the fellows were sent to the infantry to the front in Europe. But during that time, while things were going bad, they wanted doctors, so we took more tests – aptitude-type tests, I guess you would call them. So this was while I was still in engineering, but I took that test and passed it for some reason, and they said, "You ought to be a medical student."

I had about two years of school at UT before this time, and I'd had lots of math and lots of science – that's what basic agriculture is. From April to December '44, they sent me to the University of Pittsburgh to take premed. So that's what I did, and I liked it – it was a nice place, and I enjoyed it. At the end of that time, in December 1944, I got married to a lovely girl right here at the church in Knoxville. All my friends were in the military, so my male attendants were officers of the church who were too old to get in the military. Then I was scheduled to go to the Medical College of Virginia, but the semester didn't open until September. So from December to September, they sent me to Camp Pickett, Virginia, and I worked in a military hospital there in a psychiatric unit. Then I started medical college in Virginia in August '45, and I was there for six months.

One of our patients was Red Skelton, the comedian – he and Bob Hope entertained the troops, mostly in Italy. So he was the most famous of our patients, I guess. Most of the traumatized troops we got at Camp Pickett had been in the war in Italy, on the Italian front. But we had dentists, too. During World War II, they had field hospitals, and the dentists were out there and a lot of them saw a lot of trauma – I mean psychologically traumatized, and most of them were GIs. Also at Camp Pickett, for a while I was a medical corpsman for German prisoners. But my brother was killed during the Battle of the Bulge in January while I was stationed there at Camp Pickett. He was in the 82nd Airborne during the war. He saw action in North Africa, Italy, Sicily, and, of course, at Normandy, and he survived all of that until the Battle of the Bulge. So I asked them to relieve me of duty from the German POWs. I didn't want to face the Germans at that time – I was a bit traumatized myself. That was when they assigned me to the psychiatric unit.

You know, during the war, the enemy wasn't the Germans – it was Hitler and the Nazis; that's who we were fighting. That's why we can defend the Germans today because the Germans, of course, are very smart people – they're competent, wonderful people. So it wasn't the German people; it was Hitler – he was the enemy and what he stood for. The Japanese are different – their whole culture is different from ours. But the German culture is not different from ours, just their ideology. I wonder what would have happened had the U.S. lost the war – I figured that Germany and Japan would wind up fighting each other. Wouldn't it have been dreadful? If the Americans hadn't won that war, there's no telling what in the world would have happened – they had to win the war, they just had to.

When the atomic bomb was dropped, I was at Valley Forge General Hospital, which is in Pennsylvania, right outside of Philadelphia. We were transporting some dentists who had been on active duty in Italy and some others who were severely traumatized psychologically. So we were in an ambulance taking them up to a psychiatric hospital in Valley Forge on that morning. There was a storm taking place with lots of lightning and thunder, and these poor guys thought they were back in combat. We had quite a time with them; back in the ambulance, they were very upset. And we read the headlines that morning that the atom bomb had been dropped in Japan. At first I thought it was a fake – I didn't know there was such a thing. I thought the newspaper was kind of exaggerating – the atomic bomb – who had ever heard of such a thing? But, of course, they were right, and it was made right here in Oak Ridge. And all the time I was at UT, the Manhattan Project was going on over there in Oak Ridge, and nobody knew what it was. My wife-to-be lived on Magnolia Avenue at that time, and they had a boarder who worked at Oak Ridge; he would leave every morning and come back at night, and he would never tell anybody what he was doing. People noticed there would be trainloads and boxcars going into Oak Ridge that would always come out empty, but nobody in the world could figure out what was going on. We had heard after the war was over that Oak Ridge and Knoxville together would make an area as big as Atlanta – that was the rumor at that time. I guess there had to be people who knew, but people like me didn't know what was going on. I guess if you had asked the Russians, they could probably have told you what was going on, but we didn't know. Security was very tight, and, of course, at that time Oak Ridge was a military post, and they had military guards there during the whole war.

When I was discharged in March '46, I couldn't afford to continue to go to the medical college in Virginia, so they transferred me to the medical college at The University of Tennessee in Memphis so I could get in-state tuition. I got the GI Bill there, and that was the only way I would ever have gotten through medical school. My father had died of cancer when I was in high school, so it took a long time and a lot of medical expense, and we had no money. If it hadn't been for the Army, there's no way I would have become a doctor. I couldn't afford it. I got married and was a big pfc making $35 a month, but I got the GI Bill. They paid for my education and my books. My wife worked in Memphis, and we lived in the housing project in Memphis. We had one child born while I was in school in Memphis. It was hard for a while, but the Army GI Bill paid my way.

I was in family practice in Fountain City for many years, and then I went in the emergency room at St. Mary's – I was in charge of the emergency room at St. Mary's for ten years. Then I was medical director at Shannondale Nursing Home, and then I opened up an emergency clinic for five years. Then I became medical director at the walk-in clinic at Interfaith Health Clinic, where I stayed for three years. And would you believe I now work at Y-12? I work one day a week for seven hours – that's a great job. See, the workers there have to have annual physicals just to be sure they're getting along OK. I just wanted something to do because I retired a long time ago from active medical practice, so they called me up one day and asked if I would be willing to come out there and work some. When you're eighty years old, it's good for your ego, or your self-esteem or whatever you want to call it, for somebody to call you up and say they need you. Their medical director retired fifteen months ago, and they have a bunch of nurse practitioners out there, but, by law, a nurse practitioner has to have a licensed medical doctor to look over their work. They have an acting medical director, but he has to go to meetings and other things, so they wanted somebody else over there. So I've enjoyed going there; it gives me something to do one day a week.

I did get drafted again during the Korean War, and I went in as a doctor. And, again, I had a lucky assignment because I was sent to Germany in the Army of Occupation during the Korean War. You know they still have troops in

Germany today. In fact, they send their people from Iraq and Afghanistan to a military hospital in Ramstein, Germany. They also still have a big military establishment in South Korea today, at this minute.

The interesting thing is the fact that they were sending people on through school during World War II so we could come in the Army later on as trained personnel to do whatever had to be done. Of course, we could have gone to war – we got drafted and took infantry basic training, so, sure, we thought we were going to war. We took basic training very seriously, and then I took an easy examination and they sent me to school. I did what the military told me to do, and I got three wonderful medals – Good Conduct, American Theatre of War, and World War II Victory. I would rather have those than a Purple Heart.

Being transferred to all those different places over time, we didn't get the close camaraderie that these fellows did who were fighting and giving their lives for each other – that was a whole different ballgame from what I went through. What they went through meant a lot more than what I went through meant to me, of course. But I certainly wouldn't have been a physician if it hadn't been for the war, and I have enjoyed that profession very much. That's why I still work a little bit at Interfaith, too – I volunteer over there one day a week. Interfaith is a medical clinic that serves people who have no medical insurance. They're working people, but they have no benefits, and most of them can't afford medical care. But they don't qualify for indigent care because they're working, so they're really above the poverty range but fall through the cracks. So we see them, and they pay ten percent of what an ordinary fee would be for medical care. The biggest problem is to get their medicine because it is so terribly expensive, and so we try to give them their medicine for five dollars a prescription. It's a different feeling if you pay for something instead of getting it free. Most of my medical training was given to me by the government, and I owe somebody something. So that's what we do.

Chapter twenty-two
Frank Pittenger

Frank Pittenger was born in Boscobel, Wisconsin, on September 4, 1916. He joined the Navy in 1944 as an ensign and worked his way up to navigation officer by the end of the war. He was assigned to a refrigerator provisions ship during the war and never saw any combat.

I had a degree in mining engineering from the University of Missouri and came to Knoxville in 1938 for my first job. I was working as a mining engineer for the American Zinc Company in Mascot, Tennessee. We had a little four-room house where the company allowed my wife, Patsy, and our first son, Gaines, to live. I had a good deferment from the military, but a number of us became unhappy and decided to go into the service. I signed up as an ensign in the Navy in October of 1943 but didn't get called until July of 1944.

I reported for Naval indoctrination at Hollywood Beach, Florida, for training as a Naval officer, having only seen the ocean one time in my life. That lasted six weeks, and then I was ordered to board the *USS Polaris* AF-11 at Pier 90 in New York. It turned out to be a refrigerator provisions ship, which had just made trips in the Atlantic on what was known as the Murmansk Run. It had been built to haul beef from Argentina to New York, and it made a couple of trips before the Navy commandeered it and turned it into a Navy ship. It was a nice Navy ship, too, with about two hundred people aboard.

Our first trip was to provision about five bases in the Caribbean, then to return to Bayonne, New Jersey, for alterations for the Pacific. This work and reloading took about one month, during which Patsy and I got to really see New York City. The ship left New York City and went through the Panama Canal for the island of Saipan. This took about one month, so the island was pretty well secured by then. After provisioning that base, we returned to Bremerton in Puget Sound for another load. And after about one week, we left for Eniwetak, an atoll, where we met the Pacific fleet as it provisioned for the invasion of Iwo Jima. After reloading at Pearl Harbor, we provisioned a number of islands in the southwest Pacific before returning to Pearl Harbor. On this trip, we met the fleet in Ulithi as it provisioned for the attack on Okinawa. That was a real sight to see, this Naval fleet, with almost all of the Navy's major fighting ships, as they left Ulithi for the next battle. Then we returned to Long Beach, California, to reload for our final trip following the fleet to Okinawa.

It was a summer of uncertainty as we were ordered into Buckner Bay in Okinawa while the decision was being made on whether or not to attack Japan. Boredom was the most serious problem. One major typhoon, numerous false reports of peace, and almost nightly visits by kamikaze planes were our diversions. They ruined our shipboard movies, but they were generally shot down by our picket ships or chose larger targets than our ship. The many B-29s flying from Tinian to Japan told us that the end was near. Just a day or two after they dropped the first atomic bomb, we received orders to go home to San Francisco. We missed all of the celebration in the States on V-J Day but were happy to be headed home.

One of our regrets of the war was that we were within a few hundred miles from where the *USS Indianapolis* was sunk, but we were not directed to it for rescue. We were told that there was trouble nearby and to stand by for rescue. After a few hours, we were told there were no survivors and to proceed with our original orders. But weeks later, we heard that many survivors had stayed in the water for days before dying or being rescued.

Going under the Golden Gate Bridge was a real nice feeling. The ship stayed at anchor in San Francisco Bay until it was decommissioned. In the meantime, I got leave to go home and bring Patsy and Gaines back with me. They got an apartment, and I was able to join them every other night. We had an enjoyable fall, September to December, partying in San Francisco and seeing many friends as they returned from various stations in the Pacific.

Then I received orders to the *USS Melville*, a destroyer repair ship, in Jacksonville, Florida. Our work was mothballing destroyers in the fresh water of the St. Johns River. These orders came in early December, so we were able to spend Christmas with my family in Lancaster, Wisconsin.

The next three months were spent in Jacksonville, and I received my release from the Navy in March of 1946. As you can tell, the Lord looked kindly on me – but it was hell for many of my friends. When I got home, I went back to work at the American Zinc Company and then took a job with DuPont as a mining engineer, and then I went back to Mascot and worked for them for two or three years as an explosive engineer. But I could tell I wasn't going to do much good in that, so I gave it up and went to work for another mining company in Austinville, Virginia, called New Jersey Zinc Company. I stayed with them for about two or three years, but then I got the opportunity to start a company of my own here in Knoxville, a ready-mix concrete company. A friend of mine, Dick Sansom, had the idea and a good job as a salesman with American Limestone Co., so he wanted somebody to run it. So I went to work.

Being in the war gave me a different perspective on news reporting and what they do these days as far as reporting a war. Back then, they told the public in the news nothing but what they wanted them to hear. If it was bad news, they sheltered it from them. Now everything is talked about on television.

Chapter twenty-three
Walter Pulliam

Walter Pulliam was 29 when he volunteered for the Army and served from 1942 to 1945, mostly as a correspondent for *The Stars and Stripes*, the Army's daily newspaper. He often wrote from the front lines but said he never had any close calls.

After receiving my University of Tennessee degree in English and history in 1936, I was a reporter and religion editor for the *Knoxville News-Sentinel* until World War II. In 1942, after Pearl Harbor, I volunteered for the infantry. I was sent to North Africa and served in a replacement headquarters company, assigning officers. Near the end of the North African campaign, I was reassigned to *The Stars and Stripes*, the Army's enlisted men's daily newspaper. It started during the Civil War and was revived during World War I. The Mediterranean edition of *The Stars and Stripes* began publishing shortly after our invasion of North Africa, and its staff was made up entirely of enlisted men, all professional journalists, with one officer who was promoted from the ranks. Most of the staff was from New York, Washington and the West Coast. Tom McRae, news editor of *The Atlanta Constitution*, and I were the only staff members from the South. Our staff included such writers as Stan Swinton, later vice president of The Associated Press; Klaus Mann, son of Noble Prize-winning novelist Thomas Mann; Howard Taubnab, music critic of *The New York Times*; Merrill

Whitsey, sports editor of *The Washington Star*, etc. We published with the Army as it advanced from North Africa into Sicily, and then Italy, covering the front lines. We had teams of editors and reporters who went with the advance echelons of the Army to capture the leading newspaper plant in any city we took, which is where we would print *The Stars and Stripes*. In some cases, the plants had to be taken by force.

We had two correspondents killed in combat, one at Anzio and one during the invasion of southern France. We published as a morning newspaper, and toward the end of the war, had more than a million daily circulation distributed by horseback, helicopter, Jeep, and plane, and sometimes on foot, to front-line troops. I wrote from the front lines at various times, sending my stories back by courier. After we captured Rome, I was granted a private interview with Pope Pius XII.

Toward the end of the war in Italy, I was assigned in Yugoslavia with Tito's Partisans. I became acquainted with Tito and had lunch one time at the White Palace in Belgrade. After peace returned to Europe, I traveled extensively over the continent, reporting on conditions following combat. On *The Stars and Stripes,* I held the rank of sergeant, but we did not wear insignia of rank. We were accredited war correspondents and only wore a correspondent patch.

In North Africa, while in a replacement headquarters, we witnessed numerous air raids when German planes attacked North African harbors. As *Stars and Stripes* correspondents, we were often with the front-line troops, slogging through the wet – often frozen – mountains of Italy, while we were under artillery fire. But I did not have any close calls. The day after I turned my Jeep over to another correspondent, it was hit by a mortar shell. The other *Stars and Stripes* correspondent was unhurt, having jumped in a ditch before the mortar shell hit.

As our armies advanced into northern Italy and reached the Arno River just south of Pisa, an American advance artillery company was holed up in an old barn within sight of the Tower of Pisa. A *Stars and Stripes* correspondent, who was a friend of mine, was with the company. Men could be seen walking around the top of the tower, assumed to be German spotters. The artillery captain in charge considered shooting down the tower, which was within artillery range. After long debate and after consuming a lot of wine that had been captured, he gave the order. About that time, an artillery colonel rode up in a Jeep and said, "Boys, I know what you are thinking. Don't do it." He canceled the order. He knew of the criticism we had gotten from earlier destroying the historic Abbey of Monte-Casino. Twenty minutes later, there would have been no Tower of Pisa.

After the war, I returned briefly to the *News-Sentinel*, then became a staff reporter and later assistant city editor of *The Washington Post*. Since I was doing essentially the same thing in the service, I had no trouble readjusting to civilian life. My outlook on life was unchanged. I returned to the Knoxville area after buying the weekly papers at Harriman, Lake City, LaFollette and Jellico.

I am often asked what Marshal Tito was like. Unlike Hitler or Mussolini, he was not very demonstrative, wearing a simple marshal's uniform. He was easy to interview. He could speak all major European languages, was a good pianist, knowing all the classical European composers, and was an amateur photographer. He had a German shepherd dog, which he told me he captured from a German officer. "The dog," he said, "likes me much better than his Nazi master."

Chapter twenty-four
Paul Richards

Paul Richards was born in Whitewood, South Dakota, on September 29, 1913. He joined the Navy in 1943 and worked as a doctor aboard various ships. The war ended just before he left the United States, but he spent a lot of time treating the sick and injured overseas.

I joined the service in September 1943 under the V-12 program, so I could finish my medical education. I was under the V-12 program in the Navy until June 30, 1945. Then I went on active duty with the Naval Reserves. First I went to the Great Lakes Training Center for indoctrination. Then we were ordered overseas to the Pacific, so I went to San Francisco to get my transportation. I was supposed to leave there on August 15. Of course, I was there when the war ended. So I got in on the party they gave, which was one of the biggest parties I've ever seen.

Even though the war was over, the Navy continued on their wartime footing – there were still wartime precautions because they were afraid that a lot of the Japanese submarines didn't get the message. So the next morning, I left San Francisco at Mare Island Naval Station, took an LST, and went under the Golden Gate Bridge and on to Pearl Harbor. I only stayed in Pearl Harbor a short time, four or five days, and then they gave me orders to go to the 7th Fleet. They put me on a ship to go there, and, of course, it was still a time when they kept everything secret. Nobody knew where anybody was. No one was supposed to know; it was on a need-to-know basis.

Anyway, they put me on a ship and I went to Midway. Then I went to many other places – we covered a pretty big part of the Pacific. And then I was on a Liberty ship, which was run by the merchant marines – it wasn't the Navy – and we went to Saipan. The Saipan harbor was formed by a big reef, which breaks big waves, and there were a lot of ships there – no big ships and no aircraft carriers, but a lot of ships. So we tied up there and put anchor. During the night, we had a real tropical storm – it was as black as it could be. I got out on the deck to see what was going on, and the ship had pulled loose from its anchor and was just drifting down through the harbor among all these other ships. It was out of control, and I was expecting it to run into one of these other ships; it did come close to a few. Finally it got in close to the shore, and the anchor caught. Then we stopped. But there was about twenty or thirty minutes there that I wasn't sure I'd see the light of the next day.

The next morning, I got off the ship in Saipan and stayed overnight. The following morning, as I was going down to the mess hall, three Japanese soldiers came down with their rifles. I saw them, but I didn't know what was going on. Some Marines came along and cautioned them. Turns out they were just three Japanese soldiers who discovered the war was over and were coming in to surrender. And so there was no problem.

I only stayed in Saipan three or four days, and then I went to the dispensary at the main air base, where I took care of personnel. The only thing interesting about it was that it was the place where the atomic bombs had been flown from – not our airfield, but one on down the road about a mile. It had a bunker that was heavily guarded, and a lot of people said there was another atomic bomb in there; I don't know whether it was true or not – it could have been true. I didn't stay at that Naval station too long, maybe five weeks, and then I went to Guam, where I was stationed aboard a ship, the *USS Chauncey*. It was with the 7th Fleet and one of the escorts of the aircraft carrier

Antietam. The other destroyer was the *USS Black.* I told my daughter I was listed on paper by the Navy as being a medical officer on a "destroyer group," but there were only two of them. Two of the six groups were there, but four were off around Australia, and I never got to see them. But on paper I was listed as a medical officer for a group.

Antietam did some patrolling of the Yellow Sea and China Sea and finally went into the harbor at Sing Tao, where it unloaded Marines, who then went ashore and disarmed all the Japanese military there. They took their arms, loaded them on the ships, and sent them back. We weren't there too long, but the Marines stayed there. The aircraft carrier we were escorting went back out into the ocean and after a couple of weeks ended up in Guam. The destroyer was being sent back to the United States, but they said they needed doctors there, so I got off in Guam.

At Guam, they put me on a Liberty ship and sent me back to Pearl Harbor. I was there for four or five days, and then they put me on a plane for Okinawa, for a Seabee outfit. But when I got there, the place was deserted – the Seabees had been disbanded. So they put me in a temporary tent, and after a few days, I was assigned to a Seabee outfit that was building roads on Okinawa.

When I was in Okinawa's capital city, which was then a city of about one hundred fifty thousand, it was built with concrete, bricks, and stucco, partly because they didn't have much wood and partly because it stood up to earthquakes better – they have earthquakes fairly frequently. But that town had been leveled completely – you never saw anything like it – there wasn't a piece of a wall more than three or four feet tall still standing. And the people of Okinawa had been rounded up and put in compounds, which were barbed-wire fenced areas. It was mostly old men, women and children because most of the young men had been killed or captured or taken off to Japan. They were corralled, and their living situation was horrible – they lived in boxes, but the fortunate ones had canvas and made a tent out of it. Some of them were out in the open, and it was pretty cold. It was so cold, my boots froze. It's kind of pitiful to see people in that kind of situation.

I was there for a few weeks, and then I got orders to go to the 96th Seabees, who were in Sing Tao, China, where I'd been previously. They flew me from Okinawa, over the Great Wall of China, down to Shanghai. On the trip there, we got low on gas and just barely made it. From the air, we saw that the Shanghai airport had been bombed. Everything in that country had been bombed – destroyed – and we had no radio, no lights, no nothing at the airport. But we did manage to land.

Well, after we headed south, the weather was really bad. You could get above it by going about thirty-five thousand feet, but when you would come down, the fog and clouds were so thick, you couldn't even see two feet out the windows. And, as I said, there was no radio and no radar, and we knew it was mountainous country down there, so we were afraid to come down too low for fear of running into a mountain. While we tried to locate where we were, the pilot came on and said we only had a few minutes of fuel left and that we had to come down and try to land with the motors running. So we did come down to five thousand feet, then to two thousand, then to one thousand, then to one hundred, and then he told us to get into a crash position, buckle up, and tuck our knees up to our heads. Then he said, "Prepare to crash," but then he let out a big scream, "I see it! I see it!" And we were coming in beside the Shanghai airport. It was kind of a rough landing, but we made it. And as we pulled up beside the airport, we ran out of gas. Turned out perfectly all right, but it was kind of scary for a while. I tell my daughter that when I think about it, I don't remember being scared, but I'm sure I was.

In Shanghai, I had to wait for transportation, so I stayed on a ship on the Wangpu River, which was kind of unusual. These people on the sampans would spend their entire lives there – they had a high tide there, which meant that in the morning, the tide would go out, and these sampans would just float on out to the sea. Then they'd fish out there all day, and the tide would turn around and bring them back in, so it was unusual. Of course, they were very poor people.

Then I was put on another ship and went up the coast to Tsingtao, but they missed the harbor – about fifty miles past – and they had to turn around and come back. I finally got to Tsingtao again, and I reported to the 96th Seabees. We were building an airport there – actually, rebuilding one the Japanese had there. When I got there, 'about the first thing the commanding officer said was, "Where have you been? We've been expecting you for three months!" And I said, "I've been on Okinawa and various places." We checked the orders, and it turned out someone had written them out for the 9th Seabees instead of the 96th Seabees, so they sent me first to a unit that had been disbanded. They finally sent me to the right one, and I stayed there until I came home.

I mostly treated people who were sick with minor injuries; there were all kinds – colds, pneumonia, stuff like that. The ships were pretty well equipped. I was on the ship by myself – I had three corpsmen who assisted me, but I was the only doctor.

Things were very bad in China. Of course, China had been a backward country anyway, and then the Japanese came in there and took over the whole country – they had just looted the whole country. And then the war came along, and with the Japanese and the Americans fighting, everything else was destroyed, so they really didn't have much infrastructure. One of the main things was they didn't have much food. You'd see people eating grass, if they could find any grass, but our company had rations and the mess, so we ate reasonably – Spam and so forth. Our garbage was taken out every three days or so; people learned the days we'd dump it, and there would be several hundred people out there waiting for our garbage to come. The trucks would try to get in there, and they'd climb all over the trucks before they'd get in and sometimes get hurt. Then they'd dump the garbage and people would fight over it; they'd fight over a piece of bread because they were starving.

While I was overseas, my wife wrote regularly, but when I traveled around a lot, it took a long time to get the mail. It was hard for the mail to catch up with me, but when it did, I'd get several letters at one time.

When I got home, it wasn't too bad for me to adjust back to civilian life. When I went back, I had a medical education, so it wasn't too hard. When I got home, I set up a practice as soon as I finished my pediatric training. Then I came here, to Knoxville, in 1950, and I retired in 1992.

During the whole war, I never did see any actual fighting, I never carried a weapon, I never shot at anybody, and nobody shot at me, so I didn't have anything too exciting. But being in the war made me realize what a good country we have. I realized how important it is to have plenty to eat, a warm place to sleep, and I think most people don't realize that until they don't have it.

Chapter twenty-five
Rob Schmid

Rob Schmid was born in Knoxville, Tennessee, on May 7, 1923. He joined the Army Air Corps on April 6, 1943, and trained to be a twin-engine pilot. Rob was on a ship on his way to Okinawa when he heard that the United States had dropped the atomic bomb on Japan. By the time his unit reached shore, the war had ended.

You had to volunteer to go to the air force if you wanted to be a pilot. I signed up on December 4, 1942, and apparently there were about fifty of us from The University of Tennessee who all signed up and all got called up at the same time about four months later. If you got drafted, maybe you could get in the air force, but usually you had to volunteer to get in. One reason is they paid you more money, which was called flight pay. So, a private got fifty dollars per month, but if you were in the cadet program, you got seventy-five dollars per month. It sounds like just a little bit of money, but back then, it was quite a lot of money.

So, anyway, we got called up in April from UT and got sent down to Keesler Field in Biloxi, Mississippi. We stayed there for just a month, which was kind of a quick basic training. Then they sent us to what they called a college training detachment. The main reason was that they had so many in the pipeline waiting to get into training, it was kind of a place to hold them until they got an opening for them.

So, we were over here at UT for about four months; we got there in May and left there in August. While we were waiting, we went to class. A lot of the stuff I took at that time I got credit towards graduation when I came back after the war. What was funny was that I was in school when I got sent off thinking I'd be gone for a long time, but I got sent back to UT in about thirty days. So we were at UT during the summer of 1943 – it was a hot summer. They put us in the college gym with cots, and it sure was hot.

Then we were sent to Nashville, where we took a lot of tests that they used to decide whether you'd go for pilot, bombardier, or navigator training – or you might get washed out. If your test didn't turn out like they thought it should, they would send you to, maybe, gunnery school. We were in Nashville for about a month when I got picked for pilot training, and they sent a whole bunch of us to Montgomery, Alabama, for preflight. Preflight was to get used to the whole Army deal and learn drilling and all that stuff. We were down there from the first part of October until the middle of December.

But they still didn't have room for us to start into flight training. We were there with not much to do, so they gave us a three-day pass to come home for Christmas, which was lucky. We got back in January, and in the middle of winter, they sent us to Florida – I was lucky. They sent us to Avon Park, which was in the citrus belt of Florida. There we took primary and got about sixty hours in. Then we went to basic training, which was in Macon, Georgia. We were there for two months, from April to the latter part of May or June. Then, we got sent to Valdosta, Georgia, for advanced flight school. When you finished basic, they decided whether you would then go to single-engine or twin-engine aircraft. Single engine is a fighter plane, and with a twin engine, you could be in either a two-engine or a four-engine bomber, like the B-17 or B-24.

We graduated and got our wings and our commission August 1, and from there, we got sent to Montgomery, Alabama. They were just then getting the B-29s. There were only a few of them at that time, and they didn't even have them overseas yet. But we got sent up to Cortland, Alabama, which is in northern Alabama, for transition school, where we learned to fly the B-24s.

From there, we were sent to Lincoln, Nebraska, to pick up a crew. In fact, we stayed there a couple of months; we were still moving slow. While we were there, we got a pilot, co-pilot, navigator and bombardier. So you got your crew and they sent you to a place so you could train together, which in our case was in Mountain Home, Idaho. It was out in the desert, about fifty miles from Boise. We were there from March to June.

At first they said they were sending us to fly a B-32, which is a bomber they just started making. But then in a week or so, they changed their mind and said they were going to send us overseas to Okinawa to get ready for the invasion of Japan, which was supposed to happen November 1. So we were sent to Salinas, California, where we stayed about a week or ten days, and then we were taken up to San Francisco, where we headed out overseas on a slow-moving boat – it took about four weeks.

We were sent out in July, but at that point, everybody thought it would be another year before the Japs would surrender. There was no indication that they were going to drop the atom bomb. But they dropped the atom bomb the first week in August, and then the Japs surrendered after they dropped another bomb on them. We got there at the tail end of everything. If we'd been back in the States another two or three weeks, we probably never would have gone over because there was no need, the war was over.

What was funny was that we were on this ship going overseas, and it came on the loud speaker that they'd dropped an atomic bomb. Well, nobody even heard of an atomic bomb. We knew they were making something secret in Oak Ridge, and at the point when I went in the Army, they were building it, but nobody had any idea about what they were making. So it was a complete surprise.

When we were in Okinawa, it was just an airstrip; the rest was countryside. At the other end of the island, they had these old castles. But they were literally torn to pieces. There was a little island right across from where we were where Ernie Pyle got killed. He was a writer, a war correspondent and a GI's GI. Everybody liked him. He had been in Europe and then decided to go to the Pacific, and he got killed over there.

But this was a good time to be living, bringing everybody together. You had a common enemy who was going to kill you if he could.

Korea had been dominated by the Japanese for about 40 years, and they were all armed just like Japan. Since they didn't need B-24s anymore, they sent us to troop carrying crew on C-47s. So we flew around and hauled people up to Korea or Japan, the Philippines, or wherever they wanted to go. The Russians came down from the north. If we hadn't been in Korea, the Russians would have taken over the whole country. At that time, communism was a big item for everybody, and the Russians weren't cooperating. We would fly over there to take stuff over for people in Japan and down south or wherever we needed to send somebody. If we hadn't been there, the Russians would have overrun. The main thing we did was keep the Russians out.

So we were kept in Korea until the summer of '46, at which time we finally got to go home. They used the point system to determine how quickly you got to go home. We got points for different things, like every month you were overseas, you got a point; every month in the Army, you got a point; if you had decorations or whatever, you got so many points; and this and that. Of course, we had just gotten over there, so we weren't one of the first ones by a long shot to go home. It was the next summer before we got to go home.

When I got home, I went back to school. The GI Bill paid all your way through school, and, if you weren't married, you got I think sixty dollars per month from the government. So, it was a good deal – I was still living at home with my parents. It was really one of the best pieces of legislation they ever did because it educated so many people who would normally never have gotten an education. It showed in how our country prospered after the war. I was in business administration. I graduated in the spring of '46. I was overseas exactly one year; I came back on the exact date that I went over.

Being in the war taught me leadership. I was nineteen when I went in, and I grew up probably a lot faster than if I hadn't gone in and stayed at home. You make a lot of friends in the Army. One of them I visit every year. He's in Athens, Georgia, and his name is Scruggs. And since my name is Schmid, the first letters are close in the alphabet. They put us together alphabetically, and we stayed together through flight training. He went to single engine and I went to twin engine, so I lost contact with him for a while, but we re-established it after the war was over and have kept in contact ever since.

It wasn't hard at all coming home – I was glad to be back. It was kind of like going to camp every day. Anyway, the experience is something you never forget. It was a unique experience, and I'm glad I did it. It was an education.

Chapter twenty-six
Warren Sylvester

Warren Sylvester was born in Scituate, Massachusetts, on June 11, 1924. He joined the Army Air Corps in 1942 and was trained in topographic drafting and photograph interpretation. He spent most of his time in Italy and some in North Africa. His time in the service earned him a Good Conduct Medal, a Rifle and Carbine Qualification Medal, and three campaign ribbons.

I joined the Army so I could stay out of it. In most any war, there is a way to delay going into it, either like Clinton did or whatever President Bush did. There was a program that if you were in college and your draft number came up, you were allowed to finish that semester and then go as a group to wherever you were supposed to go. At the time, I was in Northeastern University as a mechanical engineering student. All the guys in my class went to Fort Devons in Massachusetts. The famous thing about Fort Devons is that is where the Patriots football team started. So we were inducted, and they forgot about us for about a week and a half. We didn't get any clothes or any underwear or anything. We were just walking around in our civilian clothes for a week and a half.

Finally, they found out where we were. And just as soon as they found we had Army clothes on, they put us on KP immediately – that was the first thing they could think of to do with us. So I guess we messed around there for a while – long enough to get a week's leave before we were to be assigned somewhere. I lived in Scituate, Massachusetts, at the time, and I went home for about a week.

I was born with flat feet. Anytime I go to an orthopedic doctor, they say, "Oh, you've got really flat feet." I know that. It didn't keep me out of the service, but there was a typical problem that I had with my feet. The first time I went on sick leave, they told me to soak my feet in cold water, which, of course, did not work. Then, the next time I went on sick leave, they told me to soak my feet in hot water. And the next time I went on sick leave, they said they would make an arch for me, and they taped my feet up. Of course, if you take a shower two or three times, that tape comes off. Then, the next time I went on sick leave, they finally took pity on me and put leather wedges in my shoes – in the soles and then the heels. That worked out pretty well, except the nails would come through in the soles of the shoe, which got uncomfortable. Of course, during all that business, I lost training time, so they switched me to another unit, and I started all over with the feet and the cold water and the hot water and the taping. It finally got to the point on the Achilles heel that I could hear it squeaking – it got pretty bad. The only time I could really, if you want to call it, take advantage of it was when I finally got sent overseas in a replacement area in North Africa. See, I was an air force person in an Army replacement depot, and they took advantage of us fine fellows. One time, we were on a hike and I kept falling back because of my feet, and I finally ended up near the back of the road. I could see way ahead that the column was turning around, so I decided that I would just step out of line, sit down and cool off, and wait until they came back. Of course, at that time, this sergeant came along and told me to get back in line. I told him, "I can't." So I deliberately didn't obey a noncom's command and got away with it. And when the column came back, I picked myself up and got in the front of the line, and by the time we got back to the base, I was the last one in again. My feet just didn't do a lot of good.

I was sent to Jefferson Barracks, which is just south of St. Louis and used to be a Civil War training place for Union forces. It wasn't a very modern facility. When you went on sick leave there, they had a rule that you had to pack up all of your clothes in your barracks bag in such a way that they wouldn't wrinkle. They were trying to discourage people from calling in sick, and that worked pretty well. But Jefferson Barracks was just a damp, cold hellhole, and I was susceptible to getting head colds. There would be stuff that would come into my eyes at night, and they would mat together, and I couldn't open up my eyelids until I got all that stuff off. They finally put me in a hospital. Apparently, my body temperature is just a little bit higher than normal, so they kept me in the hospital too long. By the time I got out, I was so weak that I couldn't do the calisthenics, so they put me back in the hospital. But, I got through the basic training, and I didn't have to cheat too much on that.

Then they sent me to Fort Belvoir, Virginia. I had quite a bit of math and drafting in school – at Northeastern University – so they sent me to a topographic school in Fort Belvoir. The idea was that they would teach me how to draw maps to go between the Germans and the Americans, which I though was so amusing. See, I wasn't supposed to have rifle training, but I was going to go out in "no man's land" to draw road maps. One time, while I was at Fort Belvoir, I got really scared – I mean really terrified – because some GI came in the barracks where I was staying, and he must have been pretty drunk. First of all, he was in the wrong building, and then he assumed that my bunk was his, and I just didn't know what this drunk guy was going to do. Was he going to try to get in bed with me? He finally made enough noise that somebody got up and threw him out of the building. I never knew what had happened to him.

My math teacher in high school was a second lieutenant in the Navy and was stationed at Fort Belvoir. My mother and father came down, and we spent a couple of days with him. It was sort of amusing that during high school, he was my teacher, but he now had a Navy uniform on and I had my private class A uniform – there was a difference on how you handled each other. That was good to see someone I knew in high school.

Before we went overseas, we had to go through rifle practice and that sort of thing, and I qualified for a rifle and a carbine. We also had to fire a Thompson sub-machine gun just to feel how strong the kickback was. But when I got through basic training and overseas training, they sent me someplace in Virginia, and we got on a boat. We had to climb up this cargo net, which was sort of scary. I was with a group of people on a freighter – I wasn't on an ocean liner with a bunch of people – there were probably only about one hundred men on this freighter. Part of this freighter was full of trucks and stuff, and part was full of men and hardware of some other kind. I think we were sort of apprehensive when we were in the convoy going across the Atlantic because they could always hit the convoys. But no convoy ships were lost through that whole mess. We mostly slept out on deck during that voyage, and I didn't get seasick except one time – I was leaning against the mast, and I'd watch it go back and forth across the sky, and that almost got me sick.

They didn't tell us where we were going, but we went through the Rock of Gibraltar and landed in Oran, which is in Morocco. When we got there, and because we were air force people, we got knocked around a little bit by the Army replacement people. One thing is they had us make a mattress bed; they told us there was a big pile of straw, so we made a mattress out of straw. The bunks were made of two-by-fours, but the mattress springs would crisscross back and forth. That was the same way the continental people did it during the Revolution, but their bedsprings were made out of rope.

Going from Oran to Tripoli, they transferred us by railroad somewhere. In WWI, there were railroad cars, but everything in Europe is small. So they had railroad cars that were meant for eight horses or forty people. Before we got on that train, they wanted us to wear our full Class A uniforms. It was pretty hot, and we all had our full overcoats on. I thought it was pretty stupid to be out in this hot sun with overcoats on.

So, me being smart, I took off my overcoat, folded it up, and put it in my pack. I thought that was the way to go. Well, just a soon as I got that done, a truck came along and picked up all the barracks bags and took off, so I didn't have my barracks bag anymore. In the desert area, it would get really cold at night; just as soon as the sun is gone, it's freezing. I didn't have any blankets, and I didn't have my overcoat. But there was a guy in my group who was smaller than I was, and he was willing to share his overcoat with me, so we didn't freeze too much.

When I was out there, they'd stop the train every once in a while so all the guys could get off and relieve themselves and then get back on the train. One time, they stopped and everybody piled out, and then the train started moving again almost immediately. One of the guys didn't get back to the boxcars. He was in the middle of nowhere, urinating and running, which is not the easiest thing to do. So he didn't get back on the boxcar, and we watched him disappear in the distance. It took him three days to finally catch up, and I don't know how he did it. I thought he was going to be killed by Arabs or something like that.

I was finally assigned to go to Italy, and it rained for four days in a row. I was supposed to fly to Italy in a small airplane – I think it was called a B-25 or B-24. So we piled on this airplane. That was going to be my first airplane ride, so I thought that was going to be great. But, the way the weather was – just full of holes in the air – the plane just kept falling into these holes. It got so bad that all of the seats along the fuselage collapsed, and the luggage got loose. And I got sick. I can't imagine being any sicker than I was on that flight – it was really pretty bad. When we finally got there, it was beautiful, clear weather.

We went to Foggia Air Base, which is in southern Italy. So the intelligence detachment that I was a part of had these aviators with P-38 planes and cameras, and they were given the assignments to photograph certain areas of Italy. They'd be on the front lines, and when they'd bring the film back and make prints, it was then our job to find out where these guys actually went. They had good topographic maps, and you could find pretty well, with the techniques we had, where the plane had actually taken pictures – where the photograph was. We would plot those on a piece of acetate, and that information would be sent out to photo interpreters so they could find out where the place was. I sent some of those things back home from Italy, and they are somewhere in the attic, but I haven't been able to find them. But, I'm sure these photographs were all tactical, in that they were involved in recent campaigns. They would use those photographs, and, quite often, they would cover the same areas. Our group was pretty close to the front lines, so there wouldn't be much delay with the photographs. Every time the front moved, we photo interpreters moved. We mostly stayed along the coast and had some really nice resort areas to live in while we were drawing our work. Most of our work was at night because by the time the pilots got back with their photographs and they were developed and printed, it was late afternoon or nighttime.

I didn't do any photo interpretations; I was just locating where the photo prints were on a map. What we were going to do was take all the photographs that we had and tear them up in certain ways to make a big mosaic. Then we would have this mosaic of all the photographs to compare with the map sources. And we did a fine job; it looked really nice. When we got it done, an officer came along and said, "This looks great, but you left out a whole mountain." This was because of the distortion of the prints – it just disappeared, so we had to redo it.

Before we went to Florence, I was given several days off, so I went to Rome and walked around for a while. I went to Venice during the same time and really enjoyed it. When we got up to Florence, I didn't have a camera – not many people did – but I found a print later of where I lived for a year and a half. In Italy, they did a lot of work with waterfalls and fountains and so forth. You know, I took a trip to Germany some time ago, and I drove down into Florence, and I was able to find this place. So, apparently, the classic thing if you had an estate like that was to build a great big wall around it. That villa was called Castello.

This one fellow who was a buddy of mine was from upper Maine. He spoke French, and it didn't take long for him to speak Italian, so he got to know a lot of people. Well, Italian women, at least the better types, are really proud of their fur coats. Well, the father of these girls we met was a publisher in Livorno, which is on the west coast of Italy. He had been put in jail by the Italians and then got out and was put in jail by the Americans and Allies because of his political views. But he kept his family together. These two buddies of mine somehow met these people, and they were just in there like an extra family. I was off every Thursday afternoon, and when I got to know those people, I went in and visited them every Thursday. There's one thing on my service record that says my two buddies and I were restricted to the barracks for three days – apparently we got home late one time. We would also take that family whatever rations we could. See, the Italians didn't have much – whether they had a lot of money or not, there just wasn't much to eat – so anything we could we brought to them.

When you went through the food line, you got so much food plopped in your mess kit. After you ate what you wanted, you'd go down through this line, throw away any leftover food, and get your mess kit cleaned in this super hot water. I remember one day when I was not feeling well, I just didn't want to eat the food that was in my mess kit. So, unfortunately, all these Italian civilians, mostly women, were outside the fence, and here I was throwing away perfectly good food, and they needed to eat. That was sort of a sad thing for me to throw away good food.

I never learned much about speaking Italian, but I was finally able to understand the language pretty well. My brother married an Italian girl named Ida, and I got home before he did. One day I was up at their house, and Ida was speaking Italian to another. One of them was criticizing the sugar bowl on the table because the bowl was too small. So I said to them, "Why don't you just get a bigger sugar bowl?" That was the first time they knew I could understand Italian, even though I couldn't speak it. They were more careful after that about what they said.

I was never in combat, but my brother got into France on D-Day plus six days. He was put in an engineering group that was scurrying to find bivouac areas and water. He was in "no man's land." He and his sergeant got turned around some place and got captured for something like half a day. That was sort of scary, but the Americans were coming forward, and he was uncaptured. So, in the distance we could hear bombers and that sort of thing, but there was never combat in my group. One time, this friend of mine volunteered to go as part of our unit to the fighting. I don't know what he did, but he came back with an Italian Beretta pistol. But the scariest thing for me was that time when the drunk soldier almost got in bed with me.

The Italian army gave up while I was in Florence. And we got some of the Italian soldiers sort of attached to our group as laborers. Their idea was that if they could follow along with us to the more northern parts of Italy, then they could get a free ride home. When we were heading toward the Po Valley, where Bologna and Milan and those cities are, this one guy convinced us that it would be nice if we took him to his home village, and we thought that was OK. When we came upon this dirt road at his hometown, he was standing up like he was Mussolini on these trucks. We finally got into the center of town, and everyone just loved us because we were liberators. But there was a sort of strange feeling because it turned out that, while he was away fighting, his wife had taken up with another man. It got to be sort of quiet, but they still got out plenty of Chianti and vino for us. Several of us – not me – got sick. It was a grand reunion.

After the war was over in Italy, somebody got up a tour of Switzerland, and I jumped in on that. They allowed us to take about thirty-five dollars into Switzerland. That was a great tour and the first time we had any dark beer. We really enjoyed that beer. See, the beer the Army gave us wasn't very good beer, but it was wet.

I had been overseas a year and a half. When we went back to the United States, I was on a converted cruise ship, and it wasn't a very good experience. They'd built up all these bunks and had only about eighteen inches between them. And it took so long to get your food that by the time you got through the line, it was time to get in line again to get your supper. It was good to be going home, but the voyage wasn't very good.

The rumor was that just as soon as we got back to the United States, my group would be retrained and sent to the Pacific. That sure didn't appeal. So I was glad that the bomb was dropped. See, when I got home, I was given a thirty-day pass, which was extended to forty-five days, and then they finally wrote a letter that said to come on down and get a discharge. It was during that interim time that I was home deciding what I was going to do when I was finally discharged.

I ended up as a pfc – private first class. I think that's my biggest disappointment because I worked my tail off on that Map Service. I know I did twice as many sorties than anybody else did. But these guys who went off drinking with the sergeants and all got the promotions. The suffering on my feet paid off reasonably well, though – I got money to buy new shoes.

When I got discharged, it was out of Miles Standish in southern Massachusetts. The trains were still running, taking GIs home. So, I got my barracks bag, got on the train, got into Scituate, Massachusetts, picked up my barracks bag, and walked home. There wasn't any greeting committee; there were no parades and no bands. I just walked home, walked up to the front door, and knocked on the door. I kept the field jacket that I got, and I can still wear it if I take the lining out – I've added just a few pounds since that time.

My father, who was a veteran of the First World War, said that they wouldn't keep me because I had flat feet. But they decided to keep me. Then he said, "They'll never send you overseas." But I took overseas training and went overseas. Then he finally got it right: He said, "When you get discharged, make sure they go over all of your records and make sure that all the 'T's are crossed and all the 'I's are dotted." So, I'd been plagued with these flat feet; it's just been a horrible thing with my feet. When I finally got the attention of some second lieutenant on discharge, I made sure that everyone was aware of what my service records were. I ended up with a ten percent disability for a service-aggravated injury. Right now, ten percent is worth about eighty-five dollars per month, but at that time, because of the way the GI Bill was for going to college, with a ten percent disability, I not only got more monthly pay, but also any supplies I needed I could get for nothing. So that ten percent worked out pretty well.

I had met a fellow in Florence who was an architect, and I guess just talking to him and working with my father, I decided that I would try to get an architectural degree. At that time, the Rhode Island School of Design was gearing up for all these guys with the GI Bill, and they expanded their school to include an architectural school. When I went to Rhode Island School of Design for an architectural degree, I got all my supplies – paper, triangles, T-squares, and such – for nothing, because I was such a good guy. I still have a serious problem with my feet, but at least during the five years I was at the school of design, I was able to be rich and have all those supplies. I thoroughly enjoyed being in the service.

I never kept in touch with anyone I was in the service with. Most all the people that I went into the Army with were from the Boston area. As soon as I graduated from the Rhode Island School of Design, I eventually came down to Knoxville, which is quite a ways from New England. Every time I moved, it was sufficient distance that I had to get a bunch of new friends. And I was very neglectful in writing to people. But during the war, I corresponded quite a bit. I have someplace in my attic all the letters that I wrote home, but I can't read them because my writing is so bad. In WWII, they had a system where you'd write something like a telegram, and they would reduce that in size and ship a whole bunch of them back home. So if I got a letter, I'd send one back. It wasn't e-mail, but you could keep them informed about what was going on.

From the standpoint of having to be in the service, not being in combat, screwing up my feet and getting paid for that, and then having the GI Bill come along, I was able to get decent supplies. Everything pretty much worked out well. When I graduated from the school of design, that particular year was the same time that all the other GIs graduated, and I had a serious problem getting a decent job. Through the architectural school, I had a couple of offers, but I didn't think they were worth my effort. At that time, the Map Service in Washington, D.C., wanted to expand, so they opened up a facility in Providence, and I got in there the first day. The problem with that – although the money was pretty good – is it got to the point that I realized I was in a Map Service without using the architectural degree. The longer I stayed with the Map Service, the less things I had to sell as an architect. So then Pratt and Whitney put out a notice that they wanted to take people with engineering backgrounds to Hartford and train them to be aircraft engineers. I thought that was at least in an engineering mode, so I jumped on that. I got in on that first class, and when the group graduated from the aircraft school, they selected three people to go to Oak Ridge, and I was one of them. The funny thing there was that the music people in Oak Ridge had a lot of influence on who to hire for the engineering groups, and of the three people who went to Oak Ridge, two of us played French horns. So I got a pretty good job working on the nuclear-powered aircraft because I played French horn. I really think that's a true situation – my educational background was enough to get them interested, but the ability to play the French horn got me the job.

They were designing atomic-powered aircraft engines there, and they started to pull people back into Hartford. It was my understanding that, after all the training we had, they were going to put us back into piston engines, and I thought that wasn't too good. So I resigned from that and decided to stay in the Oak Ridge/Knoxville area. I've been here ever since.

I got a job with K-25. Then there was a big buildup of people in Oak Ridge, and I got caught up in the reduction – I was out of a job again. But there was a fellow in a sports car club that I was in who worked at TVA, so I eased in there. And I worked twenty-five years in the architectural department at TVA. Right after I got off the K-25 thing, I married a Knoxville woman here. She has since died.

Things just sort of flowed from being born to being eighty years old. I didn't have any great triumphs, but things just sort of flowed from one activity to another – and kept me alive in food and money and sports cars. I'm happy with what I've been doing – I don't think I'd want to start over again. My whole life has been reasonably pleasant.

Chapter twenty-seven
Jim Talley

James Talley was born in Knoxville, Tennessee, on September 12, 1924. He joined the Army Air Corps in April 1943 and served as a navigator. On his twenty-second mission, he had to bail out of his airplane when it exploded during the Battle of the Bulge. His time in the service earned him a Purple Heart and an Air Medal with Oak Leaf Clusters. He later became a distinguished Knoxvillian through civic work and membership in numerous business, religious, and social activities in the community.

I was a senior at McCallie military school in Chattanooga, and we didn't know who Pearl Harbor was, or where Pearl Harbor was, or what Pearl Harbor was when it happened on a Sunday. But when it happened, we all realized that, being in the class of '42, we would be prime candidates to be going into the service. So I was looking forward to getting into the service. I came to The University of Tennessee following my graduation and really only had about two quarters when the war came along and interrupted my college career. So I really don't have any college, but the good Lord has blessed me, and I have had some good jobs, some good friends, and a good wife along the way, and life has been good to me.

Anyway, I decided immediately that I wanted to go into the service. I also wanted to go into the Air Corps because of some friends of my sister, one of whom was a four-star general in the air force and one of my heroes. He flew the P-40 over China-Burma-India, and so I always wanted to go into the air force. Most of my gang started thinking about getting orders right after the first of the year in '43. I waited and waited for my orders, and I even called the War Department one time and said, "Where are my orders? I'm ready to go."

So I volunteered, and I did get my orders and left along with a lot of my buddies at First Presbyterian Church, including Bill Tate, Rob Schmid, and several others. We all left here on April 6, 1943, from the L&N Railroad Station and went to Keesler Field, Mississippi. My mother's initial reaction to that was, "You are so fortunate – the camellias and the beautiful flowers are just great, and you will love seeing all the pretty flowers and everything." Well, I never saw anything but sand, pine trees, helmets, leggings, canteens, rifles, and what-not. I was there for a month for basic training, and I don't think I ever saw anything higher than a pfc. But it was good for us, and we learned a lot about the Army and the air force.

From Keesler Field, I went to Memphis, Tennessee, to an outfit, or a program, called the College Training Detachment – CTD. Actually, that's one of the best things the government ever did – I didn't realize it at the time, but they used college training detachments to put guys who were getting ready to go into the air force into these little colleges. It not only helped the colleges stay in business because all the men were gone, but it was a reservoir of people to go into the service as time went on. So I spent three months at Memphis State College, which has now changed names. I learned about drilling, meteorology, physics and aeronautics. I had gone to a military school for five years before entering the university at McCallie in Chattanooga, so I was pretty well oriented to the military. I liked the military, and I always have.

During my three months there, according to rumor, they found ground glass in the spinach one night. So they sent us the next day to Kansas City, Missouri, to Rockhurst College, which is a Jesuit college – a delightful place. Kansas City is a wonderful city, too, and I was there for two months. Then we all went to San Antonio, Texas, for classification. That is where it was determined whether you would be a pilot, a navigator, a bombardier, or a washout. Everybody was scared to death down there. I used to bite my fingernails as I was growing up, but I knew ahead of time what was going to happen, so I quit biting my fingernails. And the first thing they did in classification was to tell you to put your hands on the table, and they checked to see if you bit your fingernails. If you bit your fingernails, they didn't want you in the air force.

So I got through the classification down there, and Bill Tate and I were inseparable. He and I were buddies all the way through – roomed together and everything. But Bill Tate and I were classified for all three – pilot, bombardier, and navigator – and we could have any one we wanted, but we were called in front of a board and told at that time there was an extreme shortage of bombardiers and that they wanted us to be bombardiers. Well, we were scared to death to go against their wishes, so we said, "OK, we'll go to bombardier school." So we went to bombardier preflight school at Ellington Field in Houston, Texas. We were there November and December, and about a week before we were supposed to graduate, they posted a notice that there was an opening in Coral Gables, Florida, at the University of Miami for two hundred navigators. So we decided we would become navigators instead of bombardiers and we turned our names in. Fortunately, we were approved to become navigator cadets, and off we went.

We arrived on Christmas Eve in Coral Gables, Florida. Some of our other buddies ended up in places with snow all over, and we were so delighted to be in Miami. When we got there, instead of the normal hazing and so forth that the upperclassmen did to the new cadets, it was, "Gentlemen, welcome to Coral Gables. We are so happy you are here. Merry Christmas. We won't be doing anything for about four or five days, and the maid will make up the beds in the rooms. Leave your shoes outside your room if they need shining." And they woke you up every morning with Glenn Miller's "Sunrise Serenade" over the loud speaker. I mean, it was the country club of the U.S. Army Air Forces at Coral Gables. So we were very happy, and we were there training for several months in the old flying boat. Of course, none of my buddies could believe what I was doing, but ten navigators at a time would go on a night training or a daytime training mission in flying boats – seaplanes. They would take us down to the Seaplane Base in a beautiful striped awning trailer, and you would see all the views of Miami, and we would do our training and come back. That's what they used to say was "hog heaven" for us.

So we stayed in Coral Gables in navigation school for about five months. Then time came for graduation, and I pinned Bill's wings on him, and he pinned my wings on me. And we were ready to go to war. And I'll never forget, at the final meeting, we were all in a theater somewhere for graduation, and this colonel said, "Well, gentlemen, time for graduation. I have good news, and I have some bad news." That is not always good to hear, as you know. And he said the bad news is that this was no longer for air transport command – that this was heavy bombardment. That's kind of what I thought it was going to be anyway, to tell you the truth. And he said the good news was we had a choice of flying in B-17s or B-24s. Well, I had always been in love with B-17s – I just thought that was a beautiful airplane. So Bill and I both picked B-17s, and we were given a short delay after graduation to stop by home for a little while, which we did. I think that's about the time Mrs. Talley and I became engaged. We were engaged when I went overseas.

Then we went to Dyersburg, Tennessee, for a couple of months for training, where they put the crews together. There were ten men on a B-17 crew – pilot, co-pilot, navigator, bombardier, radio operator, engineer, two waist gunners, a ball turret gunner, and a tail gunner. The crews flew together for a couple of months to get used to each other and practiced formation flying, bombing, navigation flights, and gunnery missions. At the end of that training, we were sent to Kearney, Nebraska, to pick up a brand new B-17. It had two hours on it – it was just off the assembly line. We were to fly from there to Grenier Field, New Hampshire, at night, and they told all the navigators to sleep that night onboard ship because we'd be navigating over the ocean for the next two or three days. So I went to sleep and woke up early the next morning as the sun came through the astrodome on the front – the little bubble up here. I looked in the cockpit, and the co-pilot had his head back and the pilot had his head forward, and they were both sound asleep. We were flying along on automatic pilot, so nobody knew where anybody was. Then they woke up and they said, "Where are we? Well, I thought you were going to fly..." That was my first real test on navigation, and thank heavens, I found a barn that had the name of the town on top of it, and we got on to Grenier Field and stayed there for a couple of days.

Then, in the summer of '44, we flew from Grenier Field to Goose Bay, Labrador – the most beautiful country I have ever seen. It had beautiful lakes, and one of the chief navigation points was a crystal-clear blue lake where a B-17 had tried to land and you could see it through the water – I don't know if that was a good place to pinpoint where you were. Well, we got to Goose Bay, stayed there a couple of days, and I got a real education on gambling in the service. They had poker games every night. All these officers had never seen each other in their lives, but sometimes the pot in the center of the table was ten thousand dollars – I mean, there were big bucks being bet and spent in poker. Fortunately, I didn't play poker.

A couple of days later, we took off for Reykjavik, Iceland, which was a long way – a lot of ocean, a lot of icebergs, no navigation help whatsoever, no radio beams, and you couldn't use the radio because the Germans had submarines up there that were sending out artificial radio beacons to try to pull you off course, which happened to several people on the way up. So we took off single ship. I was all of nineteen years old at the time, and that's a long way with a lot of responsibility guiding a ship. There were two or three times I had to change course because I got a wind that was drastically different from the predicted wind the air transport command had forecast. My pilot and I got to know each other real well there on whether to take the heading that I recommended or use what they had forecast. So he said, "Well, I'm going to go with you. You're supposed to know what you are doing." I knew what the wind was, and it was almost one hundred eighty degrees different from what we had been told it would be. Over that long a flight, it makes a tremendous difference.

So off we went to Reykjavik, Iceland. We passed the southern tip of Greenland, and in a few days, we took off for England. It was another long trip, and we had a choice of landing at Nutts Corner, Ireland, or Bovington, England, or Aberdeen, Scotland. We ended up in Nutts Corner, Ireland, which is the most beautiful scenery I have ever seen. We stayed there a day or maybe a couple of days and then flew to Bovington for combat training. And combat really did hit me in the face when we got to Bovington. The first day there, we were in a meeting with all the officers, and this major called us to attention and said, "Gentlemen, welcome to combat." I thought, "That doesn't sound too good to me." He said, "I want you to look to your left and look to your right. Two of the three of you will get home. Whoever does and whoever doesn't depends on who listens to what you hear this week in combat training." Boy, you could have heard a pin drop in that meeting.

During that week, we learned about the radio stations called bunchers and splashers; we learned about aircraft identification; and we learned about conditions of flight and anti-aircraft. We were there for about a week, and then we were flown on C-47s to our base. My base wasn't the same one that Bill Tate ended up with. In fact, there was nobody there that I knew. I was in Bedford, England, just six miles northeast of the base called Thurleigh, and we, of course, anglicized it, and it became Thurli. I was with the 306th Bomb Group, and I ended up in the 423rd Bomb Squadron Bomb Group (H). I was in a little barracks called "Number Ten Downing Street," which was named after where Mr. Churchill lived in London. Somebody had painted "Ten Downing" on the front door.

On my first mission, I was nineteen – I wasn't twenty until the next day, on my second mission. I didn't know at the time that Fred Vance was a paratrooper; so we passed each other on the way in but didn't know the other was there. Some of my missions included bombing in Kassell, Germany; Koln, Germany; Stralsund, Germany; Schweinfurt, Germany, which was the place we went to that made ball bearings; Hamburg, which was a big port in Germany; Merseberg, Germany, which was an oil refinery; Berlin; and Frankfurt. Koblenz was my last mission.

List of Jim's twenty-two bombing missions:

1. September 11, 1944: Lutzhendorf, Germany
2. September 12, 1944: Ruhland, Germany
3. September 17, 1944: Volkel, Holland
4. September 19, 1944: Unna, Germany
5. October 2, 1944: Kassel, Germany
6. October 5, 1944: Koln, Germany
7. October 6, 1944: Stralsund, Germany
8. October 7, 1944: Ruhland, Germany
9. October 9, 1944: Schweinfurt, Germany
10. November 6, 1944: Hamburg, Germany
11. November 8, 1944: Merseberg, Germany
12. November 9, 1944: Metz, France
13. November 16, 1944: Eschweiler, Germany
14. November 21, 1944: Leewarden, Holland
15. November 29, 1944: Misburg, Germany
16. December 5, 1944: Berlin, Germany
17. December 6, 1944: Merseberg, Germany
18. December 11, 1944: Frankfurt, Germany
19. December 12, 1944: Merseberg, Germany
20. December 15, 1944: Kassel, Germany
21. December 18, 1944: Kaiserslautern, Germany
22. December 28, 1944: Koblenz, Germany

A sergeant would come in and knock on the door when you were going to fly a mission. There were twelve of us living in one little barracks, and I could almost tell he was going to grab the doorknob before he ever grabbed it. He would come in, cut the light on, and say, "Lt. Talley, you are flying in zero-five-five; breakfast at three; briefing at four; 2,780 gallons of gasoline; it's going to be a long mission." And I would think, "I don't know if I want them to call my name or whether I don't." I knew I had twenty-five or thirty missions to fly at that time. I had a superstition that I always had to put my right shoe on first. But one day I got to the mess hall and was eating breakfast at three in the morning, and I realized that I had put my right shoe on after my left shoe. So I went all the way back, took both shoes off, put my right shoe on first, and started all over again. Superstition was a big thing over there for most everybody – they had little things they liked to do for good luck.

Anyway, my first mission was fairly uneventful, but the second mission was a real doozy. This was probably one of the worst missions the 8th Air Force ever flew. We went all over the place that day, and it was done on purpose because we were trying to get the Luftwaffe to come up and attack us. Germany was running low on oil and gas at that time. So when we took off, we went north and went way up the ocean. This bad mission to Ruhland, which was referred to us as "the cook's tour of Germany," was done to pull the Luftwaffe up off the ground. We did knock down quite a few fighters that day, but we were off course. Fighters hit us before we got to Berlin, and we ended up in a bad battle – we lost three ships that day due to fighters.

We had a temporary pilot that day because my first pilot was riding as a co-pilot. But he called me and said, "Pilot to navigator, where are we?" And I said, "Captain, if you will look down, you will see the Brandenburg Gate. We are right over Berlin." He said, "Oh, let's get the hell out of here." And I said, "I'm all for that." So we went on from there and bombed the target at Ruhland, which was an oil refinery. Then, after we turned, it so happened there was not another B-17 in sight that was flying – we were totally scattered all over the sky. But we went on to the target and bombed single ship, and as we turned off the target, we found some other crippled ships. So we got in with them, and there were eleven of us from different squadrons. My pilot said, "We're taking over the lead." All the other navigators were lost, and I knew generally where we were, of course. I said, "OK." So we took over the lead, and here I was, nineteen years old, on my second mission, and I was leading eleven B-17s from deep Germany. We were down close to Munich – we were way, way far from home. We were about twenty thousand feet, and there were no fighters around. I told the bombardier that I wanted to sit up over the bombsight and get this group back. So off we went, and every now and then, I would have to change the heading ten or fifteen degrees to the right or the left, then back to the right and back to the left, and just as we got to the French coast, I realized we were about to fly over Dunkirk. There was still a pocket of Germans there that we hadn't run out. So we changed course and got on back home, and my pilot thought I was the greatest navigator that ever lived. It was later on that I said, "Well, I was actually staying out in the fields and over the woods because I knew they wouldn't have any flak guns to shoot at us. If we got over cities, we would be shot at. All I did was stay out in the countryside." But he thought that altering to the right and to the left was brilliant, so I let him keep on thinking that.

At the time, I was scared to death. I thought, "My Lord, if some other fighters had hit us or something, I don't know what we would have done." But it was just us, eleven ships trying to get back to England. Some had engine trouble and some had bad flak damage, and we had holes. I still have in a picture frame a piece of flak that came through the ship and almost took my head off. I bent down to pick up something, and this shell came through right where I was sitting. And this piece of flak lodged in an engine cell outside the plane. We were lucky to survive that mission. There were very few missions we would fly that we were not shot at, and flak would get so thick and so black at times that you couldn't see a flight of planes that had flown through it ahead of you. It looked like a big, black cloud. And when you went through that, it hit the plane, and sometimes it would do a lot of damage and sometimes not much damage – but it was a very frightening experience to go through those heavily defended targets. The flak was so thick it was jokingly said that it looked like you could walk on it. Someone compared flying combat in the 8th Air Force to taking a cold shower – the first time you do it, if you stay in the shower, you get used to it, and it's not so bad. But we would fly a day or maybe two missions in a row, and then the weather would move in, and we would be down for two or three weeks and have that time to think about going back up again. And it would be initiating yourself to combat situations again. It was kind of nerve-wracking to be doing some, then quit, then do more. But it was an interesting thing. My first pilot and I were big buddies, and we went through several German air raids in London blackouts, and we'd see the German planes flying over and the spotlights and the anti-aircraft – it really was an experience. We were so loved by the British people, who thanked us for coming over to help them win the war. And that was a pleasant experience. I can still hear, "Thumbs up, mate. Good show, mate. Thanks for coming over," and that kind of stuff.   And, of course, there was a saying the British had over there: "Over-paid, over here, and over-sexed." That's what they said about the U.S. air force, which isn't really true, but that's what they said anyway.

My last mission was on December 28. We had been to a target at Koblenz, which is where the Rhine and the Moselle rivers join. This was during the Battle of the Bulge, which started on December 16. That also happened to be the same day that Maj. Glenn Miller, who had the orchestra, disappeared. And America was more concerned about Glenn Miller disappearing than we were about the Battle of the Bulge. Nobody knew how serious the Germans were there, and we almost lost the war there. We were unable to fly for a long time because the weather was so bad. Finally, we got off the ground and bombed at Koblenz, which was a railroad marshaling yard that was supplying the Germans in the Battle of the Bulge with munitions and people. We had some enemy opposition but didn't feel that we would have any problems flying back. All of a sudden, the ship blew up. We were twenty minutes away from England, from our air base across the channel. We were heading for the base when the ship blew up, and I've never seen such a mass of fire in my life. I went up to the nose of the ship – navigators fly up in the nose of the ship with the bombardier – and I got over the bombsight, which is as far away from the fire as I could get. I could never get in that little nook and cranny again, but I was up there then. And God told me that I could stay there and burn up, or I could crawl back through those flames and get out. And I did.

When I got through the flames, I realized that my parachute was over near the drift meter, so I picked it up, and the end of it was smoldering where it had been on fire. I put it on and went back through the fire again. I don't know what my bombardier was doing – I think I saw him on the way out. But I dove out, and the chute didn't open for the largest part of the flight down. I realized I had the D ring in my hand after I pulled the ripcord. And I thought, "This is going to look real pretty on a plaque over my fireplace." Then I got busy and started opening the chute by hand. It opened, and I spent several weeks in the hospital. I had first- and second-degree burns about my face – the rest of me was covered with uniform. I had lost a flying boot when my chute opened, and I cracked my left ankle when I landed. It's like landing barefoot; all I had on was a little felt medium boot from the inside of the heavy flying boots that flipped off me. So I had a very close call with death – that was the worst mission I ever had. We were not expecting the fire; we were not expecting the explosion. All the crew got out except the bombardier – he jumped out without a parachute and fell to his death from ten thousand feet. Yes, it was horrible. I've had nightmares about that.

The explosion was caused by an electrical short that burned through an oxygen line return. People came out and looked at what was left but couldn't tell what caused the electrical shortage. We assumed it was a little hit from a piece of flak or something, but it was also an electrical shortage.

The war was winding down about that time. Actually, the war in Europe was over on May 8, and this was December 28, so it was about four months before the end of the war. Well, when I got out of the hospital, I invited some older Red Cross people to come to a luncheon that I paid for to thank them for what they did for me during the war. After the worst missions, the Red Cross would greet us on the ground with a couple of ounces of scotch whiskey when we got off the plane. It impressed me how considerate they were. Also, when I was in the hospital, I had a bad condition known as operational fatigue, or combat fatigue. I was in a couple of the nursing homes operated by the Red Cross, and those ladies taught me how to play ping pong, and I ate good food, went to movies, walked through a garden, and listened to pretty music – it really glued me back together.

So I came home with the Purple Heart, the Air Medal, and two Oak Leaf Clusters. I think there was an Air Medal for the first ten missions you flew, and every five missions after that, there was another cluster. It was for successfully completing a combat mission; it really wasn't for heroism like the Silver Star. There was nothing heroic about anything I did – it was just kind of routine flying.

While I was overseas, my mother wrote me every day, and my wife – we were engaged at the time – wrote me about every other day. And when I got home – this is sort of embarrassing to tell – my mother found a whole bunch of letters that she had written me but I hadn't even opened. I kept them, but I have no excuse at all for not reading them. It didn't bother her too badly, but it bothered me thinking that I had these letters from my mother that I hadn't even read. Her writing wasn't really easy to read anyway, but that's no excuse. I also didn't write back very much. I did communicate somewhat, but I really didn't take much time to write. I didn't have much to tell them anyway, and you couldn't tell a whole lot about what you were doing or where you were going, so I wasn't a very good correspondent. I plead guilty on that.

I had a little New Testament that Dr. McGukin had given me from First Presbyterian Church, and I kept that in a locker all the time – it was kind of a security thing for me. I would hear from the church every now and then. Jean and I were born into the First Presbyterian Church, and we've been there all our lives – it's home to us. And I have lived in Knoxville all my life; I never lived anywhere else and never wanted to live anywhere else.

When I came back, I went to work in a woolen mill that my family owned. I also got involved in a lot of civic work. Adjusting back to civilian life was pretty hard. Being in the war taught me how to appreciate life. I came so close to death so many times while I was flying my missions and when the ship blew up and my parachute didn't open. I wouldn't even get into an airplane for ten years after the war – I was petrified of flying. I think I rode the last train to New York – I used to have to go to New York on buying trips when I was with the woolen mill. And I know the war has affected my health in a way. My hands have started shaking pretty bad, and I really relate that to an emotional reaction – I feel it made me more nervous than I would normally be. But it hasn't been a problem for me at all; I've been able to overcome whatever it was. I don't sleep too well, but that's just me. I used to lay awake and think about the missions that I flew the first year or two or three, but I don't do that any more. So I don't think I have any serious aftereffects, but it did affect the way I appreciate every day that I am alive.

And now I'm spending most of my time going to funerals – all my friends are dying now. I had this great class at McCallie; there were ninety-nine in my graduating class, and I think there are twelve of us left. And, of course, every time I cut on the TV, they remind me that at least a thousand veterans a day from World War II are dying. I'm trying to postpone me being a statistic for a while anyway. But I'm happy, I love people, and I hope people love me. I have nothing bad to say about my experience in World War II. Overall, I think my experiences in World War II have helped me. When I came back, I taught Sunday school here at First Presbyterian Church for about ten years, and I could really put myself into the lesson. I usually tried to tie a personal experience from my time overseas into my Sunday school lessons.

I think I would have been miserable if I hadn't been in the service. Nowadays, when the war is mentioned, I think it's kind of a damper on my friends who were not in the war – or even those who were in the war but never saw actual combat. There's a tremendous difference between a man who has been in mortal combat a few times and a man who's never faced death or been shot at. It's hard for me to describe, and I don't know if you can understand it. I actually looked a German pilot in the face as he was coming by our plane, and I was shooting a .50-caliber machine gun out of the side of the ship. And, I swear to you, I saw him face to face as he came by – he was looking at me and I was looking at him – and I thought, "That guy's trying to kill me." I can see it now, and that black cross on the side of his plane was a mile high – it was just frightening. And I didn't have time to be too afraid because there were other planes around. He may remember that, too, if he is still around; I don't know, but I've thought about it.

Chapter twenty-eight
Bill Tate

Bill Tate was born May 1, 1923, in Lynnville, Tennessee. He joined the Army Air Corps in 1943 and became a navigator. During his fourth mission, he had to bail out of the airplane and landed near a German prison camp. He was captured and stayed in the camp for seven months, during which time he kept a journal that he still has to this day. He wrote about daily occurrences and documented his favorite poems and songs, the names and addresses of his friends, various recipes, his earnings, detailed lists of his rations, Christmas and Easter menus, and other tidbits he wanted to remember. He was a second lieutenant when the war ended but later rose to lieutenant colonel when he became an Air Force Academy liaison officer. His service earned him a Purple Heart.

I was in ROTC at Knoxville High School and for a short time at The University of Tennessee. I liked the military – I didn't really want to go to war, but I felt it was my duty. So I volunteered, and Jim Talley and I went to basic training in Memphis, Tennessee. They called them CTDs – college training detachments – and in effect, it was to get us a little more indoctrinated into the military.

Jim and I were roommates, and we ended up as cadet officers. We had about two hundred cadets broken up into squadrons. We went from there to Kansas City, Missouri, where we lived in an old apartment hotel – it was real luxury. We both dated a little bit and had a good time besides going to school, waiting for the time when we would go to navigation school. Then we went from there to San Antonio, Texas, where we went through classification, which determined whether you would be a pilot, a navigator, or a bombardier.

At the classification center, we stood up before a panel of officers, and they said you had maybe a fifty percent chance of graduating from bombardier school, a thirty-five percent chance of graduating from pilot school, and a thirty-five percent chance of graduating from navigation school. We were scared to death; we didn't know what to do. So Jim and I stood there for a few minutes, and I said, "What do you want to do?" He said, "Well, let's take the best odds and go to bombardier school." So we said that's what we wanted to do, even though we could have done any of the three according to the test. So we had what they call preflight. If you graduated from preflight, then you had the choice of navigation, pilot, or bombardier school, where you actually flew. So we went to preflight down in Texas, and one day an announcement was made that if anyone wanted to go to advanced navigation school in Coral Gables, Florida, step forward. Jim Talley and I were the first two out there. So that's where we went to navigation school, the University of Miami in Coral Gables. We flew old Pan American clippers, which flew at about ninety miles per hour. We had Pan American navigators that taught the flying part, but we went to class to learn to use the computer and do the plotting and everything. I had a good time in Coral Gables – met a cute little girl down there. We were there about three or four months, and it wasn't long before we were sent to Dyersburg, Tennessee, and from there, we went to the classification center.

We were graduate navigators at that time, so, of course, we were put on different crews. We took off one morning – I'll never forget this – we took off about five o'clock and were headed toward Labrador. When we went to this base, we went singly, and that is where I really tested navigation. I saw a lot of icebergs, and we could see Greenland hundreds of miles away just as clear. It fools you because you think, "Well, we've got it made, there's Greenland." Greenland was really hundreds of miles across there, but you could see it.

Our second destination was Iceland, which was just a little postage stamp. The pilot called and asked what our ETA – estimated time of arrival – was and I gave him a time, and that time came and went. I couldn't see a thing, and the crew couldn't see a thing. They would say, "How we doing?" And I would say, "We're all right, right on course, right on time, right on time." I'll tell you when I saw that tiny little dot of Iceland there, I said, "Thank you, Lord." I had a good friend who was a navigator and got lost – he just disappeared. There is no place else to land out between there and northern Ireland.

We spent a night or two in Iceland. It was so cold – my feet are still cold. In a couple of days, we took a brand-new B-17 to England, thinking, "Gosh, we ought to be in good shape." But when we got to England, they took away the B-17, and the one we flew was an old-timer. But, anyway, we left Iceland and headed to northern Ireland, and we spent a few days there. Then we went by boat over to the mainland, and from there, we went to our base at Horham, where we flew practice missions. This was the 95th Bomb Group, and our crew was assigned to the 336th Bomb Squadron.

An orderly would come in the barracks and wake us up at four in the morning. They said, "Granny's drawers are flying," which meant the flag was flying, showing that we were going on a mission. There were nine of us. One of the crew members was taken off because they didn't need him in the waist of the airplane. When you're flying in formation, you only need one man in the waist of the airplane. We started with a waist gunner on each side, but when we flew missions, we just had one waist gunner, so there were nine members in the crew. The bombardier sat in the very nose of the airplane at a little table.

The Norden bombsight was a tremendous aid of developing how and when you were going to drop your bombs to hit the target, because the bomb doesn't go straight down; it goes with the momentum of the airplane. So this Norden bombsight, which was a deep, dark secret, was what we had, and our bombardier would actually fly the airplane. The pilot would give up the controls, and the bombardier would turn these little dials, and when the crosshairs cross, drop the bombs. The bombs were in a bomb bay; the doors would open and the bombs would drop.

We flew three missions and there was what was called flak. They were long-range guns, and particularly as you got close to the target, there were a lot more guns. You could see puffs all around you, and you could hear the shrapnel hitting the airplane. On our fourth mission, which was a Tiger tank factory in Berlin, we were hit badly by flak between the number three and number four engines. The pilot started yelling, "Bail out!" So we started getting our heated boots off and getting our GI shoes on so we could walk, just getting ready. There was a little door near my compartment, and I waited for the pilot to come down. As I waited, he rang the alarm bell, which meant we were in serious trouble, so out I went. After seven of us had bailed out, the co-pilot went to the back of the plane to be sure all had gotten out. Then he called the pilot on the intercom to tell him that everybody was out and just two of them were left on the plane. The co-pilot then told the pilot that he was going to bail out, but the pilot told him to wait just a minute. He said he had the engine feathered. If you have an engine that is "running away," it gets faster and faster because the wind of the other three engines is forcing that engine's prop to turn more and more. So to feather that engine took quite a bit of doing. So the co-pilot came back and got into his seat, and the pilot and the co-pilot got the plane back to England, though the seven of us had already bailed out. We didn't know that for a long time, but finally later on, somebody said, "Did you know that your plane got back to England?" I said, "What?!" I never saw the pilot or co-pilot, so I just thought they had been killed or captured.

So anyway, when I went out, I had on a pair of GI shoes because the flight shoes are fur lined and you can't walk in them on the ground. So I had the GI shoes on so I could try to get away from whoever would try to capture me. As soon as you pull that chute strap, then your chute opens and there you sit, and if there were German fighter planes close by, they would just shoot you. Just after that chute opened, I hit the ground – I didn't even have time to look up and see if it was open. So I laid there a minute trying to get my parachute off so I could try to run away or go somewhere where nobody was after us. I was on the ground and I heard shots, and I felt a bullet go in my side. It must have been a low-caliber bullet or gun because these people were farmers. I prayed for God to take me to Heaven. I was convinced I was going to die that instant!

Luckily, I landed near a prison camp, and the guards from the prison camp ran the civilians off so they didn't finish me off. I'll never forget walking toward that prison camp and seeing all these prisoners of other nationalities – none American. They were cheering like I was a great hero coming to rescue them. And here I thought I was going to die. They took me into this little commissary. I pulled up my shirt, and I looked around and saw a hole. The medic there kept pulling my shirt up and he kind of laughed. The bullet had ridden between my skin and ribs and come out the back. It didn't even get into my lungs or heart or anything – just an inch or two, and I sure wouldn't be here talking to you.

I spent the night there, and the next morning, two guards motioned that I was to put all my stuff in my parachute and walk. Before we started walking, they gave me a tetanus shot. I begged them not to because on my dog tags it showed that I had had a tetanus shot. There are two kinds; one was not as strong as the other, and I had had a lot of trouble as a kid with a tetanus shot. So when I started walking, I could just barely go, much less carry that parachute with all that stuff in it. We got into some woods, and a guard motioned for me to walk up this path, and I said, "Well Lord, I didn't get there yesterday, but I'm coming today." I thought, "They're just going to take me in the woods and shoot me." I put my parachute down, and one guard handed his rifle to the other one and picked up my parachute and carried it all the way through the woods. He had a good heart. And from there, I went

through various places on trains and so on, and finally we
ended up at Staliq 1. There were thousands of American
officers in this camp and a lot of British officers also. I think
there were maybe ten thousand in that camp.

I was assigned to a room with twenty others. There
were twenty bunks, but there were twenty-one of us, so I had to
sleep on a bench for a while. But after about a month, they
separated all the Jews and Jewish American fliers from the rest
of us and put them all in one barracks. We thought they were
just going to shoot them – the Germans just hated the Jews and
killed a lot of them. But a concentration camp was a lot
different from a prison camp. A concentration camp killed
Jews and they didn't give them any food. So I got this Jewish
American air force man's bunk. They just sent them into
another area of the camp we were in – I don't know if it was
just to scare them or what, but they were still there after the
war when we were liberated.

Excerpt from Bill's war journal:

> The doctors and Col. Zempke have been in 3 of the concentration
> camps in this area, and they are in the most horrible conditions
> imaginable. The people in these camps are underground and have
> no windows or lights of any kind. Some of them have been here up
> to 9 years – How they have stayed alive seems impossible. They
> are living corpses, and hardly any of them are expected to live. The
> ones that worked were fed 1/8th loaf of bread, 1 cup of coffee, and
> 1/2 bowl of turnips. Up until now I had a slight sympathy for the
> Germans, but now I have none whatsoever.
>
> 9 May – Today I visited one (of) these camps, and this one was a
> big barracks with electric fences & barbed wire entanglements.
> There were hooks in the basement where some of the Germans'
> victims had been hung up like slaughtered cattle. But some of these
> people had been hung up by their chins while they were still alive!
> There were 4 new graves, and the Lord only knows how many
> more there will be before it's over. How anyone could treat another
> human being like some of these have been treated is impossible for
> me to grasp. The kids around here are playing with leather whips
> that were used on some of these people. One little boy here is 14
> years old & has been in this living hell for 7 years!

We had very little to eat. We had a few Red Cross packages and Germans gave us some bread, but mostly it was sawdust and potatoes. We saved up food for a month for Christmas, and when it came, we sat down and looked at that food – but we couldn't eat it. It didn't take anything to fill our stomachs up because our stomachs had shrunk so much.

There were two men in there who were first cousins who had never met but ended up in the same room in the prison camp – it was really an amazing coincidence.

The camp was horribly boring. The YMCA sent in a lot of books, and we did have a library where you could take a book out to read. You could walk around – there was plenty of room to walk in this compound where we were. So you could get plenty of exercise if you made yourself do it, or you could lie in your bunk all day. A lot of the guys just laid there; they didn't want to do much. I had this little Testament that First Presbyterian gave me, and I still have it, even though it is absolutely falling to pieces. That was the one thing the Germans didn't take from me after I was captured – they let me keep that little Testament and my toothbrush. There is not enough money to buy that little Testament from me, and I still read a little of it just about every night.

Some of the Germans were just maniacs; they believed in Hitler so much that they thought he was going to capture the world for Germany. There was the SS, which was sort of military intelligence, but they were also very, very cruel – if they got hold of you, you were in trouble. Then you had the regular soldiers. They were people who just had been conscripted, like the two guys who carried my parachute when I was in such bad shape. And there were the Luftwaffe, which were the flying portion of the German army, and it was highly organized. Those people thought Hitler was God, and they worshiped him.

After we were there for seven months, it was around the first part of May, and my birthday is May 1. Right on May 1, the Germans left the camp. They vamoosed because the Russians were coming, and they sure didn't want to see those

Russians. They were wild, just like savages, and the Germans were scared to death of them. So they flew us to a camp just for people who were prisoners that had been released. We stayed there a little while and then they put us on a boat to New York. Then I was put on a train and sent to Camp Gordon, Georgia. When I got down there, I was told to go upstairs, find a bunk, and that if I wanted to sleep for twenty-four hours, to do it, or do anything I wanted to do.

Jim Talley and I were so close, and I didn't even know if he was dead or alive, but I was thinking about it. The next morning, I walked down the steps and out the door, and Jim Talley's little convertible was across the street – an unbelievable coincidence. Neither one knew what had happened to the other. He had gotten home earlier than I had, and he drove down to Camp Gordon, where he was discharged. I rode back with him to Knoxville, and he said, "I want you to be in my wedding." He was getting ready to get married.

After I got home, I went to work for the Tennessee Valley Authority – I was a file clerk – and I remember that there were two or three of us talking the morning after the atomic bomb was dropped. Nobody dreamed of the power and what it did to Nagasaki and Hiroshima. It was just unbelievable; it just flattened everything. So it took several days for anybody to have a conception of what happened and what it really did. Of course, the Japanese immediately surrendered, and it saved a lot of American lives.

Adjusting back to civilian life took a while. I don't know how to explain it, being in a situation like I was and coming back. Well, it made me a lot closer to the Lord. You never knew from day to day whether you were going to be with Him or if you were not a Christian and going to Hell. I sure didn't want to go to Hell.

After the war, I lived just about two blocks from the fraternity house, which is where I met my wife. She came to this church, too, but she was about three years younger than I. So, you know, three years when you're twenty years old makes a lot of difference. Now we've been married fifty-nine years.

And we have three wonderful children – our oldest daughter is in her fifties, and our twin boys are in their late forties. I can't believe that time has gone by so fast. We have two wonderful daughters-in-law and six grandchildren.

I never finished at UT; I got married instead. I went for about two years, but I think you get sort of into a mood when you live for the present, and I was so much in love and she was too, so I said, "Let's get married. We can go to school afterwards." But I didn't. I did for a while, but I went to work in my brother's real estate office. When I think back at it, I'm glad I didn't go back to college. I'm sure I would never have met my wonderful wife and had my wonderful children and wonderful grandchildren. I would have had an entirely different life.

After the war, I became an Air Force Academy liaison officer. We worked with guidance counselors and worked with people in high school and some in college who wanted to go to the Air Force Academy or Annapolis and make a career out of it. There were several of us, and we would meet with these boys – some girls, too – and tell them what they were getting into. The Air Force Academy is tough physically. I told the fellows that I worked with that the best thing you can do is run two or three miles a couple of times a week because the air out there is so rarified, it's quite different than it is in Knoxville – not as much oxygen. I had several fellows that I worked with graduate, and they had to stay in the Air Force for three years. One of them became a pilot for one of the airlines.

I retired after twenty years, so I've been retired now ten or fifteen years. But the Veterans Administration is working on whether they want to award us some funds to make up for what we went through. I had my feet tested, and I have some nerve damage in my feet – they are freezing cold all the time. They sent me to a veterans' hospital, took all these tests. And I have to eat about every two hours, day and night, twenty-four hours a day. I wake up at night, eat and go back to sleep. I had a nervous breakdown in 1972, and that's when it really got bad,

on top of everything else we had been through. To get through
that, I prayed a lot. It really brought me closer to the Lord.

I can't emphasize enough that having terribly hard
times and having to live not on a bed of ease sure brings you
closer to the Lord. Most people don't have things like this
happen to them, so they don't always know what it means to be
a Christian or how much they need the Lord. I don't think I
would have survived without Him.

My favorite poem in that journal is called "Prisoner of
War," and I can still recite it:

> Kelly, get your barracks bag,
> The shipping list is here.
> We're sailing in the first tide
> For home and yester year.
> But Kelly stirred no muscle
> To join the homing flocks.
> He was parked behind a tiny stove
> Beside a Red Cross Box.
> Kelly, we're a sailin',
> The bitter war is done.
> It's off to the states, Boy,
> To sweethearts and to fun.
> But Kelly turned a deaf ear,
> His stubbornness uncleft,
> "I should go anywhere
> With all these groceries left."
> It's a sad story they tell these days,
> Along the Bowery street;
> Of Kriegsgefangenen Kelly
> And his parcels full of meat.
> Now some love adventure,
> And some love curly locks;
> But Kriegsgefangenen Kelly
> Loved a faithful Red Cross Box.

Chapter twenty-nine
Vince Torbett

Vince Torbett was born in Knoxville, Tennessee, and joined the National Guard band when he was in high school. During World War II, he played with the band and became a flight instructor. He attended The University of Tennessee after the war and was called back into the Army when the Korean War broke out. He stayed in the Army until 1965.

When I was still in high school, in 1940, I joined the National Guard because they were forming a band for the 191st Field Artillery. We got called to active duty in February of '41 on account of World War II. And after about a year, I left that outfit and went to the aviation cadet program because I wanted to fly. I graduated in June of '43 and got assigned as a flight instructor. But after two or three weeks, they didn't get the orders, so I was sent to the navigation school in Texas to fly for the school. I did that for the rest of the wartime until I got discharged in '45.

How I got to be an instructor was because, when I was in basic training, I got fascinated with doing two-turn snap rolls. I did all my other maneuvers, but I got really fascinated with making two-turn snap rolls. So one day, the instructor told four of us to all follow him, that he was going to watch us do the same maneuvers he did through his mirror. When we took off, I was right behind him, and after he did several maneuvers, he did a snap roll. And I said, "Uh huh!" So I went into my procedure, and fortunately my two-turn snap roll turned out absolutely perfect. And as soon as I did it, he peeled off, and we followed him down to the field, where we landed and went to the parking area. Before I even closed up, he was slapping the hood on the back and said, "Don't shut it down." He opened it up, crawled in, and said, "Now take me back up to where we were." So we went up, and as it turned out, for thirty minutes, I was instructing my instructor. That's the reason I think they assigned me as an instructor when I graduated, and that's probably what saved my life – because I spent the rest of the time flying for the navigation school. I would just fly while they were training.

In the band, I played cornet or trumpet. We were a band for an Army unit, and whenever we had parades or something, the band was out front. And we made concerts for the people to enjoy and so forth.

When I got out of the service, of course, I went to the university. I was going to get a civil engineering degree. Well, I took that for about two and a half years, and then I thought I wanted to be a dentist. So I backed up, took all my premed stuff, and I was waiting to go to dental school when the Korean War broke. I got called back into the service, and then I stayed in the Air Force flying and also in civil engineering functions until 1965.

I had three children while I was in the service, two sons and a daughter. After I left the service in '65, I went to the university, and I was an assistant to university architecture for about six years. At the time, the university was in a large expansion program for several years, and that's what made it really interesting and exciting. But after they quit their massive production program, I got kind of interested in retiring. And I've been tiring ever since.

Chapter thirty

Fred Vance

Fred Vance was born in Knoxville, Tennessee, on August 20, 1915. He has been a member of First Presbyterian Church all his life. During the war, he was a member of the 82nd Airborne Division and spent most of his time in North Africa, Sicily, Italy, and Germany. His time in the service earned him a Bronze Star. After the war, he stayed in the Reserves for 28 years, reaching the rank of major.

I went into the Army in 1941 and was assigned to the 82nd Airborne Division. I was first assigned at Fort Benning, and then I went to Fort Bragg and stayed there a year or so. I remember walking down a road called Longstreet Road, which was a long road by Fort Bragg. We started walking and walking and walking – I guess it totaled twenty-five miles, but it might have been more – and then we heard that the 8th Army Artillery was going to fly a whole lot over our heads. But that wasn't just hearing – that happened. They were close enough overhead that you felt like you could reach up there and tickle their belly as they went by.

At Fort Benning, I started running short on money to keep up with my social life, so I learned to parachute – because they'd give me one hundred dollars more money. Then we went to England, and I had a girlfriend or two there. But I was of the age when you're supposed to; I wouldn't have been normal. When I had some leave time built up, some of us

decided to take a vacation. So we went into the west side of
Liverpool, and we took a nice vacation for three or four weeks.

Then we went down to Casablanca, which is when we
took these little-bitty boxcars and rode around the top of North
Africa to where we were going to make the first jump. Then we
went into Sicily, and the people there thought we weren't
exactly their friends and started firing. We lost forty-three
airplanes, with about twenty-five men in each plane. When we
got up there, we did a whole lot of walking. And the more we
walked, the more tired we got.

I was also in the backbone of Italy, from the northern
part, right along the backbone, to about Naples. We went all
that way by foot. Luckily I got an assignment that required me
to ride in a Jeep; otherwise, it was by foot.

Then we went up into Germany – the Germans didn't
like anybody but themselves. Then we started to head north for
the canal in Germany, and that's where we found the Russians.
The Russians would rather shoot you than look at you, and they
did some of that. But I remember one time the Russians invited
us to come up and visit with them and drink their schnapps. I
was afraid I might get mad at some of them, and that would be
bad, so I didn't go.

I remember going to a concentration camp in Germany.
I guess there were a couple of hundred people laying in there,
just dying. Of course it was up to us to do something about it,
so we did. We got them out of there. I also remember hearing
Hitler on the radio. There were a lot of words, and I didn't
understand them because he was speaking German – but he
sounded unhappy, and I'd say he was.

I remember one time they started firing at us while we
were carrying a lot of ammunition, food, water, and stuff like
that. I remember jumping off some terrain into a low place, but
then I saw a better low place. And no sooner had I hopped over
to that new low place but a shell landed right above what I
jumped out of. There were other times when it was necessary
to get down in a foxhole – you just hoped you would get out of
it – and it happened time and again. I was also in the Battle of

the Bulge, and one of the worst things I remember is it was cold. We did have good boots and socks, but even so, you could get cold. But we shot at them, and I hope we got a few of them – actually, I'm hoping we got a whole lot of them.

I was still in Germany when the war ended, and I remember because I read a sideboard that said "Berlin 65 kilometers." When we heard the war was over, we all got in the schnapps and were celebrating – but that's not bad, even for us Presbyterians.

After the war, I wasn't in Germany very long, maybe four or five months. We were just keeping everything quiet and making sure nobody got out of line. One day, we saw a lot of refugees coming down the highway from Berlin, just miles and miles of them. You could look down the road, and as far as you could see, it was refugees. You know why they were coming our way? We fed better – our rations were a whole lot better than the rations of the Russians.

During the war, I wrote my family a lot because I didn't have anything else to do. We had V mail, and it got back and forth all the time without any problem. But I didn't keep any pictures or mementos from the war – because I wasn't sure I was going to get out of it.

Before we went home, I remember we had a lot of ammunition with us and didn't want to take it back with us, so we fired it all up. That way, there wasn't any left over to carry back. We were in combat a total of two and a half years.

When I got home, I stayed in the Reserves for a total of twenty-eight years. I didn't need the GI Bill because I had already gone to school. So I worked for the Tennessee Department of Employment Security, the state employment office. And I still read the Bible every day – that's just part of living, especially at my age.